Kalecki's Economics Today

Michal Kalecki was a Polish economist who independently discovered many of the key concepts of what is now identified as Keynesian theory. His contribution to macroeconomics was late in being acknowledged, but his work can be seen to have resounding influence on some of today's economic problems.

The analyses presented in this book serve to scrutinize Kalecki's theories and show both their significance for explaining the working of modern economies and the areas that need adaptation to changed circumstances. Crucial issues in the present world economy covered in this book include:

- the pattern of cyclical recession and financial crises
- historically high levels of unemployment and poverty
- neoliberal economic policies

With contributions from such scholars as Philip Arestis, Malcolm Sawyer and Jan Toporowski, this impressive book will interest students and researchers involved in economic policy, macroeconomics and the history of economic thought.

Zdzislaw L. Sadowski is Professor of Economics at the University of Warsaw, Poland.

Adam Szeworski is Professor Emeritus of Economics at the University of Warsaw, Poland.

Routledge Frontiers of Political Economy

1 **Equilibrium Versus Understanding**
Towards the rehumanization of economics within social theory
Mark Addleson

2 **Evolution, Order and Complexity**
Edited by Elias L. Khalil and Kenneth E. Boulding

3 **Interactions in Political Economy**
Malvern after ten years
Edited by Steven Pressman

4 **The End of Economics**
Michael Perelman

5 **Probability in Economics**
Omar F. Hamouda and Robin Rowley

6 **Capital Controversy, Post-Keynesian Economics and the History of Economics**
Essays in honour of Geoff Harcourt, volume one
Edited by Philip Arestis, Gabriel Palma and Malcolm Sawyer

7 **Markets, Unemployment and Economic Policy**
Essays in honour of Geoff Harcourt, volume two
Edited by Philip Arestis, Gabriel Palma and Malcolm Sawyer

8 **Social Economy**
The logic of capitalist development
Clark Everling

9 **New Keynesian Economics/Post-Keynesian Alternatives**
Edited by Roy J. Rotheim

10 **The Representative Agent in Macroeconomics**
James E. Hartley

11 **Borderlands of Economics**
Essays in honour of Daniel R. Fusfeld
Edited by Nahid Aslanbeigui and Young Back Choi

12 **Value, Distribution and Capital**
Essays in honour of Pierangelo Garegnani
Edited by Gary Mongiovi and Fabio Petri

13 **The Economics of Science**
Methodology and epistemology as if economics really mattered
James R. Wible

14 **Competitiveness, Localised Learning and Regional Development**
Specialisation and prosperity in small open economies
Peter Maskell, Heikki Eskelinen, Ingjaldur Hannibalsson, Anders Malmberg and Eirik Vatne

15 **Labour Market Theory**
A constructive reassessment
Ben J. Fine

16 **Women and European Employment**
Jill Rubery, Mark Smith, Colette Fagan, Damian Grimshaw

17 **Explorations in Economic Methodology**
From Lakatos to empirical philosophy of science
Roger Backhouse

18 **Subjectivity in Political Economy**
Essays on wanting and choosing
David P. Levine

19 **The Political Economy of Middle East Peace**
The impact of competing trade agendas
Edited by J.W. Wright, Jnr

20 **The Active Consumer**
Novelty and surprise in consumer choice
Edited by Marina Bianchi

21 **Subjectivism and Economic Analysis**
Essays in memory of Ludwig Lachmann
Edited by Roger Koppl and Gary Mongiovi

22 **Themes in Post-Keynesian Economics**
Essays in honour of Geoff Harcourt, volume three
Edited by Peter Kriesler and Claudio Sardoni

23 **The Dynamics of Technological Knowledge**
Cristiano Antonelli

24 **The Political Economy of Diet, Health and Food Policy**
Ben J. Fine

25 **The End of Finance**
Capital market inflation, financial derivatives and pension fund capitalism
Jan Toporowski

26 **Political Economy and the New Capitalism**
Edited by Jan Toporowski

27 **Growth Theory**
A philosophical perspective
Patricia Northover

28 **The Political Economy of the Small Firm**
Edited by Charlie Dannreuther

29 **Hahn and Economic Methodology**
Edited by Thomas Boylan and Paschal F. O'Gorman

30 **Gender, Growth and Trade**
The miracle economies of the postwar years
David Kucera

31 **Normative Political Economy**
Subjective freedom, the market and the state
David Levine

32 **Economist with a Public Purpose**
Essays in honour of John Kenneth Galbraith
Edited by Michael Keaney

33 **The Demise of Involuntary Unemployment**
Michel De Vroey

34 **The Fundamental Institutions of Capitalism**
Ernesto Screpanti

35 **Transcending Transaction**
The search for self-generating markets
Alan Shipman

36 **Power in Business and the State**
An historical analysis of its concentration
Frank Bealey

37 **Editing Economics**
Essays in honour of Mark Perlman
Hank Lim, Ungsuh K. Park and Geoff Harcourt

38 **Money, Macroeconomics and Keynes**
Essays in honour of Victoria Chick, volume one
Philip Arestis, Meghnad Desai and Sheila Dow

39 **Methodology, Microeconomics and Keynes**
Essays in honour of Victoria Chick, volume two
Philip Arestis, Meghnad Desai and Sheila Dow

40 **Market Drive and Governance**
Reexamining the rules for economic and commercial contest
Ralf Boscheck

41 **The Value of Marx**
Political economy for contemporary capitalism
Alfredo Saad-Filho

42 **Issues in Positive Political Economy**
S. Mansoob Murshed

43 **The Enigma of Globalisation**
A journey to a new stage of capitalism
Robert Went

44 **The Market**
Equilibrium, stability, mythology
S.N. Afriat

45 **The Political Economy of Rule Evasion and Policy Reform**
Jim Leitzel

46 **Unpaid Work and the Economy**
Edited by Antonella Picchio

47 **Distributional Justice**
Theory and measurement
Hilde Bojer

48 **Cognitive Developments in Economics**
Edited by Salvatore Rizzello

49 **Social Foundations of Markets, Money and Credit**
Costas Lapavitsas

50 **Rethinking Capitalist Development**
Essays on the economics of Josef Steindl
Edited by Tracy Mott and Nina Shapiro

51 **An Evolutionary Approach to Social Welfare**
Christian Sartorius

52 **Kalecki's Economics Today**
Edited by Zdzislaw L. Sadowski and Adam Szeworski

Kalecki's Economics Today

Edited by Zdzislaw L. Sadowski
and Adam Szeworski

Routledge
Taylor & Francis Group
LONDON AND NEW YORK

First published 2004
by Routledge
11 New Fetter Lane, London EC4P 4EE

Simultaneously published in the USA and Canada
by Routledge
29 West 35th Street, New York, NY 10001

Routledge is an imprint of the Taylor & Francis Group

Typeset in Bembo by Wearset Ltd, Boldon, Tyne and Wear
Printed and bound in Great Britain by MPG Books Ltd, Bodmin

British Library Cataloguing in Publication Data
A catalogue record for this book is available from the British Library

Library of Congress Cataloging in Publication Data
A catalog record for this book has been requested

ISBN 0–415–29993–4

Contents

Contributors

Arestis, Philip, Professor of Economics, University of East London.

Bhaduri, Amit, Professor, Centre for Economic Studies and Planning, School of Social Sciences, Jawaharlal Nehru University, New Delhi, India.

Chilosi, Alberto, Professor of Economic Policy, Faculty of Political Science, University of Pisa, Italy.

Courvisanos, Jerry, Senior Lecturer, School of Economics, Launceston Campus, University of Tasmania.

Flakierski, Henryk, Professor of Economics and Comparative Economic Systems, York University, Toronto, Canada.

Flassbeck, Heiner, Dr, Chief, Macroeconomic and Development Policies Branch, UNCTAD, Geneva.

Kowalik, Tadeusz, Professor of Economics and Humanities, Institute of Economics, Polish Academy of Sciences, Warsaw, Poland.

Laramie, Anthony, Professor of Economics, Merrimack College, Mass., USA.

Laski, Kazimierz, Emeritus Professor of Economics, Johann Keppler University, Linz, Austria.

López, Julio, Professor of Economics, Faculty of Economics, Universidad Nacional Autonoma de Mexico.

Mair, Douglas, Professor of Economics, Heriot-Watt University, Edinburgh, UK.

Miller, Anne G., Heriot-Watt University, Edinburgh, UK.

Mott, Tracy, Associate Professor and Department Chair, Department of Economics, University of Denver, USA.

Nuti, D. Mario, Professor, University of Rome La Sapienza, and London Business School.

Reynolds, Peter, Professor of Economics, Head of the Economics Division, Staffordshire University, UK.

Sachs, Ignacy, Honorary Director of Studies, L'Ecole des Hautes Etudes en Sciences Sociales, Paris.

Sadowski, Zdzislaw L., Professor of Economics, Department of Economics, University of Warsaw; President of the Polish Economic Society.

Sawyer, Malcolm, Professor of Economics, Head of Economics Division, University of Leeds, UK.

Skarstein, Rune, Associate Professor, Department of Economics, The Norwegian University of Science and Technology.

Skuse, Frank, University of East London.

Szeworski, Adam, Emeritus Professor of Economics, Department of Economics, University of Warsaw; Warsaw School of International Trade and Finance.

Toporowski, Jan, Reader in Economics, The Business School, South Bank University, London.

Preface

The chapters contained in this book were originally papers presented at the Conference in commemoration of the 100th anniversary of the birth of Michal Kalecki. The Conference was organized by the Polish Economic Society and took place in Warsaw, at the site of the Polish Academy of Sciences, on 27–8 September 1999. Some of the papers were revised before inclusion in this book. This is indicated whenever applicable.

Michal Kalecki was unquestionably one of the great economic minds of the twentieth century. The original idea of the Conference was to bring together an international group of renowned economists known for having devoted much of their academic work to the study of Kalecki's ideas related both to theory and policy, in order to arrive at an assessment of the relevance of these ideas to the modern world which changed so very significantly since his times. This presupposed taking up such issues as that of the role of financial markets and of liberalization of capital flows – the basic factors which brought about substantial changes in the working of present day capitalism – with the purpose of trying to identify their influence on economic growth, unemployment and income distribution. Interestingly, in spite of the fact that such issues could not have been dealt with by Kalecki, as they emerged only after his death, the discussions at the conference revealed in Kalecki's theories much relevance for the world of today.

In preparing the book, the editors felt that it should make interesting reading to those willing to follow and compare the differing approaches of individual contributors, who all seem to consider themselves in a sense Kaleckians, but remain fully independent in their own thinking.

Acknowledgements

The editors, while thanking all the contributors for their cooperation and understanding, want also to acknowledge with appreciation the contributions made at the 1999 Warsaw Conference by participants who are not represented in the present volume because the subject of their papers as presented at the Conference, though of much interest, went beyond the immediate scope of this book. These were: Lord John Eatwell, President of King's College, Cambridge; Stanislaw Gomulka of the London School of Economics and Political Science (whose paper was published elsewhere); Noemi Levy-Orlik of the National University of Mexico; Soltan S. Dzarasov of the Russian Academy of Sciences; and Marcin Wyczalkowski, former Senior Adviser of the International Monetary Fund, now retired.

Acknowledgements have also to be addressed to those participants who only took active part in the discussions without presenting papers, among whom a notable place must belong to Paul Streeten from USA, Gabriele Pastrello from Italy, as well as to Jerzy Osiatynski, the editor of the much appreciated *Collected Works of Michal Kalecki.*

Apart from what is mentioned in the notes, individual contributors expressed in their chapters specific acknowledgements which should be quoted here. Tracy Mott thanked especially Philip Arestis and Amit Bhaduri for helpful comments and suggestions, some of which he used in revising the original draft of his chapter, of course absolving them of any responsibility for what he has done with their suggestions. Jerry Courvisanos gave special thanks to Julio López for his comments on an earlier version of his chapter, while keeping all responsibility to himself.

Needless to say, special acknowledgements have to be addressed to the Polish Economic Society for the initiative and organization of the Conference which brought about valuable analytical material largely presented in this book.

Introduction

A note on the changing approaches to Kalecki's ideas in the world literature

Adam Szeworski

Michal Kalecki, the eminent Polish economist, died in Warsaw in the seventy-first year of his life, on 17 April 1970. His intellectual legacy includes writings on all the three main types of economies characteristic of the world of the twentieth century, i.e. the capitalist, the socialist, and the less developed economies. These writings were brought together and expertly commented upon by J. Osiatyński in the *Collected Works of Michal Kalecki*, edited in Polish in 1979–88 and translated into English in 1990–7. Expressed in numbers this legacy contains about 550 items – books, articles, reviews, notes, etc. – all of them meticulously enumerated by the editor, for the period of 1927–87, in the bibliographic annex to the last of the seven volumes of those *Works*.

It is interesting to note that a considerable part of these writings – at least 80 items – was published after Kalecki's death. From among these only 18 were reprints in Polish (including single volumes of *Collected Works*), while the rest was composed of reprints or translations in English (22), Spanish (17), Italian (9), Portuguese (6) as well as Japanese, Turkish and Tai. The actual number has been still growing owing to new reprints or translations which have continued to appear in different parts of the world.

Still more numerous and fast growing in numbers after Kalecki's death have been various publications referring to his theory. For instance, at least 250 such publications in English were registered since 1971 in the international database of Silver Platter Information, Inc., *EconLit 1969–2001* which is far from complete. These numbers should be looked at against the relatively weak diffusion of the knowledge of Kalecki's scientific achievement during his lifetime. In fact, his economic theory (not always correctly understood), and even his name, were known internationally mainly to a rather narrow circle of British economists connected with the universities of Cambridge and Oxford, where he had been active from a few years before the world war until its end, and to some other economists who had had the opportunity to meet him in later years, during his work for the International Labour Office in Geneva and for the United Nations in New York, preceding his coming back to Poland in 1955.

It is unquestionably unusual that such an abundance of publications, including Kalecki's own writings and those of various other authors referring to his theory, appeared during more than thirty years which elapsed since his death and kept appearing at a relatively high annual rate over the last two decades. The causes of this phenomenon deserve perhaps a closer look. An important explanatory factor seems to be the spreading of interest in his economic theory in the less developed countries. While economists of developed countries expressed growing interest in the relevance of his views on the capitalist economy in the changing conditions of the real world, the interests of those of the less developed countries, particularly in Latin America, but also in India, were focused primarily around his contribution to the theory of economic planning and development economics. As a result, it seems justified to talk of a worldwide posthumous discovery of Kalecki as an independent original theorist.

Let us, however, say first a few words on the reasons for that 'delay' in the scientific career of the man counted today by many renowned authors among the most eminent economists of the past century. These reasons, as explored by some authors, seem to have been rightly summarized in the phrase that 'Kalecki was not born at the right time, did not live in the right place and did not write in the right language'.

Indeed, his earliest innovative outline of the modern theory of effective demand, presented in his *Essay on the Business Cycle Theory*, was published by a research institute in Warsaw in Polish, already in 1933. It was not accessible to English readers until in 1966, when its English translation, together with five other important essays on related issues, appeared in his *Studies in the Theory of Business Cycles, 1933–1939*. The book was edited with the introduction of Joan Robinson who already earlier had underlined the publication date of that *Essay* which preceded Keynes' *General Theory* by a couple of years. This gave rise to the discussion on the possible priority claim of Kalecki to the fatherhood of the modern theory of effective demand, commonly attributed to J.M. Keynes, as well as to another discussion on the superiority of his theory over that of Keynes, claimed by a large part of the present day post-Keynesians.

For the rest of his lifetime there was no essential change in Kalecki's position in the economic profession. Although his three main books, in which his earlier outlined theory was successively developed to its final form, i.e. *Essays in the Theory of Economic Fluctuations* (1939), *Studies in Economic Dynamics* (1943) and *Theory of Economic Dynamics* (1954), were all published in England, the significance of his theory remained known to and understood by a rather limited number of economists. In general, due to its apparent similarity to the Keynes' *General Theory*, which was enthusiastically praised and extolled in the early post-war decades, and, on the other hand, due to the Marxian ingredients in his theory, he was commonly counted among the left-Keynesians.

As far as his native country, Poland, is concerned, his theoretical work was also scarcely known, and limited mainly to the older, pre-war generation of economists. In the post-war period his name was not even mentioned in academic textbooks of political economy owing to his imputed Keynesianism and his dissent from the official Marxist–Leninist theory of the socialist economy. A certain change in this regard took place only in the early 1970s – as it may be judged from references in writings of various authors to Kalecki's theory – owing to the posthumous edition in England of two books containing reprints of his essays or chapters of his books, selected by himself as his main contribution to economic theory, i.e. *Selected Essays on the Dynamics of the Capitalist Economy* (1971) and *Selected Essays on the Economic Growth of the Socialist and the Mixed Economy* (1972).

But the real breakthrough in his position seems to have finally taken place owing to the English edition of his *Collected Works*, whose seven volumes appearing successively in 1990–7 were reviewed by competent well-known economists in the widely read English periodicals.

In the meantime, two important factors have contributed to that essential change. The first of them was, without any doubt, the fundamental discussion which developed inside the Keynesian school as a result of growing dissatisfaction with Keynesian policies and the related criticism of the underlying theory; these were deemed responsible for the wave of inflation which came upon the world economy in the 1970s. In this connection, much interest went to Kalecki's theory which was found to compete with orthodox Keynesianism. As a result of many comparative studies it has been finally recognized – at least by those known later as post-Keynesians – as superior in many aspects to the original theory of Keynes, and consequently adopted and integrated into their research programme, to become finally the central body of their revised theory.

The other closely related factor which largely contributed to the diffusion of Kalecki's theory and its advance to the present position in economics at the world level, were two periodicals, the *Cambridge Journal of Economics* and the *Journal of Post Keynesian Economics*, founded respectively in 1977 and 1978 which in their statements of purposes declared explicitly their adherence to Kaleckian theory. In the case of the former it was said that the source of the adopted position was 'the belief that the economic approach rooted in the traditions of Marx, Kalecki and Keynes has much to contribute to the understanding and treatment of current economic and social issues . . .' Similarly, founders of the *Journal of Post Keynesian Economics* laid stress on innovative theoretical work that could shed a fresh light on contemporary economic problems. This was specified by Joan Robinson in the conclusion of her leading article in the first issue of the *Journal*:

> We now have a general framework of long and short period analysis which enables us to bring the insights of Marx, Keynes and Kalecki into coherent form and apply them to the contemporary scene.

In fact, the annals of both periodicals, representative of the post-Keynesian

School in Britain and the USA respectively, have been plentiful of articles, notes on, and references to, the Kalecki's writings.

The growing interest in Kalecki's theory has been reflected particularly in the number of books, individual and collective, or special issues of periodicals devoted to the discussion of its contents and relevance to the changing economic conditions. At least some of them deserve to be mentioned here.

The first, in chronological order, was the special issue of the *Oxford Bulletin of Economics and Statistics*, No. 1, 1977, containing commemorative essays of seven former collaborators of Kalecki. The next, responding specifically to the growing interest in less developed countries in Kalecki's writings on economic planning, was the collection of his essays in the volume edited by J. Toporowski in 1986, entitled *Selected Essays on Economic Planning*.

Of particular importance are the collective volumes which appeared successively. First, *Kalecki's Relevance Today*, edited by M. Sebastiani in 1989, containing the collection of 19 papers presented to the symposium held at the University of Perugia in 1986 which was intended 'to mirror the variety of arguments treated by Kalecki, as well as the diversity of the scientific circles which are interested in his thought'. Second, *Michal Kalecki (1899–1970)*, the collection of 15 previously published papers of various authors on the influential work of Kalecki, edited by M. Blaug in 1992. Next, edited by J. King in 1996 *An Alternative Macroeconomic Theory: The Kaleckian Model and Post-Keynesian Economics*, a collection of papers of nine authors who survey the principal components of Kalecki's theoretical system and promote his claim to recognition as a dominant influence on modern non-neoclassical economic thought. Finally, *The Legacy of Michal Kalecki*, two volumes edited by M. Sawyer in 1999, comprising 55 previously published papers relating to the work of M. Kalecki, including 11 papers by Kalecki himself, and 44 papers which explore, develop and/or evaluate his work.

The latter is the last and most comprehensive collection of reviews and opinions on Kalecki's work. It is worthwhile to quote the summary of its contents to show the broad range of the main areas of interest in his work. It is composed of nine parts. In Volume One the first part devoted to general issues is followed by:

- ii Effective demand, investment, profits and distribution of income;
- iii Pricing and the degree of monopoly;
- iv Cycles and growth; and
- v Political economy of full employment.

In Volume Two we find the following subjects:

- vi Money and finance;
- vii Taxation;
- viii Socialism; and
- ix Development.

From among other collective editions of this kind due notice should be given to the special issue of the *Review of Political Economy*, Vol. 11(3), 1999, comprising 10 essays in commemoration of the 100th anniversary of Kalecki's birth.

The present book is a follow-up of this succession of previous publications which is intended to shed some fresh light on a selection of crucial issues of the contemporary world economy in both its economic and social aspects. The ground for this discussion is provided again by the theories of Michal Kalecki, whose characteristic feature was his high sensitivity to social aspects of the economic mechanism and for whom the primary concern of economic theory and policy was unemployment. It is interesting that this is exactly what seems to be increasingly relevant in the greatly changed economic system of today. Various contributions contained in this book help to explain the reasons.

Part I

The overview

1 Kalecki and Keynes revisited

Two original approaches to demand-determined income – and much more besides

D. Mario Nuti

Introduction

In 1962–3 I had the privilege of attending Michal Kalecki's lectures at the Warsaw Higher School of Planning and Statistics (SGPiS), as it then was, on the dynamics of a capitalist economy. From Warsaw I moved directly to King's College, Cambridge, where I often heard Joan Robinson speak of Michal Kalecki as the man who had discovered the General Theory before Keynes, as she also fully acknowledged in print (1952, 1964, 1966a, 1976) and in correspondence with Kalecki. Such a generous recognition was put forward also by some few others, such as Oskar Lange (1939) and Lawrence Klein. Kalecki's pre-1936 writings 'created a system that contains everything of importance in the Keynesian system' (Klein 1951: 447); Klein (1975) makes the even stronger statement that 'Kalecki's greatest achievement, among many, was undoubtedly his *complete* anticipation of Keynes' *General Theory*' (emphasis added; see also Klein 1964, 1966). No recognition ever came from Keynes, or from any of his close associates such as Richard Kahn. Apparently Kalecki had sent to Keynes, before the *General Theory* was published, a German version of his 1933 paper on the business cycle, which Keynes returned to him with a note explaining that he did not know German[1] – others of Keynes' immediate circle certainly did and the resources of the College and of the University make this a curious response; it rankled then and it still rankles today. In 1937 Joan Robinson wrote to Kalecki: 'It must be rather annoying for you to see all this fuss being made over Keynes when so little notice was taken of your own contribution' (reproduced in Patinkin 1982).

In his 1936 review of the *General Theory*, Kalecki was the first to claim similarity of, and priority in, discovery for his 1933 essay: 'The statement that investments determine the total size of output, I have proved in a manner similar to Keynes in *An Essay on the Theory of the Business Cycle* (Institute of Research on Business Cycles and Prices, Warsaw 1933), pp. 114–16' (Kalecki 1936: 268). He also wrote: 'I pointed out the independence of changes in output from shift in nominal wages also in the *Essay on the Theory of the Business Cycle* (1933)' (1936: 260). But he did so in two footnotes, and in another extremely discreet and concise claim in his Introduction to Kalecki (1971): 'The first part includes three papers published in 1933, 1934 and 1935 in Polish before Keynes' *General Theory* appeared, and containing, I believe, its essentials'. Otherwise he never pressed the point. I believe he was much too proud to feel the need to assert it and a claim not spontaneously and universally accepted could only diminish his greatness. After Kalecki's death, Don Patinkin (1982) denied that Kalecki could be credited with anticipating Keynes' *General Theory*: 'Kalecki came significantly closer to the *General Theory* than did the Stockholm School. . . . At the same time, I cannot accept such claims [as those of Klein and Joan Robinson]'.

As a side note I will argue that while Kalecki and Keynes have in common a theory of national income determination based on effective demand and driven by investment, and the important policy implications that descend from it, each of them followed a distinctive intellectual route, used very different building blocks and covered distinctly different additional ground. It is not a question of establishing priority in discovery, but of crediting both of them with equally original, central contributions to modern macroeconomic theory.

Different departures

Kalecki's and Keynes' personal backgrounds were very different (on Kalecki's biography see Kowalik 1964). Both knew from direct and personal experience the cyclical nature of capitalist economies, but from different viewpoints. Kalecki was the son of a manufacturing entrepreneur who went bankrupt, and was therefore familiar with the world of production, the investment process and the risk of investing in production on borrowed money. Keynes came from an upper-middle-class family and had direct operational experience as a civil servant and as a financial investor who operated daily in the financial markets, on behalf of King's College and for himself (sometimes more successfully than at other times; he died rich, but he was close to ruin more than once).

Their intellectual formation was also very different. Kalecki was an engineer who lacked the financial means to complete his university degree, was versed in the mathematics of difference and differential equations, a self-taught economist who had not been influenced by the kind of conventional economic theory against which Keynes rebelled and campaigned. He made little use of choice theory and marginalist thinking. He was influenced by Marx's reproduction schemes, by the class categories of people and incomes (capitalists and workers, profits and wages) typical of the Marxian and English classical tradition, by Rosa Luxembourg and Tugan-Baranowsky. He had worked with Ludwik Landau on the construction of Polish national income statistics. Keynes was a mathematician who specialized in probability theory, which like Frank Knight he found useless in the assessment of business risk. He had an Eton and Cambridge education. He was taught economics by Pigou and Marshall against whom he reacted.

The very titles of their main works display the main differences in their approaches and concerns. Keynes had a theory of employment based on interest and money, Kalecki laid bare the dynamics of capitalist motion.

Common features in approach and propositions

Both Kalecki and Keynes disregarded the role of money wages in labour employment, regarding real wages as determined by producers' price setting; indeed they were both prepared to contemplate even a possible direct rather than inverse relationship between employment and wages. Both followed a bold, macroeconomic and aggregate approach to the theory of national income and employment determination, taking national income identities as their starting points. Both regarded investment demand as the driving force of the capitalist system and assigned a crucial role to government expenditure in macroeconomic policy to supplement investment and net exports when national income was in under-employment equilibrium, regarded as the normal state of the world. But similarities end here. Their investment and consumption functions were different; different too was the theory of interest and the role of monetary policy; the spillover effects of their theories led to important and original developments in entirely different areas of economic investigation.

Investment functions

Kalecki had a very complex view of the investment process, distinguishing between investment orders, investment output and actual deliveries of investment goods. Investment orders depend on the ratio of profits to the capital stock, and the long term interest rate. Thus for Kalecki, contrary to Keynes' approach, investment profitability is not a marginal concept derived from discounting prospective cash flows, but a current average ratio projected into the future. Such ratio is an increasing function of the degree of utilization of productive capacity – thus making Kalecki's investment function behave as a flexible accelerator or capital-stock adjustment equation. Short-term interest rate does not matter as much as in Keynes because for Kalecki the rate affecting investment is the long-term rate, which moves more sluggishly than short-term rates, and because increasing risk from the use of borrowed money, and the ensuing danger of bankruptcy, soon stops investment even at low interest rates. Current investment output is the result of lagged past decisions; investment deliveries raise (lower) the capital stock according to whether they exceed (fall short of) the equipment going out of use, feeding back onto current profitability and new investment orders. Expectations play no role, other than in current average profit rate being projected into the future.

For Keynes, on the contrary, current investment depends on both the marginal efficiency of investment – i.e. the internal rate of return on prospective investment projects, ordered in terms of decreasing efficiency – and current interest rate. The marginal efficiency of investment is something which exists solely in the minds of entrepreneurs, it embodies their 'animal spirits' and is subject to sudden changes according to 'the state of the news'. Instead of the long-term interest rate being mildly affected by the current rate, as in Kalecki, for Keynes the current rate depends on expectations about the future normal rate of interest to which the current rate tends to revert (i.e. the interest rate 'hangs from its bootstraps').

Consumption functions

For Kalecki consumption behaviour differs among income categories: capitalists' consumption consists of a fairly stable amount which is constant over the cycle, as capitalists are constrained by their entire wealth and not by current income; they also consume a small – if any – share of current profits. Workers are presumed to consume all they earn. It follows that the marginal propensity to consume c can be approximated by the share of wages in national income, and indeed Kalecki's multiplier – which he seldom uses – is expressed as 1/(1 – wage share) instead of the conventional Kahn–Keynes $1/(1-c)$.

For Keynes, aggregate consumption depends primarily on aggregate income, regardless of its distribution, which comes into play in post-Keynesian (one should certainly say post-Kaleckian) income distribution theory (see below).

The basic models

For Kalecki:

$Y = C + I$ where Y = GDP; C = Consumption; I = Gross investment

$Y = W + P$ where W = Wages; P = Profits

$C = Cc + Cw$ where Cc = capitalists' consumption; Cw = workers' consumption

$Cc = A$ or $Cc = A + b.P$ where A = constant and b is a small fraction;

$$Cw = W$$

$$A + W + I = W + P$$

$$P = A + I$$

Thus profits are determined by capitalists' (fairly constant) consumption and (variable, indeed cyclical) investment expenditure. A fall of money wages would leave demand unchanged if prices fell by the same proportion, and would result in a demand fall and therefore income fall if prices were rigid. Kalecki (1934) specifically considered an open economy in which exports played the same role as investment in driving demand and employment, while government expenditure was viewed as 'domestic exports', with imports as leakages and – *ceteris paribus* – a trade balance deterioration arising from an increase in government expenditure.

Investment decisions *Id* are a function of average profit ratio and long-term interest rate:

$Id = Id(ltr, P/Y)$ where ltr = long-term interest rate
$P/Y = f(Y/K)$ where K = capital stock

For Keynes:

$I = I(r)$ r = interest rate
$M = L(r, Y)$ M = money supply, L = money demand
$C = B + c.Y$ B = constant, c = marginal propensity to consume

'For Keynes prices are determined by money wages, investment is determined by the interest rate and the marginal efficiency of capital, the interest rate is determined by liquidity preference' (Joan Robinson). Lower money wages – as in Kalecki – do not necessarily promote employment unless they are accompanied by higher investment, which in Keynes might occur through their impact on the real quantity of money and therefore the interest rate.

For Keynes the central position is taken by the interest rate, as confirmed by the *General Theory*'s full title. He is under the influence of Sraffa (*General Theory*, ch. 17, plus the convention of measuring income and money in wage units).

We are confronted with similar conclusions originally and independently drawn, arising from different starting points, different intellectual and technical backgrounds, different values and above all different building blocks, i.e. different theories of aggregate consumption, investment and the role of money. There is sustained originality in both; there is a very great deal that we can find in Kalecki that is not in Keynes, and vice versa. It is inappropriate to regard them as in competition for the same achievements.

Exclusive originalities

Kalecki has a theory of distribution, reviewed above. Indeed he has two distribution theories, the other depending on the aggregate degree of monopoly or aggregate mark-up although, as Nicholas Kaldor used to say, this is not satisfactory: for every product a mark-up theory of prices must specify price leadership criteria (in which enterprise's costs matter), the relevant degree of capacity utilization (costs varying with it) and the mark-up determination. Keynes neither has nor needs a theory of distribution. What is known as the neo- or post-Keynesian distribution theory is actually a neo-Kaleckian reformulation of Kalecki's first theory of distribution, with profit share instead of absolute profits and a more flexible hypothesis about the magnitudes of propensities to save out of profits and out of wages.

Kalecki has a theory of cycles, indeed a number of theories of cycles that are increasingly refined over the years (including a theory of political business cycles) culminating with the approaches further developed by Nicholas Kaldor and by R.M. Goodwin. Keynes' model is compatible with business cycles and – with the addition of an accelerator or other ingredients – can be and has been turned (beginning with Paul Samuelson and Roy Harrod) into a theory of cycles. But Kalecki had a theory of cycles of his own, driven by investment demand, as early as 1933; he also had growth solutions as special cases of his cycle models.

Finally, Kalecki exercised his talent in diverse other areas of economic research, primarily development theory and economic planning, both in less-developed countries and in centrally planned socialist economies. In particular, his theory of the socialist economy was a strong denunciation of its excessive propensity to invest – excessive with respect to non-inflationary conditions, to population willingness to abstain from consumption for future gains, to the sustainability of income and consumption growth (see Nuti 1989). Had Soviet and central–east-European leaders heeded Kalecki's advice the history of the last 15–20 years in the socialist block would have been very different.

Keynes has a theory of expectations – sometimes self-fulfilling, sometimes self-falsifying (in the Preface to a reprint of the *General Theory* he wrote that if he ever were to re-write it he would distinguish carefully between the two cases). Expectations – he explains – are important because demand for future goods does not have to be expressed in current markets. Today we would say that markets are incomplete (most forward/future markets are missing) and in any case sequential (i.e. even if futures markets were complete, one would not have to transact in them today for markets reopen daily, indeed never close in the global economy). The volatility of expectations is a major ingredient of his approach, and a key to the understanding of his view of financial markets.

At the same time, fairly simple 'reversionary' expectations govern for Keynes the medium-long normal level of the interest rate, which is the foundation of liquidity preference. Right or wrong, relevant or irrelevant at the end of this century, this is a great original feature and a cornerstone of Keynes' theory of effective demand: the notion of money as a potential 'bottomless pit' absorbing purchasing power which otherwise would be expressed as demand for current goods. An intriguing attempt to link the monetary interest rate to real 'own' interest rates for commodities can be found in the controversial chapter 17 of the *General Theory*.

Finally Keynes, like Kalecki, made diverse contributions to other areas of economic theory and policy, before and after the *General Theory*, from fiscal policy to the shaping of the international monetary system.

Patinkin (1982) argues that Kalecki did not use the marginal method, the multiplier and the notion of under-employment equilibrium, did not consider money markets and did not seek to integrate value and monetary theory. That Kalecki – like post-Keynesians – used marginal notions only sparingly should not be regarded as a defect. He did use the multiplier, but in a different formulation (see above) consistent with his own consumption theory; he was interested in the impact of investment not only on demand but also and primarily on capacity; besides, the multiplier was Kahn's (1931) and not Keynes' creation. Kalecki was more interested in economic dynamics than in the comparative statics of income determination, which he however obtained as a by-product of his dynamic models. Kalecki did not consider financial markets as fully as Keynes, nor did he attempt to integrate value and monetary theory, but his merits were to develop macroeconomic dynamics and to integrate it with distribution theory, while Keynes did not attempt either. It is equally immaterial to criticize Keynes for no theory of distribution, of economic cycles and growth. While Kalecki should not be credited with the '*complete* anticipation of the *General Theory*' (Klein 1975; emphasis added), certainly Kalecki's remarks about anticipating Keynes' relationship between money wages and employment and 'the statement that investments determine the total size of output' are the most admirably restrained and understated of claims. The significant intersection of the sets of their original contributions to the determination of employment and income, and their different, original and fundamental contributions in so many other areas, place Kalecki and Keynes as the founding fathers of modern macroeconomic theory.

In the last 20 years economic theory and policy have been dominated by what Joan Robinson called 'pre-Keynesian economics after Keynes'. The recent international financial crises, the undeniable cyclical patterns of world development, whether or not synchronized, the widespread delusion that ending world unemployment is just a matter of enforcing wage flexibility, demonstrate fully the continued relevance of Keynesian and Kaleckian propositions. The time has come for a joint revival.

Note

1 Personal communication from Mrs Ada Kalecka.

2 The relevance of Kalecki's 'Political Aspects of Full Employment' to the twenty-first century

Philip Arestis and Frank Skuse[1]

Introduction

In 1943 Kalecki published a path-breaking paper (Kalecki 1943b) entitled 'Political Aspects of Full Employment', a paper that took a somewhat pessimistic view of the prospects of a return to full employment in the capitalist democracies in the period following the cessation of hostilities. It was followed by other papers (Kalecki 1944a, 1945) in which he gave more detailed consideration to the types of policy initiative that would be needed to steer such economies towards the full employment goal.

The purpose of this chapter is to consider the arguments presented by Kalecki and consider their relevance, with particular regard to the Eurozone and the UK economy, over 50 years after their original publication. This revisiting occurs in an environment in which the problem of unemployment has become a less important priority of governments, replaced by the desire to control inflation at almost any cost and pursue 'sound' public finances. One indicator of this can be found in the Maastricht Treaty and its imposition of convergence criteria in terms of interest rates, inflation rates and public finance ratios, but not unemployment. A further change in the environment concerns the greater extent of linkages between economies, particularly financial interdependencies, which can be seen both within the Eurozone and, more broadly, in the context of increasing globalization.

This chapter has four sections: a summary of Kalecki's position on the problems of achieving full employment; the relevant changes that have taken place at the international level since the time Kalecki formulated his thesis in the early 1940s; the relevance to the twenty-first century of Kalecki's political barriers; and a concluding section.

Kalecki's thesis

The central tenet of Kalecki's argument in the 1943b paper was simple. Technically the means to achieving full employment existed. His own theories, and those developed contemporaneously by Keynes in the 1930s, emphasized the crucial role of effective demand as the determinant of activity and employment levels. Particular emphasis was placed on the impact of investment spending in influencing fluctuations (Kalecki, 1933a; Keynes, 1936), a point developed in Kalecki's work on business cycles (see for example Kalecki, 1943b). These arguments carried with them the powerful corollary that in order to push an economy towards the point of full employment, it was sufficient to create the appropriate level of aggregate demand. Kalecki argued that not only was it possible by this means to *create* full employment in the short term (a point of common ground with Keynes) but also to *maintain* it over time. In this regard it could be argued that he was incorporating long-run dynamics more explicitly than Keynes (see Sawyer, 1985: p. 194).

The real problem of militating against full employment in either time scale is a political and institutional one. Kalecki argued that the interests of the capitalist class are such that they will object to government involvement in creating and maintaining higher levels of employment. Political and social pressures are thought to impose significant constraints on the achievement of these objectives. Kalecki (1943b) argues strongly that although governments have the potential to influence economic magnitudes relevant to creating full employment, this prerogative would not be utilized effectively. This is entirely due to the 'power of vested interests' upon which Kalecki placed so much importance. More recently Kaldor (1983a) gave support to these ideas when attempting to throw some light on the reasons behind the objection to Keynesian economic policies. He too contended that the changes in the power structure of society, which came about as a result of Keynesian economic policies, were responsible for the antagonism towards these ideas.

These constraints on economic policies are viewed by Kalecki (1943b) as being rooted in the objections to full-employment by the 'industrial leaders' or oligopoly capitalists. In general terms these emanate from the oligopolists' dislike of government interference in the private sector and the consequent erosion of private capital's influence. They are as follows. First, there is the objection to government subsuming the role of private capital by becoming involved directly in production (e.g. through publicly owned industry and state investment). Such intervention is seen as involving direct confrontation with the traditional interests of private capital as it simply replaces what is regarded as legitimately within their interests by state activity and socialism. Capitalists also see it as a threat to the health of profitability and investment since government intervention would crowd out the 'efficient' and wealth-creating private sector by the 'inefficient' public sector. Second, there is the objection to government spending on public investment projects and subsidies on consumption. This dislike is essentially based on arguments like 'not spending more than one's means', 'the need for sound finance', 'the need to balance the budget', and similar arguments. In the case of subsidies on consumption, the argument is associated with the 'moral principle' that 'The fundamentals of capitalist ethics require that you shall earn your bread in sweat – unless you happen to have private means' (Kalecki 1971a: 140). The third objection relates to the social and political changes resulting from the *maintenance*, rather than creation, of full employment. His argument here is in terms of workers 'getting out of hand' due to full employment reducing the fear of unemployment, a situation which the 'captains of industry', or their managerial representatives, would not be prepared to tolerate. Rentiers would have a common interest with owners of capital since the inflationary pressures, which are associated with full employment, would disadvantage them. Kalecki suggests that under these circumstances there could very well develop

> a powerful bloc . . . between big business and the rentiers' interests, and they would probably find more than one economist to declare that the situation was manifestly unsound. The pressure of all these forces, and in particular of big business, would most probably induce the Government to return to the orthodox policy of cutting down the budget deficit.
> (Kalecki 1971a: 144)

We may also cite Kaldor (1982: xxi; 1985: ch. 2) here, who refers to the cheap money policies pursued in the period after 1945. Banks and other financial institutions in the City objected to those policies calling for a more 'active' and discretionary monetary policy, an example of the pressures alluded to above (see also Cowling 1982 and Steindl 1952). There is, still, another significant element in Kalecki's (1943b) analysis. As attempts to cure high levels of unemployment lead to budget deficits, powerful industrial and financial interests insist on a return to the tenets of 'sound' finance, and attempts to reduce the deficit lead inevitably to a slump. However, in a democratic system, the consequent growth of unemployment is electorally unpopular, and as the next election approaches pressures to relieve unemployment grow very strong. A period of expansion follows moving the economy towards full employment, but at some point fiscal conservatism re-emerges with its attendant pressures for contraction. In this way a business cycle determined by economic forces is replaced by a political business cycle, a proposition that prompted Robinson to argue that 'Just now the political trade cycle seems to be taking a more violent form than ever before' (Robinson 1972: 5; see also Feiwel, 1975).

In what follows we group Kalecki's ideas into three categories of objections, for the purposes of subsequent analysis:

i an objection to government involvement in the manipulation of aggregate demand *per se*. It deprives capitalists of power in the sense that governments no longer have to have regard in policy decisions to maintaining private-sector confidence. Capitalists consequently lose a constraining influence on government;
ii an objection to the impact of government expenditure aimed at expanding aggregate demand. If the state undertakes investment spending it is in

competition to private interests and crowds out private investment by taking over what capitalists regard as their legitimate sphere of activity. If, however, expenditure takes the form of a subsidy of consumption this breaks the ethic of the market capitalist system according to which reward, at least of labour and employment, should be related to effort expended;

iii an objection to the commitment to the *maintenance* of full employment. Establishing this over the long run is argued to alter the balance of power between employer and employee in favour of the latter. Capitalists, Kalecki argued, see some level of unemployment as a normal and desirable feature of a market capitalist system.

In subsequent 'Three Ways to Full Employment' (Kalecki 1944a) and 'Full Employment by Stimulating Private Investment?' (Kalecki 1945), Kalecki elaborated on the ways in which governments might endeavour to move an economy towards full employment and considered the likely impact of these measures.

Kalecki argued that institutional change within a developed capitalist system is a necessary precondition for any realistic chance of returning to a world of full employment and maintaining it on a consistent basis. This means, of course, that in the absence of this necessary condition, achieving full employment may not be a realistic objective. He also argued that the sufficient conditions for raising employment levels can be identified. He suggested that governments in capitalist democracies have three basic methods available to stimulate demand: direct creation of demand through state investment and/or forms of subsidy of consumption; stimulating private investment; redistribution from high to low income, i.e. towards that section of society with higher propensity to consume.

Kalecki was generally pessimistic about the ability of investment, in either the government or private sector, to act as the motor for the move to full employment and as sustainer of it. There would always be a finite volume of feasible projects available for state investment, possibly inadequate to the required expansion of demand. It is important to note here Kalecki's insistence that only investment projects which are economically viable should be undertaken. There is a clear rejection of the use of socially unjustified projects as means simply of creating jobs. In the private sector difficulties would be likely to emerge in encouraging private investment. Kalecki's argument is that it would require cumulative support if full employment is to be maintained over the longer run. There is clearly a floor to interest rate reductions designed to stimulate investment and the result would be the impossibility of generating adequate investment over the longer run. This led him to conclude that using investment demand as the stimulus to full employment could only be achieved through greater direct state involvement in production which is precisely what is resisted by the capitalist class. Kalecki is thus led to the conclusion that the most effective policies to bring about full employment will have to involve some form of state subsidy of consumption in order to raise demand. This would need to be reinforced by the even more politically sensitive redistribution of income from high income to low income sectors of the population.

Before we leave this section it might be appropriate to ask what the meaning of full employment might be. One possible definition is that 'Full employment meant everyone working who wanted to work at a wage equal to but not necessarily more than his or her marginal product' (Eisner 1996: 106). Is this still an operational definition of full employment? Can we even think in terms of a definition that indicates some global match between those seeking work and the number of vacancies available, ignoring any mismatch between the nature of the vacancies and the labour available? Or should we, following Sawyer (1995a), accept that full employment does not mean a job for everyone of working age but that full employment implies some limit on the length of frictional employment suffered by any one job seeker. Consideration must also be given to the idea that the supply of labour may itself be influenced by demand and that long periods of unemployment may themselves cause the reduction in the supply of labour as people cease seeking work. What possibly appeared to Kalecki in 1943 as a precisely definable concept is clearly not capable of unambiguous definition. This becomes particularly important in a situation where flexible labour markets cause the creation of low paid, poor quality, often part-time jobs (see Wells 1995). How do we interpret the decision of people not to offer themselves for such employment: are they *choosing* not to work in a meaningful sense of that term or would they prefer to work if an appropriate position was available?

Full employment is inevitably a fluid concept, and difficult to define precisely, for it rests on a notion of who 'should' be working and rewarded as a result. It seems, like Sawyer (1995b), we should accept a definition that involves matching vacancies and offers subject to an arbitrary maximum period in unemployment, bearing in mind that this already begs some questions. Even on this definition, it is clear that the UK, along with other capitalist economies, has not achieved full employment for many years.

Relevant changes since Kalecki's time

Given the purpose of this chapter, it is imperative to consider the principal ways in which the economic landscape has changed since Kalecki put forward his thesis on the political constraints to achieving and maintaining full employment. They are as follows:

i The dominance of purely financial motives over real forces, both inside the national economy and in foreign exchange markets, has made speculation a considerably more potent force than in the days of Kalecki's contribution. This has had a significant impact on the operation of markets, and on their instability, helped by improvements in communication that make interconnections between markets more immediate. More importantly, though, speculation has been helped by the conscious attempts of governments worldwide, inspired, and in certain cases even imposed by international financial institutions, especially the IMF, to implement financial and capital account liberalization. Over the last 20 years in particular, country after country adopted these policies only to experience financial and banking crises, some more serious than others depending on the strength of their institutional framework. The evidence is overwhelming in indicating that liberalization of this kind leads directly to greater volatility. Indeed, capital account liberalization has fostered new financial instruments which made speculation easier and faster (Michie 1999). Hedge funds in particular, with their highly leveraged positions, borrowing up to 50 times their own capital, have promoted herd-like behaviour accentuating speculative bubbles and irrational exuberance. These waves of speculative activity have taken place in an era when the economies of most countries were sufficiently robust to withstand the resultant destabilizing forces. In some cases, however, as in south east Asia recently for example, these waves had a significant impact on the real economy;

ii the sea change in the focus of the objectives of economic policy. More precisely, the objectives of economic policy of the 'golden age' of capitalism (i.e. 1950s and 1960s) namely full employment and healthy growth rates, balance in external economic relations, and modest redistributive policies, have been displaced by the dominant objective of ensuring the confidence of 'markets'. The main job of the government has thus become to ensure that markets work efficiently and with minimum interference. At the microeconomic level, government action has been limited to supply-side initiatives in areas such as education, training, infrastructure, research and development, and in attempts to remove inflexibilities in the labour market. At the macroeconomic level, governments have given priority to running balanced budgets, thus downgrading the importance of fiscal policy, assigning to it a mere passive role. It has been replaced by an emphasis on monetary policy, which is upgraded to a prominent role. The direct involvement of government, however, has been weakened by policy being placed increasingly in the hands of independent central banks. They are given the sole objective of price stability, and interest rate manipulation is the primary instrument. For example, in the case of the Bank of England Monetary Policy Committee, interest rate reductions since autumn 1998 have produced an effect that is helpful to the real economy, the *justification* for these reductions has been consistently in terms of the inflationary outlook. Beneficial effects on aggregate demand have been a coincidental side effect rather than a basis for the reductions. A further example is found in the institutional and policy arrangements of the Eurozone and the role of the European Central Bank (ECB), where again the emphasis on price stability and interest rate manipulation to this end is of primary importance. Galbraith labels these changes appropriately enough as 'the surrender of economic policy', and suggests that 'To accept a balanced budget and the unchallenged monetary judgement of the Federal Reserve is, by definition, to remove macroeconomics from the political sphere' (Galbraith 1996: 60). This is another aspect of an important shift since the time of Kalecki's writings, namely the attempt to take economic policy out of politics, thus throwing into question the notion of a 'political business cycle';

iii we now have an international monetary system that is characterized by dominant players who are only prepared to consider deflationary policy options: high real interest rates, lower Public Sector Borrowing Requirements (PSBR), squeezes on welfare spending, and in more general terms, avoidance of deliberately expansionary policies because financial markets see them as 'inflationary'. This has been accompanied by the removal of capital controls, which has generated pressure for high real interest rates as the price of avoiding a flight of capital. In Europe and elsewhere, capital markets have had a dominant role and brought with them an inherent tendency to generate deflationary outcomes. This creates an additional form of conflict in that the interests of financial capital clash with those of industrial capital. For example, during 1999, the Bank of England Monetary Policy Committee has been under pressure from industry to keep reducing interest rates. At the same time, as financial markets are concerned at the possible re-emergence of inflationary pressures they have been seeking the opposite;

iv a further key change since Kalecki's time has been the extension of the market ideology outside the confines of the individual national economy to embrace the system of national economies. Globalization has increased the vulnerability of individual economies to external forces and limited further the ability of governments to operate in isolation from global market forces. This too accords with Kalecki's ideas of an inbuilt deflationary bias to the system. This problem is particularly acute in the case of developing countries where recurrent volatility in international financial markets has had devastating effects, not helped by their poorly developed national institutions. Kalecki insisted that this need not be the case. In an open world economy 'no country will experience difficulties in balancing its foreign trade if all countries maintain their expenditure on goods and services at a level adequate to secure full employment with no export surplus in existence' (Kalecki 1946b: 323). This could be arrived at if each country maintained full employment 'based on domestic expenditure and on net foreign expenditure financed by international long-term lending' (ibid. 327). These were ideas related to the establishment of international financial institutions, the aim of which would be to provide enough short-term and long-term lending facilities to help overcome foreign exchange difficulties

(Kalecki and Schumacher 1943; Kalecki 1946b), rather than allowing market forces to dominate;

v the enormous growth in the volume and international mobility of capital along with changes in technology permit funds to move around the world with substantially lower transaction costs, and, more importantly, almost instantaneously. Furthermore, the organization of markets away from bank-based institutions and more towards market-based financial systems, has given financial markets a more impersonal and more fluid character. Consequently, international financial capital has assumed significantly more strength in relation to single governments, making it difficult or impossible to control capital movements in the modern world. Similar problems were actually identified and discussed both during the Bretton Woods era (for example, Tobin 1966) and before it (for example, Kaldor 1939). Keynes (1946) recognized the dangers for an organized international system of capital mobility and responded with a variety of proposals aimed at restricting international capital movements. With the dominant market ideology extending into international capital markets, these difficulties have become more evident, bringing greater market volatility as the expectation of a devaluation produces a flight of capital of dimensions that central banks in any one country are unable to control. Consequently 'national central banks take a step down, becoming single banks in a world-wide system, not at the "centre" any longer' (Hicks 1967: 60). To a significant degree, central banks no longer possess the type of control necessary to intervene successfully in financial markets. In addition central banks are less willing to exert the type of control over banks that was taken for granted at the time of Kalecki's writings on the political constraints, operating largely in a lender of last resort role to a banking system which expands credit money in response to demand. The degree of co-operation necessary to re-establish control over financial markets represents a formidable obstacle to redressing this shift of power.

Modern relevance of Kalecki's thesis

This section considers the relevance of Kalecki's thesis as summarized above more than 50 years after it was published. In doing this, emphasis is on the experience of the UK since the coming to power of a New Right influenced government in 1979. We also draw on the experience of the European Union and on the more recent experiment of the Economic and Monetary Union (EMU) in Europe. We start with a consideration of the relevance of Kalecki's view on the objection to government involvement in manipulating aggregate demand.

Objection to government involvement in manipulating aggregate demand

The first element of Kalecki's argument concerns capitalist anxiety at losing the disciplinary effect of unemployment if the state succeeds not only in achieving full employment but also in maintaining it. This argument seems to be of continuing relevance 50 years on as evidenced by governments' willingness to accept higher levels of unemployment at all stages of the cycle. It is also part of the shift that has seen the discussion of unemployment shift away from aggregate demand management problems to questions of labour market flexibility and adjustment, and re-assertion of the argument that wage control is the key factor in raising levels of employment. Such a view is entirely consistent with the general notion of an excess supply of labour acting as a brake on real wage growth. Indeed it may be that the nature of unemployment and the existence of long-term core and structural unemployment means that higher levels may be necessary to exercise this disciplinary effect. Britton (1996) indicates that growing unemployment through the 1960s was not obviously the consequence of deficient aggregate demand but more due to an upward trend in non-accelerating inflation rate of unemployment (NAIRU). This becomes, in the sense of Kalecki's argument, 'acceptable' to both capital and that part of the workforce, which remains in employment. There is further evidence from the 1980s that even at the peak of booms the level of unemployment was rising. For example, the lowest level of *long-term* unemployment between 1979 and the early 1990s (occurring in the third quarter of 1990) was 40 per cent above the corresponding figure in 1979 (see Skuse 1995).

Kalecki appears to have had in mind what may now appear a rather simplistic version of the impact of unemployment on 'discipline', namely that any increase in its level would have the required effect (although not in the sense of different levels of unemployment being associated with differences in the pace of wage inflation). From a modern perspective we would wish to add that the history of the level of unemployment and its structure are as important as its absolute level. Hysteresis effects become relevant. Related to this we should distinguish between the 'insiders' and 'outsiders' (Lindbeck and Snower 1987) and their differential impact. Changes in unemployment among outsiders may not have the disciplinary impact that Kalecki envisaged, meaning that insiders may retain influence and wage bargaining power despite rising unemployment. The consequence of this is that very savage increases in unemployment may be needed to maintain the disciplinary threat of dismissal and consequently it may be in the interests of capital to oversee even higher levels of unemployment on a periodic basis to maintain the credibility of the disciplinary threat. However, what Kalecki does appear to be suggesting is that a period of *sustained* full employment will have a significant impact on both inflationary pressures and the difficulty of maintaining discipline.

Associated with the relocation of the causes of unemployment within the labour market itself has been a systematic attempt to limit the rights of organized labour in the UK. This too is at least consistent with Kalecki's argument as to the desire of capital not to be party to a shift in the balance of power unless of course it is in their favour. Ironically, given the reduction in trade union power together with the steady decline in union membership in the UK and growth in the numbers of self-employed, it may well be that any future return towards levels of full employment would not have the effects that Kalecki argued capitalists feared.

Experience within the EU and more recently the Eurozone is relevant here. The creation of an independent central bank within the Eurozone, with the unique objective of pursuing price stability, has meant that fiscal policy has been restricted to maintaining a balanced budget (Arestis and Sawyer 1999b), thus effectively ruling out the discretionary use of demand management policies. Any hope of achieving higher employment levels is left to supply-side forces, effectively labour market flexibility. Kalecki is thus completely vindicated: any direct government involvement in the economy is likely to exacerbate labour market inflexibilities and should thus be avoided. Thus within the Eurozone, and elsewhere of course, the objective is to re-establish the disciplinary impact of unemployment by making labour markets more flexible. Market forces become dominant and government involvement in achieving and maintaining full employment is sidelined. Policies such as those pursued by the French government in the early 1980s are ruled out by the demands of sound finance and labour market flexibility.

Objection to government expenditure as a policy instrument

The second aspect of Kalecki's argument concerns the objection to the *direction* of spending undertaken by government. This would appear to be as relevant in the eve of the twenty-first century as when Kalecki first wrote. The UK has seen changes which have significantly altered the balance between public and private sector provision in a wide range of activities as the result of the massive programme of privatization. The private sector and private shareholders have taken over what had previously been regarded as public provision. Such changes have taken place in a range of areas from public transport to health provision. In addition, successive governments since 1979, in the UK and elsewhere, have increasingly looked to involve private sector capital in what previously would have been public projects and to shift the public/private balance in favour of the latter. This phenomenon has been repeated in a number of economies with major de-nationalization programmes both within the EU (e.g. France, Spain and Greece) and elsewhere (e.g. Australia and New Zealand).

The consequence of these changes is that large areas of investment spending have been returned to private hands and in addition the monopoly position previously enjoyed by public utilities has in many cases been eroded as competition has been allowed. Within the UK, British Telecommunications is perhaps the most obvious example, but competition is also evident in both rail and gas industries. Investment decisions are now taken by (even though regulated) private companies based largely on straight commercial criteria, and government has effectively ceded most of the influence it previously exercised over investment levels in these industries. In addition many of these newly privatized businesses have seen reductions in employment levels as significant numbers of staff have been made redundant (e.g. British Gas, British Telecommunications) in the interests of efficiency, or perhaps more significantly, shareholder dividends.

The Eurozone experiment is of relevance in this context too. Members of the Eurozone are subject to the rules of the *Stability and Growth Pact*, which increases the restrictions imposed on them to use fiscal policy. It calls for fiscal positions normally to be balanced or even in surplus, and provides an early warning signal when the budget deficit reference value of 3 per cent of GDP is at risk of being breached. A country, which fails to keep its budget deficit within this stipulated limit will have to pay in the first instance a penalty in the form of a non-interest bearing deposit. If the situation persists the penalty becomes a fine equivalent to between 0.2 and 0.5 per cent of GDP, depending on the size of the 'excess' deficit. It is assumed that any fine would be levied in respect of the *ex post* budget deficit since budget deficit forecasts are subject to both error and to manipulation (though this would also apply to deficit outcomes). Assuming the prospect of fines is effective and credible, governments would aim for deficits substantially below 3 per cent of GDP in each year, regardless of the stage of the business cycle. This is designed to avoid unforeseen events pushing the actual deficit over 3 per cent of GDP. If a government is running a budget deficit near to the 3 per cent of GDP margin, then a degree of approval would have to be obtained from the EU for any actions involving expenditure which would take the deficit over 3 per cent. Any budget deficit, which does occur, would have to be financed by borrowing, which, however, is itself subject to restrictions. This constraint on the budget deficit effectively precludes the use of national fiscal policy for active demand management purposes.

Objection to full employment

There can be little doubt that the question of unemployment has been relegated in importance as a key objective of economic policy and replaced by the need to control inflation (see, for example, Arestis and Skuse 1989; Skuse 1995; Britton 1996). Indeed it can be suggested that in addition to the constraints identified by Kalecki, the experience of the 1970s led to the emergence of a fourth constraint. This is the fear of inflation and that this has proved as powerful a brake on pursuit of full employment as Kalecki's original trio (see below for more details). Related to this has been a questioning of the ability of governments to bring about full employment by manipulation of demand and a greater emphasis on the labour market as the explanation for higher levels of unemployment. This is associated with resort to supply-side policies and attempts to make labour markets more flexible. Thus a fundamental question mark appears over Kalecki's starting point that a government does in fact have the means to create full employment in the way that he envisaged. Governments in many democratic capitalist societies have abandoned this approach. The argument advanced is that greater flexibility in labour markets is the essential prerequisite to removing unemployment and that the government cannot achieve this objective through reflationary expansion of demand.

Central to the New Right agenda has been greater reliance on market mechanisms and a concerted attempt to reduce the extent of government involvement and provision. This has manifested itself in an unwillingness to consider active fiscal policy designed to engineer changes in aggregate demand for fear of increasing inflationary pressures and a greater reliance on monetary policy in various forms as the measure to control macroeconomic variables. It is not however clear that this is entirely captured by Kalecki's argument that government must do nothing to undermine business confidence, at least in the real economy. It would appear to be more related to the desire to avoid at all costs following a policy that risked threatening the new policy priority of controlling inflation. Indeed it has been argued that it is in the interests of capital for governments to use aggregate demand management in a way that is contradictory to Kalecki's argument. As Dow (1964) argues, the low levels of unemployment experienced in the 1950s in particular are in part due to government willingness to use discretionary fiscal policy appropriately to create an environment of stability in which private investment could occur. More importantly for the argument here, this high level of demand and employment would not have occurred 'if the world of business had not acquired some confidence that governments could and would so intervene when necessary' (Dow 1964: 364; see, however, Matthews 1968, 1970 and Stafford 1970 for a different view). What changed between the 1950s and the late 1970s was the breakdown of the immediate post-war consensus between labour and capital (Britton 1996: 7–8) and the replacement of the presumption in favour of the 'right to work' by the 'right to manage'. Capital saw its interests best served by the operation of more flexible labour markets and a change in the balance of power between labour and capital which is entirely consistent with Kalecki's arguments.

On the other hand, the increasing globalization of capital and importance of multi/transnational firms does place pressures on the government to pursue policies, which help to maintain business confidence. The UK government throughout the 1980s and 1990s was concerned to attract inward investment, most notably from Japanese car manufacturers anxious to establish capacity within the EU. This became of particular importance due to the decline in manufacturing industry experienced by Britain in the first half of the 1980s. Unwillingness on the part of the Conservative Government to sign the EU

Social Chapter is another example of the change in balance of power between capital and labour.

What has clearly changed since Kalecki wrote is the power of market ideology, and this helps give 'business/industrial leaders' more leverage over the state. It is not an argument couched in terms of the impact of government on the state of business confidence. It is rather a more ideologically based and direct assertion that the market will provide the best solution and that the state should dismantle direct intervention in order to give freer rein to these forces. Increasing globalization becomes relevant again. It has enhanced the power of business vis-à-vis government and workers, and has taken place in parallel with the development and implementation of policies designed precisely to reduce the power of trade unions (Sawyer 1999b). Furthermore, financial globalization has enhanced the power of financial markets in relation to central banks. The rapid growth and frequency of the flow of funds between national currencies has created an environment where national economic policies are more difficult to implement and have also become less effective.

Where Kalecki's confidence based argument may have greater relevance in a UK and Euroland context is with respect to financial markets. The power of an internationally open market makes it important that governments be seen to adopt policies that will be well regarded by financial markets, and not cause destabilizing liquidity flows in the age of deregulated markets. While it is difficult to disentangle all of the factors causing price movements in financial markets, casual observation throughout the first half of the 1990s indicates that it was not uncommon for markets to react adversely in response to falls in unemployment levels, even when the absolute level remained high. A desire to avoid destabilizing such markets may well act as a significant lever on government policy and reinforce the priority of an inflation target over concern at employment levels. The Labour Government's decision to delegate interest rate determination to the Bank of England and similarly the objective of price stability given to the ECB, strengthen this argument substantially. Furthermore, it is not so clear that the Bank of England and the ECB have felt similarly constrained with respect to the real economy. As already indicated, there has been a willingness to use interest rate policy in a way that is counterproductive to confidence, investment and employment, i.e. in a way that is contrary to the interests of industrial capital, and designed to limit expansion at the first sign of possible upward pressure on inflation.

A new constraint: fear of inflation

The analysis undertaken in this section clearly implies that a fourth constraint has been identified. This is the fear of inflation. This has probably become the most powerful constraint in turning governments and policy-makers away from concern with the goal of full employment and so powerful has its impact become that even left leaning governments place the inflation target on at least an equal footing to that of employment. This has occurred for a number of reasons.

In part the reason is historical. Kalecki's argument was developed at a time when memories of the Great Depression and falling prices were strong. The inflationary spectre was not a serious threat. In fact, taking on board a longer perspective, the experience of the previous century had been that of broadly speaking stable prices, with the exception, of course, of hyperinflation associated with war or its immediate aftermath. It is also consistent with Kalecki's understanding of how a developed capitalist economy functions. A key part of his theoretical apparatus is that up to the level where labour *and* equipment are scarce, 'short period supply curves are horizontal or mildly rising for most commodities' (Kalecki 1944a: 361). Kalecki wrote as though there were generally no capacity constraints in an industrialized economy and that such an economy he saw as demand constrained. Shortage of capacity was a problem of developing countries (and under specific circumstances in industrialized economies, notably period of war). He argued that employment levels short of full employment, and capacity utilization short of full utilization would be non-inflationary. Thus problems of inflation would arise at 'over full' capacity as unit costs rose pushing down real wages. It can be argued that Kalecki saw inflation as arising from capacity utilization as a proportion of full capacity, rather than employment levels relative to full employment. Then if inflation is correlated with unemployment, it arises from a correlation between inflation and capacity utilization, and between capacity utilization and unemployment. Consequently, it follows that if government demand creation 'stops short of increasing effective demand over the full employment mark, there is no need to be afraid of inflation' (Kalecki 1943b: 348). Such insouciance in connection with inflation was borne out by the experience of economies such as the UK during the 1950 as high levels of employment were not accompanied by serious levels of inflation. Events of the 1970s, triggered by the oil price shocks and reinforced by the breakdown of social consensus between labour and capital meant that both the threat and actuality of inflation became much more real. A consequence of this was the New Right's accession to power in the UK on a platform which emphasized this aspect.

There is however a further reason that plays a part in accounting for this shift. Kalecki's original argument is couched largely in terms of the opposition of *industrial* capital to achieving and maintaining full employment. It emphasizes opposition to the impact of state intervention on private industrial interests and the negative consequences on opportunities for real investment. There is brief reference to the maintenance of full employment operating contrary to the interests of the rentier class in terms of rising prices (Kalecki 1943b: 355). The thrust of his argument remains, however, that full employment alters the balance of power, undermines 'discipline in the factories' and 'political stability' (ibid.: 351). It means that workers would 'get out of hand' [so that] the 'captains of industry' would be anxious to 'teach them a lesson' (ibid.: 355). Furthermore, since Kalecki's time economies like the UK have witnessed a significant decline in the size of manufacturing and related sectors alongside a growth in the absolute size of the financial sector. As Wells (1995) shows, employment in the industrial sectors of the UK fell considerably from the mid-1960s onwards whilst at the same time employment in services, particularly financial services, grew rapidly. Measured in output terms, from 1983 to 1996, banking, finance and business services grew by 46.7 per cent compared to 28.9 per cent and 27.1 per cent for construction and production industries respectively. Finance capital thus became much more important. The decline of manufacturing and the enormous growth of the financial sector is a powerful new fourth constraint of a political nature. Given the emphasis that the financial sector places on keeping inflation under tight control, this makes governments less likely to pursue policies aimed at reducing unemployment. In any case, it can be argued that the growth in the relative importance of the service and financial sector may actually make achieving full employment more difficult. To the extent that multiplier effects in the service sector are lower than those in manufacturing, at given inflation rates reductions in unemployment would be greater in the manufacturing sector than in the service sector.

The role of financial markets as barometers of confidence has grown with the growth of the sector and economic policy has increasingly been framed within the context of the reactions of financial markets rather than in terms of impact on industrial confidence. An important criterion of policy formulation becomes its credibility as viewed by financial markets. It is on the basis of this argument that a number of central banks throughout the world have been given independence from the political sphere and the objective of price stability at the same time (including the Bank of England and the ECB). Adverse reactions by the financial markets to signs of rising inflation, often associated with publication of data showing falls in unemployment, place a constraint on governments' ability to pursue full employment and give precedence to anti-inflation measures. This is particularly important in an economy with large and international financial markets such as the UK. The result is a strengthening of opposition to inflation as the result of, in Kaleckian terminology, the captains of *finance* as distinct from captains of *industry*, who have a vested interest in low inflation.

This distinction between the two types of capital should not be exaggerated as the interests of industrial capital also suffer from inflation even in a Kaleckian world in which the pricing of goods determined by the degree of monopoly enables wage rises to be passed on and profit margins reestablished. Retained corporate earnings suffer from increased taxation at given rates of corporation tax, in view of the use of essentially historical cost methods in determining tax liability. This will impinge upon corporate ability both to distribute dividends and to finance investment. The former will have impact on those who hold equity based wealth, a group in which higher income earners predominate. Michl (1995) discusses this issue, citing US studies, which indicate that the costs of inflation weigh most heavily on upper income groups. Given that these groups are also likely to be more socially influential, and include significant representation from the captains of industry, we have another argument leading to the emergence of the fear of inflation as the fourth political constraint on full employment.

Other constraints

There are, of course, other economic obstacles to lasting full employment beyond the ones discussed above. Included in this list would be poor research and development and consequent innovation, inadequate excess capacity due to low investment, and inadequate levels of training and skills development in the labour force. In the case of open economies, there is a further awkward problem in that the balance-of-payments can be a severe constraint in terms of allowing the economy to move to full employment. Expansion of demand may be met with severe balance-of-payments deficits and undesirable movements in the country's exchange rate, so that the expansionary policy would have to be reversed.[2] Kalecki suggested that in extending loans to countries, the international financial agency responsible for world monetary affairs should have the power to direct borrowers to use the loans to increase their imports from already industrialized countries which had deficits in their balance of payments (Kalecki and Schumacher 1943).

Summary and conclusions

We have argued that Kalecki's prescient forecast in 1943 is of continuing relevance today. Indeed, we suggest that it is relevant to the realities of the twenty-first century. Clearly a number of significant changes have taken place since the early 1940s when Kalecki was propounding the ideas on which this chapter has focused. In an attempt to summarize the contribution of this chapter to these ideas, we draw on a far-reaching implication of these changes on Kaleckian economics.

In Kalecki's analysis it is the real sector which is assigned the more 'active' role, while the financial sector is 'passive' in the sense that it reacts endogenously (see also Sawyer 1999b). Given the principle of increasing risk (Kalecki 1937a), though, interest rate policies may impose constraints on the activities of the real sector.[3] While this may have been the case at the time of Kalecki's writings on these issues, the developments alluded to in this chapter have definitely changed the economic landscape substantially. The financial sector has assumed a more critical role, what with the power of financial markets and central bank independence. In effect the real sector has lost its predominantly 'active' role in relation to the financial sector. In this sense, we fully agree with Sawyer's (1999b) recent proposition that whilst Kalecki's analysis remains relevant to the realities of the twenty-first century, a great deal of analysis is required to 'modernize' Kaleckian economics.

Our contribution has been in the area of the relevance of Kalecki's political aspects of full employment to the new century. In this regard we have identified new constraints to the achievement of full employment. Contrary to the prevailing views on the role of economic policy and the role of the state in economic life, our analysis clearly implies that it remains central to the achievement and maintenance of full employment. How precisely this policy should be implemented is the subject matter of another paper.

Notes

1 An earlier version of this chapter appeared as Skuse, F.E. (1999) 'Kalecki's "Political Aspects of Full Employment" Revisited' in Daniel S.S., P. Arestis and J. Grahl (eds), *Adjustment, Convergence and Economic Policy – Essays in Macroeconomics in Honour of Bernard Corry and Maurice Peston*, Vol. 1, Cheltenham: Edward Elgar. We are grateful to Malcolm Sawyer and Paul Streeten, and to participants in the International Conference to commemorate Michal Kalecki's 100th anniversary of his birth (Warsaw, 27–8 September 1999), for helpful comments.

2 This difficulty, of course, may not be unrelated to the other problems that are mentioned in the text. More concretely, a balance-of-payments constraint could very well arise from the inability of the economy to respond to the increased demand well before full employment is reached, due entirely to the obstacles enumerated under other constraints.

3 There are two further constraints which emanate from the operation of the banking system. The first is that any inappropriate action by the banking system could easily abort recovery. For example, and as Kalecki argued, banks could respond to a recovery by raising interest rates excessively when 'the precondition for the upswing is that the rate of interest should not increase too much in response to an increased demand for credit' (in Kalecki, CW I: 191). The second is that the availability of finance is seen as a key factor limiting the growth of a firm; Kalecki puts it in the following way: 'The access of a firm to the capital market . . . is determined to a large extent by the amount of the entrepreneurial capital. It would be impossible for a firm to borrow capital above a certain amount determined by the amount of its entrepreneurial capital' (Kalecki 1954a: 91).

3 Michal Kalecki as a behavioural economist

Implications for modern evolutionary economic analysis[1]

Jerry Courvisanos

> Kalecki's innovative theoretical views now seem to constitute the cement that pulls together the various schools of the post-classical research programme.
>
> (Lavoie, 1992, p. 422)

Setting the agenda

On the 17 November 1997, *Business Week* heralded the emergence of 'The New Economy' in the USA. The term has since been used in both the mass media and business journals worldwide to signal the widespread use of microelectronics and computer-based networks as information and communication technologies (ICT) that have enabled knowledge to become the 'key' economic engine. The '. . . new intangible features of international transactions appear to form the essence of what "The New Economy" is all about' (Soete 1999: 3). Evidence from traditional trade and foreign direct investment flow data show no increase in globalization, yet, in terms of the internationalization of information and knowledge the level of intangible transactions that do not show up in balance of payments has grown exceptionally strongly (Soete 1999: 6–12). These intangibles stretch across the domains of purely financial to exchange and co-operation of information and knowledge (scientific, business, media). Thurow (1999) calls these developments the third industrial revolution.

Michal Kalecki was born at the beginning of what Thurow (1999) calls the second industrial revolution, with its huge structural changes brought about by electrification and 'Fordist' mass production based on oil. Kalecki's economic analysis is clearly based on monopoly power within the manufacturing sector; even his development and socialist economic writings reflect this second industrial revolution. All the authors who have applied Kaleckian analysis in theory and empirical evidence have done it explicitly within the context of manufacturing and related distribution (tertiary) sectors.[2] This raises the issue as to whether Kalecki's insights into analysing modern capitalism are relevant to 'The New Economy'.

A minimalist perspective to this issue would be to look at what aspects of

Kalecki's manufacturing world are still relevant within 'The New Economy'. This would *not* address the central issue of the structurally changed economy and Kalecki's work becomes sidelined. This chapter aspires to a broader dimension on this issue, by attempting to place Kalecki's insights into the centre of the innovation-based evolutionary systems analysis that is explicitly studying this 'New Economy'. In this way post-Keynesian economics can, through Kalecki, be made applicable to evolutionary economics. Since both schools of thought are part of what Lavoie (1992: 5) calls the 'post-classical research programme', this approach follows his dictum in the opening quotation.

This chapter first specifies the crucial dimensions of 'The New Economy'. Then, Kalecki is brought in from a behaviouralist perspective to analyse the process of change in capitalism towards this 'New Economy'. The chapter next outlines the evolutionary economic process underlying the endogenous technical change models that have been used extensively to explain this 'New economy'. This process is set out with possible links to Kalecki being flagged. Finally, a research agenda for Kaleckian–evolutionary analysis is proposed that should make Kalecki's innovative views continue to be relevant into the twenty-first century.

Dimensions of 'The New Economy'

Six significant dimensions to the new information-knowledge based economy are set out in this section. Together they provide the stylized facts on the type of capitalist economy that will dominate in the twenty-first century. From the epistemological position of realism,[3] Kalecki's economics will need to deal with these aspects in some form.

Technological revolution

Structural change to 'The New Economy' is identified and dated in Freeman and Soete (1997: 19) as the Fifth Kondratieff wave (1990s–?). Microelectronics is the ubiquitous and cheap key factor input into this economy, with its emergence at the beginning of the 1990s being related to the proliferation of personal computers, establishment of the world wide web, laying out of the information highways infrastructure, and development of digital networks. This is the organicist ontology dimension (Lavoie 1992: 7), which focuses on the process of technical change. Microelectronic technological revolution is the specific process by which capitalism has evolved from the 'Fordist' mass production manufacturing base to the new information and knowledge base.[4] Structural unemployment is a significant by-product of this revolution.

Innovation

The nature and extent of innovation in this new economic climate has been examined extensively by technology-based economic research. Rothwell

(1994) summarizes the research on this area, calling it the fifth generation innovation process that concentrates on ICT systems integration and networking. ICT has vastly increased the efficient means of innovation through the accumulation and transmission of data that is incorporated into a strongly collaborative network system. Global access of this technological system of innovation centrally clustered around new ICT has led to an increased rate of innovation consequent on the '. . . dramatically reduce[d] communication and information handling and processing costs' (Soete 1999: 12). This higher innovation rate under ICT, together with reduced investment delivery lags, establishes a requirement for shorter payback periods on investment commitments compared to manufacturing investment where the nature and extent innovation involves a longer time horizon.

Investment cycle

'Volatility is here to stay, but technology and globalization will spur robust growth'. This subtitle to another *Business Week* (24th August 1998) issue on 'The New Economy' encapsulates the investment cycle dimension. Keynes (1930) recognizes that waves of investment expenditure are stimulated by new technology. From a Kaleckian perspective, Courvisanos (1996) maps the investment cycle pattern between endogenous (minor improvements) innovation that is 'part and parcel' of investment decision-making (Kalecki, 1954a, p. 158) and exogenous (radical) innovation. The latter occur at severe investment cycle troughs that generate structural change, powerful burst in economic growth (boom), and strong susceptibility to cyclical downturn. Any downturns lead to expanded cyclical unemployment. Hollanders *et al.* (1999) provide empirical evidence to support this pattern. After the 1973–91 period of weak capitalist investment, the 1991–8 period has been characterized by strong investment in USA, leading to rapid growth divergence from Europe and Japan. The investment has been in mobilizing private capital stock in ICT, developing the infrastructure of information highways (process innovation) and the 'commodification' of knowledge processes (product innovation).[5]

Knowledge-based economy

Along with the physical based ICT investment outlined above is the intangible investment in the new knowledge and its dissemination needed to take advantage of all the new ICT capital stock. In the USA, investment in intangibles has increasingly outgrown those in physical capital (Abramovitz and David 1996). The manufacturing sector has become highly dependent on ICT knowledge-base for its economic activity.[6] This is evident by greater intangibles that are needed as inputs, while more services are incorporated into their final products.[7] The growing size and importance of the services sector that trades essentially in knowledge is the counterpoise of declining manufacturing (Wycoff 1996).

Information inequality

All major structural changes throw up greater inequalities. Depressed isolated regions and disadvantaged groups *within* advanced nations, and less developed nations all struggle to take advantage of the new economic developments. 'The New Economy' has exposed a large number of information-poor that exist in all these identified sectors of the world.[8] The Internet does not lend itself to organized mass action to prevent the information-rich from conducting their Internet money-making (Thurow 1999). Worse still, the culture and knowledge-base in underdeveloped economies is so far removed from the Internet as to make any 'catching-up' a ludicrous proposition (Arunachalam 1999).

Role of the state

The ICT-based globalization raises serious issues for the role of the state in intervening on its nation's behalf. Governments need to assess how to reconstruct activist economic policies. The global access of knowledge (at least to the information-rich) has favoured deregulation of the private sector and privatization of the public sector. The new specifications of the role of the state can be seen from the 1980s' financial deregulation that led (due to unsustainable financial volatility) to more prudential-oriented financial regulations on a global co-operative approach. Soete (1999: 18–22) identifies three broad policy perspectives: comprehensive industrial and regional policies with learning-type perspective adjustments; international regimes on laws and rights; co-operative global interventions (especially on the environment and the information-poor problem). Macroeconomic stabilization of inherent instability and full employment should figure as part of all three processes noted, rather as some separate box of 'fine-tuning' implements.[9]

A 'behavioural' Kalecki analysis of 'The New Economy'

The task here is to take some essential features from Kalecki's analytical exegesis and use them to explain aspects of 'The New Economy's' dimensions. From a post-Keynesian outlook, this type of analysis is generally absent in the literature.[10] Despite Keynes (1930: Vol. 2, 86) recognizing innovation in the link from cycles to growth, by the time of *The General Theory* (Keynes 1936) this aspect drops out as Keynes provides a depressing view of the long period.[11] Then, the dominant post-war Keynesian macroeconomic models were developed in a strongly aggregative way with an equilibrium analysis (to solve simultaneous equations), and making technical change exogenous. This approach to cycles and growth ignored the vast work of Wesley Mitchell that had through the 1920s and 1930s identified cumulative innovative change and breakdowns in such processes (Rostow 1990: 282–8). Following this tradition, innovation-based analysis is lacking in post-Keynesianism.[12]

Kalecki has some significant endogenous innovation-based analytical features that can provide the basis of a post-Keynesian contribution to understanding the processes in ICT-powered capitalism. The starting point is to examine Kalecki's investment cycle models from a behavioural perspective, a position first developed in Courvisanos (1996: 69–72). Procedural (or bounded) rationality is the behavioural context behind the conventions used in Kalecki's investment models. Specifically these are to do with three conventions; retention rates of profit for investment, desired excess capacity levels and acceptable gearing ratios. Underlying investment spending is the technical uncertainty due to embodied process innovation, and market uncertainty due to product innovation. At the static level of analysis, the conventions provide 'risk premium' to cover these fundamental uncertainty factors embedded within investment decision-making at a certain point in time; or what Steindl (1941) calls 'preference for safety' in a world of uncertainty.

At a dynamic analytical level, there is recognition by Kalecki that static rules will not be adequate. In Kalecki (1937a) there is a sense of 'degree of uncertainty' that alters subjectively with changing rates of capital accumulation. This means that conventions need to take account of increasing risk with rising investment: higher retained profits and lower desired excess capacity rates, with a growing concern for rising gearing ratios. The cumulative nature of this process over the investment cycle expansion will lead to a point when the increasing risk is untenable as capital accumulation rates peak. This creates the conditions for an investment downturn and reduced innovation. The behavioural element to the cyclical investment process is what Crotty (1992) calls the growth–safety trade-off, and provides an explanation to 'The New Economy' investment cycle dimension where volatility (i.e. cycle variance) increases with greater innovation.

Combining the above cyclical process with the Marxian 'laws of motion' within Kalecki's work provide an organicist macroeconomic view of the economy. Rather than reducing the analysis to mechanistic aggregate demand components, Kalecki saw 'extended reproduction' through capital accumulation that embodies technical change with cheaper extension of technological developments (Kalecki, 1939a). This process comes up against effective demand failures that reduce investment spending, and with it the innovation process. 'The New Economy' has within its own endogenous development the contradiction of both massive expansion and its unravelling. Derived from this contradictory investment process emerges greater cyclical volatility for 'The New Economy' than the old established manufacturing-based economy. Under these conditions, much of the cyclical unemployment in downturns becomes serious structural unemployment in the next cyclical upturn. Empirical patterns of innovation-based investment cycles support this heightened volatility (Courvisanos 1996: 200–3). Only increased 'regularizing' from other components of effective demand (particularly government policies or the external sector) can counteract such increased instability.

A few significant short-term aspects of this greater investment volatility from 'The New Economy' have implications for Kalecki's short-term macroeconomic analysis. The most notable is in relation to private investment being the result of past decisions. This remains intact, but as there is a shorter payback period required of investment in 'The New Economy' with firms needing to discount the future strongly with shorter foresight, then investment cycle behaviour is more pronounced (see Hillinger *et al.* 1992). Two influences emanate from this behaviour. At the infant stage of the new technology there is a tendency for short bursts of profit growth followed by short profit declines leading to more frequent cycle periods in this sector (but in macroeconomic terms not yet significant). At the growth stage, the success of the new technology creates higher expectations of quick profit returns stimulating private investment strongly into what could be viewed as an unsustainable strong investment expansion.

The impact of wages on investment and demand becomes an open question in the volatile 'New Economy'. The Fordist wage–labour nexus is where wages are both a crucial cost and a key determinant of consumption (Boyer, 1988, p. 73). In 'The New Economy' the relatively lower labour direct (prime) costs are spread over large fixed costs as scale economies are quickly appropriated (Freeman and Soete 1997: 181). This means that in the infant stage wage costs are more important than in the growth stage. As 'The New Economy' expands, the labour cost element in investment decision-making becomes much less significant. The high productivity-high earnings link in new technology ensures strong consumption demand (Martin 1994: 344). A neoclassical reduction in wage cost policy could provide some short-term benefit to infant firms, but overall it would tend to have little effect on investment, while dampening consumption and exacerbating any cyclical downturn. From another angle, this seems to support Kalecki's analysis.

Two more Kalecki macro-relations can be briefly raised. Reasonably rigid profit margins under Fordist manufacture tend to become less rigid in 'The New Economy' under innovative and volatile competitive pressures, but over time as large new monopolies become entrenched (e.g. Microsoft) profit margins again become more rigid under investment planning mechanisms. The inelastic investment–interest rate relation does not seem to need revision under the new capitalism, particularly due to the unequal access to funding discussed later on in this section.

The essential novelty (or creative) element in innovation comes from Kalecki's 'semi-autonomous' variable '*d*' in his version II investment function which is subject to long-term changes, in particular technical progress (Kalecki 1954a: 98). In his (final) version III investment function (Kalecki 1968), two innovation effects on investment are identified. First, is the exogenous effect that relates to the intensity of technological innovation; this is the major creative aspect of innovation which provides the long-term trend over Kalecki's trendless pure investment cycle. Major new technical knowledge, in the form of the microelectronic revolution, Kalecki would describe as a random shock for generating growth (Sawyer 1985: 68). However, this exogenous innovation is clearly '... rooted in the past economic, social and technological developments rather than determined fully by the coefficients of our equations as is the case with the business cycle' (Kalecki 1971a: 183). The intensity of the technical progress of a society and its path of economic development is governed by the extent of such major exogenous innovation. A ceiling on the rate of growth of capital accumulation is determined by the level of adoption of the major technology within any particular economy. This variable, to Kalecki, is 'semi-autonomous' because the level of adoption is positively related to the size of the economy (Kalecki 1971a: 175).

Kalecki provides a behavioural 'micro-level' investment motivation related to this 'semi-autonomous' variable. The motivation for introducing major technological innovations initially is '... to increase profitability by reducing production costs' (Kalecki and Szeworski, 1957: 377). Kalecki (1954a: 17–18) sees this motivation in relation to innovations' long-term influence on raising the degree of monopoly. Further, he identifies entrepreneurs who invest 'today' in innovations as having '... an advantage over those having invested "yesterday" because of the technical novelties that have reached them' (Kalecki, 1971a, p.173). This gives what Steindl (1964, p. 430) finally recognizes as an active role for innovation, with major technical change (like ICT) creating an asymmetric action that delivers a predominantly stimulating effect, lengthening expansion and shortening contraction phases of investment cycles.[13] How this occurs takes us into the endogenous effects of innovation.

Second, is the endogenous effect that relates to the speed (or rate) of technological innovation. With the endogenous effect, go-ahead entrepreneurs are induced to introduce innovations in order to gain market share and increase their profit rate over the constant average profit rate assumed by Kalecki in the pure trendless investment cycle. This innovation can be seen as 'part and parcel' of investment decision-making. At the macro-level, the ICT-based 'new Economy' has a strong Schmookler (1966) demand–pull effect so that aggregate investment expansion works through a swarming of innovatory behaviour in a step-wise process described by Goodwin (1990: 86).[14]

The final behavioural element based on Kalecki that can be applied to 'The New Economy' relates to inequality. The class analysis in Kalecki seems initially inappropriate to the new technology world where unions are disappearing as fast as new Internet entrepreneurs are appearing, leading to the seeming disempowerment (if not the disappearance) of labour. At two deeper levels this is quite inaccurate. Class analysis is theorizing in terms of groups, with inherent collective coherent behaviour involved, in contrast to methodological individualism that is an absurd reductionist explanation of complex interdependent socioeconomic phenomena. In Kalecki power centres in one group: the entrepreneurs who are '... a controlling group of big shareholders' (Kalecki 1954a: 93) that manage the firm. Such power has effects at two levels.

The first level is with the entrepreneurial function itself. Kalecki has a concise entrepreneurship quotation that challenges the (still) dominant orthodox economics position on the efficient capital market. It also questions the orthodox management-based entrepreneurship position on the central role of 'entrepreneurial ability':

> Many economists assume, at least in their abstract theories, a state of business democracy where anybody endowed with entrepreneurial ability can obtain capital for starting a business venture. This picture of the activities of the 'pure' entrepreneur is, to put it mildly, unrealistic. The most important prerequisite for becoming an entrepreneur is the *ownership* of capital.
>
> (Kalecki 1971a: 109; italics in the original)

The entrepreneurial function is significant if it leads to investment in ICT, and this means a need to explain how innovation is financed. The extreme difficulty pioneer ICT-based innovators as a group have to finance new venture creations compares with the financial 'deep pockets' of large corporations for research and development (Legge and Hindle 1997: 507). Thus, the process of innovation in 'The New Economy' is inherently unequal in terms of economic power *within* the capitalist class.

The second level is related to inequality in an 'entrepreneur economy' and its implications for information inequality. The source of inequality stems from the basic Kaleckian proposition that capitalists 'earn what they spend', while workers 'spend what they earn'. By investment, capitalists determine the extent of their own profits, with the residual in wages going to labour. Since entrepreneurs are the sub-group of capitalists that make the investment decisions, they are the causal element of volatility and innovation in the capitalist system.[15] In this sense, they determine the level and distribution of income.[16] Galbraith (1998) is an admirable book that makes the link between Keynesian demand and Schumpeterian change to look at growing US pay inequality, to which Kalecki's income distribution model would add stronger theoretical generalizations rather than the specifics of the USA in the Galbraith study.

Further, Kalecki's same aphorism can be applied in a behavioural approach to information poverty directly. The ICT-based investment spending and related endogenous innovation feeds back through profit reinvestment into greater knowledge-based economic power. This reinforces the 'creative' power of information. This 'innovation control' power of entrepreneurs to decide on reproduction of technology provides the information-rich with the financial and knowledge-based wherewithal to maintain and extend information inequality. Labour that has limited 'New' knowledge is potentially subject to exploitation in situations like call centres, or to remain in long-term unemployment (Courvisanos 2000).

The evolutionary economic process and technical change

Beginning with Nelson and Winter (1982), there has been a large explosion of research work in what is broadly termed 'evolutionary economics' (Hodgson 1997: 10–14). Evolutionary economics has reached a level of intellectual rigour, relevance, and prolificacy that it has been recently touted as the possible new economic paradigm (Bryant and Wells 1998). There are different versions of modern evolutionary economics that are examined in great detail by Hodgson (1993, 1997), Foss (1994) and Nelson (1995). This section briefly outlines the essential elements of the evolutionary process that are generally agreed to by the above reviews of the evolutionary literature, and applies them to technical change within 'The New Economy'. As this exposition unfolds, there will be various 'bookmarks' that will signal links to the Kaleckian behavioural analysis from the previous section, providing opportunities for cross-fertilization between the two research paradigms.

At the behavioural level, technical change and innovation is surrounded by technical and market uncertainty creating imperfect information. This is the starting point for all evolutionary processes, as it is with 'Kaleckian behaviouralism'. Evolutionary writers, particularly in the area of industrial organization, examine human agency within the firm that creates chance and spontaneity. This allows complexity-type analysis to be used to come up with various outcomes that are not predetermined by the assumptions of the model. These outcomes have much to do with learning processes through feedback and interaction of agents. This leads to knowledge accumulation, path-dependence and increasing rates of diffusion of innovation. Kalecki was well aware of these issues as they relate to investment, both in terms of the lags he allowed in the investment process, but even more in the analysis of the traverse within socialist investment planning models.[17]

To handle uncertainty at an operational level, evolutionists acknowledge the role of bounded (or procedural) rationality needed by agents to derive rules-of-thumb, conventions and guideposts that allow non-optimal decisions to be made. Only through operation of these rules will knowledge be extended in the inductive way that permeates the innovation culture. This knowledge then allows the feedback and interaction in behaviour that leads to learning. Essential at this operational level is the need to be flexible with the operational rules, so that learning can infuse the actions in the next iterative period of decision-making. The various static and dynamic rules in Kalecki and his socialist modelling work on perspective planning provides a strong juxtaposition to the learning processes encompassed in the evolutionary operations.

Economic change occurs via technology, both at the broad technological revolution level and also at the level of incremental innovation. This change happens as a result of the operational aspects outlined above. Change comes in a form that is cumulative, irreversible and reflective of historical time and the socio-economic forces that drive society. The cumulative process is not optimal. As a result of the learning process the technological system is one that mutates, selects and adopts certain forms of knowledge and capital stock for the production process. This is the *evolution* of the system, in the sense that economic development unfolds over time in an iterative way to reveal a changing economy. The muddled process of change is one that at times can be gradual change (especially when there is only incremental innovation occurring at relatively low levels) and other times extremely rapid and revolutionary (when there is a major technological revolution occurring with many experimentations and failures).

Kalecki can also be linked to evolutionary change by his concept of the 'semi-autonomous' variable that alters the investment function, as well as incremental innovation that is part of the investment decision. Economic growth is not a stable process for Kalecki, recognizing changes over historical time can be both positive and negative. The one aspect that Kalecki can contribute to the evolution process is the clear chain of short-term decisions that make up the long-run. This is in effect a learning and mutation process, but with recognition for the role of decision-making within the short-term horizon. Demand plays a crucial determinant in such short-term decisions. There is a tendency for evolutionary writers to concentrate on the long-run processes, without explaining the short-term decisions that effectively provide the 'learning' environment for what occurs in the evolutionary process.

Three evolutionary economic papers are mentioned here for they attempt significant linkage with post-Keynesian analysis by looking at the short-term implications of evolutionary processes. Freeman and Perez (1988) is a seminal theoretical exposition which outlines the structural crisis involved in the transition to the 'The New Economy' and shows how this increases the instability of investment behaviour along the lines examined in this chapter. In the process of structural crisis, a deep recession (of the type experienced in the early 1990s) as defined by Freeman and Perez forms a basic part of change to the new dominant techno-economic paradigm. This strikes an accord with Kalecki's process of economic growth through cyclical instability and its impact on cyclical/structural unemployment.

The other two chapters are more recent empirical-based macroeconomic modelling experiments that use post-Keynesian analytical elements. Toivanen *et al.* (1996) identifies the uncertainty and macroeconomic volatility that emerges out of investment in new technology. In the process of this change, diffusion rates of technology are linked to high growth economies with real interest rate effects not hampering this process and inflation actually speeding up this diffusion. Not surprisingly, Toivanen *et al.* views the presence of macroeconomic volatility as slowing diffusion. Verspagen adopts a short-run input–output model and shows that investment demand increases with higher technological progress, but '... this is not enough to compensate for the more efficient use of other factors (labour, intermediate demand)' (Verspagen 2002: 14). The analysis also shows that a service economy scenario yields stronger growth than an 'environment-friendly through electronics' scenario. In strategic policy terms, '. . . above average competitiveness is a powerful way of creating economic growth . . . [and] being specialized in the "right" sectors is seen to pay off in terms of higher growth . . . [although] it is not easy to determine which sectors are the right ones' (Verspagen 2002: 16, 17–18).

Finally, the evolutionary writers recognize systemic failures that result from the above processes. Smith (1998: 41–4) identifies these failures as related to (i) infrastructural provision and investment; (ii) transitional adjustments; (iii) lock-in technology; and (iv) institutional (or regulatory) weaknesses. The type and extent of specific failures under these headings is very long, extending from unsustainable natural environments to outmoded regulatory practices, to long-term unemployment, to breakdown of public health systems, etc. These failures are the rationale for public policy actions. Here too Kalecki's voice can be barely heard in the wildernesses behind optimal neo-liberalism. It was Kalecki's concerns with the structural impacts of capitalism across all such systemic failures that made Kalecki a life-long supporter of public policy planning towards a more stable and equitable society, which would in turn deliver more efficient long-term economic outcomes.

A Kaleckian evolutionary research agenda

Kaleckian behaviouralism in the form outlined above could be the foundation link to the evolutionary process needed to regain the organistic perspective of Keynes' own macroeconomics, while also making it applicable to institutions of the new ICT-based economic environment represented by Thurow's third industrial revolution. Evolutionary economists have made tentative steps to incorporate post-Keynesian elements into their models (e.g. Verspagen 2002), and to empirically show the role of Keynesian demand in the technological innovation story (e.g. Brouwer and Kleinknecht 1999). However, as noted earlier, there does not seem to be any explicit attempts by post-Keynesians to relate their work to evolutionary economics.[18]

Seven areas are set out below in the Kaleckian–evolutionary research agenda that can regain the organistic perspective, while adding a 'New Economy' institutionalism:

- i Analysis of the endogenous/exogenous innovation dichotomy and the institutional links between them. This could use the short-term causal chain in Kalecki to appreciate how endogenous innovation reacts with investment to affect cycles-cum-growth patterns. Feedbacks from structural change to short-term effects need to be also investigated. Steindl (1952) began this evolutionary project,[19] but has been rarely elaborated since then.[20]
- ii Traverse issues on the cumulative path of investment and innovation are difficult to tease out, yet they provide crucial theoretical links on how the economy moves over time both in regions where diffusion of

technology is high and regions where it is low. Kaleckians can build on much theory and empirics in evolutionary research by adding the short-term behavioural perspective on firm/industry decision-making. Kaldor's cumulative causation principle can be used to link with evolutionary concepts of lock-in and path-dependence. In this way analysis of regional development and policies can be made effective, beginning with Kaldor (1970).

iii Keynesian macroeconomic models have a strong application to real economies, where the '. . . macro-evolutionary models apply some rather strong assumptions on the macroeconomic structure, which make it hard to implement such models empirically (Verspagen 2002: 2). The demand-side approach from Kaleckian macroeconomic models can be linked to the supply-side technological change factors in evolutionary models thereby removing the reductionist element in macro-modelling and gaining better 'strategic competitive' implications. This should lead to better policy analysis, even at the cost of less predictive ability (but not necessarily any less predictive power).

iv Effective demand analysis is the Kaleckian 'competitive edge' over other economic models. Research is required to maintain this edge by extending the analysis from Fordist manufacturing-based economy to ICT service-based economy. Earlier in this chapter some tentative thoughts on the impact of this structural change on Kalecki's effective demand story were set out in relation to wage changes, profit margins, investment lags, interest rates and private investment volatility. Much needs to be done to support or reject these 'thoughts'. Such conclusions could then be applied to questions of incomes policies, taxation of profits, interest rate policy and (most crucially) ways to gain and maintain full employment in the face of intensified private investment volatility (see also seventh point below on the state's role).

v Rules and conventions set in terms of Kaleckian models have had difficulty in explaining when these rules change, the direction of change and the extent of change. When are customs replaced and by what? Kaleckians need a stronger behavioural base of the type outlined in this chapter to answer such questions. It is only through contributions from innovation-based evolutionary analysis that there can be some effective resolution of these questions of micro-level behavioural changes (e.g. Bianchi 1990).

vi 'Kalecki's theory of income distribution is one of the most debated parts of his legacy. Various aspects of this theory have been discussed, criticized, and empirically tested in dozens of articles and many books' (Kalecki 1938: 479). This theory has been an effective counter to neoclassical factor distribution and with it providing an appreciation of monopoly capitalism within the specific confines of manufacturing industry under the second industrial revolution (Baran and Sweezy 1966: 53–6). Now the task is broader, to take the two elements of Kalecki's inequality related to 'The New Economy' on financing innovation and capitalist information-rich reproduction into an understanding of information poverty. The project would be the 'New' version of labour income 'poverty'. This is the most speculative of the agenda issues, with little to go on. Even the evolutionary writers have not examined the inequality issues of 'The New Economy', except in relation to regional sectors with limited spillover effects (e.g. Caniels 1999).

vii Role of the state in 'The New Economy', as indicated in this chapter, has to be different to the manufacturing-based public policy actions in a micro-macro dichotomy. No such dichotomy can exist in the 'New' policy framework. Policy must be articulated in an iterative (or perspective) planning approach that coincides with the nature of the innovation process. An instrumental analysis to policy along the lines of Lowe (1976) is required, where the starting point is where you want to end up. A long-term strategy is set through a grass roots mechanism with short-term specific perspective plans that are monitored and reviewed regularly, as suggested by Kalecki (Nuti 1986). As the current global economy has policy-makers floundering on the way forward to re-regulation, there is 'room to move' for a new political economy to replace the one so succinctly described by Kalecki (1943).[21]

Epilogue

My task in this chapter is completed. There has been an attempt to show how Kalecki can remain relevant in a global economy that has changed so significantly since he was born a century ago. 'The New Economy' is *not* centrally based on manufacturing and all its related institutional elements that have led to much debate over Kalecki's work: degrees of monopoly, capacity utilizations, inventory adjustments, pricing with constant costs, trade union wage struggle, etc. The field of play has shifted and the rules of the game have changed, Kalecki needs to be able to play on the new field with new rules for his analysis to remain relevant for contemporary capitalism. The essence of the argument is that if Kalecki's fundamental behavioural perspectives are revived in an organic whole and linked with recent evolutionary economics research, then basic Kaleckian insights will significantly inform modern economic analysis as it has done for manufacturing-based Keynesian economics from the 1940s onwards.

Postscript, September 2002

No changes have been made to this chapter since its original version in September 1999, except for shortening of some passages and updating of references that have been published since 1999. Two years on, however, there have been some dramatic changes in the ICT sector. Notably, the 'tech wreck' which began in late March 2000, when the US index measure for the new Internet (dotcom) company shares peaked and then collapsed. This was a typical bursting of a financial bubble on the back of an overpriced new area of economic expansion. The ICT industrial revolution discussed in this chapter is still with us. Industry has not thrown out their computers, nor have they stopped upgrading quickly their new technology. All the six dimensions of 'The New Economy' set out in the chapter are still major aspects of modern capitalism. To the extent that the financial bubble burst affected business confidence in production of real technology, the investment cycle did move into a downswing affecting the macroeconomic environment with reduced employment opportunities. ICT is such an essential part of business investment in the global knowledge-intensive economy that the downswing relates to the highly volatile nature of any new industrial revolution. Of all ICT revenues 60 per cent come from the services sector that remains the main bulwark of 'The New Economy' (Needham, 2002). A recent chapter by evolutionary economist Professor Verspagen and myself has taken up the first of the research agenda items set out in this chapter (Courvisanos and Verspagen 2002). In it we indicate that the pattern of this latest business cycle reflects past patterns of effective demand failure within the context of an evolving new industrial revolution.

Notes

1 Revised with Postscript, September 2002.
2 Lavoie (1992: 94–148) explicitly sets his theory of the firm within this manufacturing context, with its 'cost-determined' pricing and reserves of manufacturing/distribution capacity. Other notable Kaleckian manufacturing-based analyses are Steindl (1952), Asimakopulos (1977), Sylos-Labini (1979), and Arestis *et al.* (1985–6).
3 See Lavoie (1992: 7) for the full 'presuppositions' in the post-classical research programme.
4 The neo-classical paradigm recognizes this new technological revolution and has attempted in recent work to analyse its effects, even if it is in a limited way. See Caselli (1999).
5 See Hollanders *et al.* (1999: 18–25) for empirical details of all three processes. It is interesting to note that Australia has also seen similar strong economic growth (4.6 per cent over the year to December 1998), but only from the mid-1990s (Huh 1999). The lack of innovation in Australia has not prevented it from quickly adopting all three forms of innovation from the USA, both in the form of consumption and investment spending (Goldsworthy 1997: 103–7). The lag in Australia's strong growth rate compared to the USA reflects this adoption time.
6 See Caselli (1999: 80, n3) on the types of manufacturing equipment arising from ICT systems.
7 For example, the wine industry is increasingly using ICT-based knowledge input to produce large and consistent wine output, while its product demand is increasingly dependent on knowledge of wines, adoption in restaurants, product endorsement in entertainment outlets, and wine-based tourism (Ruthven 1998).
8 For detailed statistics on information-poor, see UNDP (1999).
9 See Courvisanos (1996: 217–32) on how the state can 'tame uncertainty' while at the same time restructuring sectors and regions through comprehensive investment planning.

10 *The Journal of Post Keynesian Economics* (US publication) prior to Volume 21 (1998–9) has no articles centrally on 'The New Economy' or generally on the *evolution* of innovation and technology. In Volume 21, Khalil (1998–9) and Setterfield (1999) provide some evolutionary glimpses, Thurow (1998) and Appelbaum and Schettkat (1999) examine structural change, and Legge (1999) is a book review of Galbraith (1998). *The Cambridge Journal of Economics* (UK publication) dedicated a whole issue to technology and innovation (Vol. 19(1), February 1995). All the articles came from the broadly evolutionary economics approach, but there was no attempt in any of them to link their analyses to 'the tradition founded by Marx, Keynes, Kalecki, Joan Robinson and Kaldor'. Brouwer and Kleinknecht (1999) is a short *CJE* note that *does* make this type of effort. Kaleckian influences were not perceived by this author in any of the articles referred to in this note.

11 See Rostow (1990: 272–82) for an account of changes between the two books on the innovation issue.

12 Bortis' broad attempt at a political economy with institutions and behaviour is a very recent example of ignoring to handle technology and innovation in cycles and growth in any significant endogenous way *within* the processes of capitalism. Yet, then Bortis proposes economic policies related to technical change (Bortis 1997: 339–41).

13 Entrepreneurial motivation by Kalecki and Steindl in this paragraph is reflected in an untypical Kaldor lecture on the 'volatility of entrepreneurial expectations' (Kaldor 1954). This points towards the partial unpacking of Kaldor's concept of the technical progress function conducted by Nelson and Winter (1982) and with strong empirical support from evolutionary economists (see next section).

14 Brouwer and Kleinknecht (1999) provide empirical evidence from the R&D intensity in Dutch manufacturing and services firms across two years 1988 and 1992. This research lends support to the Schmookler-induced demand pull effect that creates a Goodwin-type swarming of innovations. Industries that are slow to adapt to the ICT-based technological paradigm will have a weak investment expansion cycle, compared to the strong investment expansion in leading ICT-based industries. This market power related to innovation is in evidence by Geroski *et al.* (1993) that found that profits in innovating firms make them more resistant to business cycle recessions.

15 The remaining capitalists are 'rentiers' who basically spend on capitalist luxury consumption goods.

16 See Asimakopulos (1975) and Kriesler (1987) for detailed analyses of Kalecki's income distribution models.

17 Formally the 'traverse' is 'the dynamic (out of equilibrium) adjustment path in historical time' (Kriesler 1989: 1–2).

18 I would be interested in being advised of any such attempts that I may have missed.

19 This has been recognized by the current researchers in evolutionary economists, e.g. Silverberg and Verspagen (1997: 137).

20 See Courvisanos (1996) for a recent effort along this trajectory.

21 Three recent papers by the author have attempted to tackle this crucial policy issue: Courvisanos (1998) on sustainable environmental planning; (2000) on innovation policy; (2001) on regional policy.

4 Kaleckian crucial reform of capitalism and after

Tadeusz Kowalik

My short chapter contains more exegesis of Kalecki's texts than theorizing, it belongs more to the *history* of economic thought than to the economic *theory*. I would like to reconsider Kalecki's most general views on the last century capitalism as a socioeconomic system. Or, as I call it – on the capitalist mega-system, which even now, in the era of globalization, is split into many different systems.

Kalecki's message

These remarks are mainly caused by many misunderstandings which arose from, or were created by, Kalecki's last article, published posthumously:[1] 'The observations on crucial reform' (Kalecki 1971, 1991). The controversial character of this article was already stressed by the unusual way in which it was published. Sent to the Italian political monthly review *Critica Marxista*, it was published with more than a year's delay, and not in the journal it was sent to, but in a rather more peripheral bimonthly review. Moreover, it was supplemented with a long and far going criticism (practically a rebuttal of Kalecki's main idea) written by the well known Italian Marxist economist, Antonio Pesenti.

The main message of Kalecki's article is clear even in its title: a crucial reform of the capitalist system has been – in his opinion – quite successfully implemented in the main capitalist countries. Kalecki saw this as a paradoxical outcome of the class struggle. I quote the main theses:

> Let us imagine that the strong pressure of the masses leads to such a radical reform of the system, in spite of the opposition of the ruling class, that, without abolishing existing relations of production, a new valve is opened for the development of forces of production. There will then be a paradoxical situation: a 'crucial reform' imposed on the ruling class may stabilize the system, temporarily at least. As we argue below, we have to do with just such a situation in contemporary capitalism.
>
> (CW II: 467)

And further we read:

> Government intervention in the expansion of market became an institution, making it possible to limit unemployment to a few per cent, and hence in practice to accept something similar to 'the right to work' slogan. . . . This state of affairs (along with a considerable expansion of social security) led to a certain transformation of the working class, which on the whole became radically reformist in its attitude toward capitalism.
>
> (ibid.: 472)

This 'neo-capitalism', or reformed capitalism, as Kalecki labelled it, shaped by strong pressure of the masses, was also the result of the favourable international environment, namely of the emergence of the Soviet socialist camp, and the rivalry between the two camps, each having its own superpower.

For Pesenti the very idea of even temporal stabilization of the capitalist system was unacceptable. It meant for him an underestimation of its 'internal contradictions, especially economic ones' (ibid. 612).

From political business cycle to the long upturn

Pesenti's contention was perhaps too dogmatic, but similar opinions were also put forward by numerous Kalecki's followers. They were at least surprised by Kalecki's stability thesis. Why? The simplest explanation is, because it was for Kalecki something unusual. He was for a long time well known as a theoretician very sceptical with regard to the capitalist developmental possibilities and similarly about the reformability of capitalism. In many publications he was (still is) labelled as a stagnationist, or, as in one of the newest criticisms, as a painter of a 'bleak picture'.

In a different wording, this pessimistic attitude of Kalecki has also been expressed by Joan Robinson. Evaluating Kalecki's contribution to the theory of effective demand, she stressed that Kalecki, strong in his analysis of business cycle (short-run), was not that sure of himself in his views of long-run processes. Partly because he was lacking a definite theory of investment decisions. She wrote:

> I had a running argument with Michal on this subject. He regarded my use of the concept of 'animal spirit' as somehow irrational though to me it was only a modification of the Marxian imperative: 'Accumulate! Accumulate! That is Moses and the Prophets' [Robinson 1977: x]. He [Kalecki] maintained that new inventions raise prospects of profit and accumulate investment.
>
> (Robinson 1977: 17)

By the way, this opinion of Joan Robinson is rather surprising, because one could have assumed that while editing and introducing Rosa Luxemburg's

The Accumulation of Capital, she accepted the main line of thinking of this Polish–German economist, who stressed that accumulation of savings and real investments are not automatically identical and this creates vital difficulties to the very existence of capitalism. Kalecki tried to solve the problems which were left by her.

He thus explains his criticism of Marx's approach as represented in the well-known schemata of reproduction:

> His [Marx's] system can be in equilibrium only when automatic expanded reproduction is assumed, i.e. when there is a complete reinvestment of accumulation. Such an assumption is in line with classical economics, to which Marx linked himself. From the spirit of Marx's analysis it follows that this reinvestment does not always take place, and hence there is a deviation from his schemata. This deviation, which Marx did not systematically investigate, is more consistently emphasized by Rosa Luxemburg . . . Marx's schemata were constructed in a period when the question of [insufficient] demand played a lesser role [and they] represent a certain ideal equilibrium, which is in contradiction with the fundamental and often-quoted statement of Marx on the incommensurable development of forces of production and the expansion of purchasing power.
>
> (Kalecki CW II: 559)[2]

Kalecki is still more equivocal when relating his approach to E. Domar's model rather than theory of growth:

> The idea of steady growth was well known in classical economics: savings are accumulated and transformed into investments which in turn generate growth. Innovation, which is prominent not only in Domar but also in Harrod, takes for its starting-point not accumulation changed into investment, but investment decisions, and then it is argued that investments below the requirements of balanced growth cause a breakdown, disturbing the equilibrium and giving rise to a cumulative downward movement. . . . Domar's theory can be interpreted as a pure demand model, but then it ceases to be a growth theory. If balanced growth appears in fact unstable, then it really is non-existent. . . . According to Harrod, this ends with cyclical fluctuations around the trend line, but I have tried to show that it ends in cyclical fluctuations around a quasi-static position and exogenous factors are required to ensure a lasting long-run development.
>
> (ibid.: 559)[3]

These two tendencies in explaining capitalist dynamics have lasted until nowadays. Sometimes even those who outline very gloomy prospects for capitalism tend to explain it by an animal drive for over-accumulation and over-investment. This is the main idea of a recently published book, much discussed in the West, *The economics of global turbulence* by Robert Brenner (1998).

Although it is not my purpose here to consider the controversy between Joan Robinson and Kalecki, I am tempted to think that such an 'animal spirit' might have been a historical phenomenon, quite adequate to the heroic period of capitalism, dominated by individual (Schumpeterian) entrepreneurs. Contrary to this, the mature capitalism of big corporations needs some special (or stronger) incentives for accumulation and investment. A sharp division between economic performance of the first quarter of the century after World War II, and the second quarter lies just in this. These special incentives have been created by state intervention. I will come back to this with regard to the present criticism of Kalecki's theory, but leaving aside Joan Robinson's views.

Let us try to answer the question why Kalecki decided to invent the new concept, not referring to his older notions, like 'the regime of the political business cycle' or 'capitalism of full employment' which he used in his famous, hundreds of times quoted essay 'Political aspects of full employment' (1943b, 1991). This is simultaneously an attempt to reconcile Kalecki's general pessimism with his optimistic concept of crucial reform of the capitalist economy in the third quarter of the last century.

In 1943 Kalecki distinguished (besides fully fledged wild capitalism) two stages of the reformed capitalism. The '*regime of the political business cycle*' was to mean a policy which in the 1960s obtained in England the name of 'stop and go' policy, stemming from the belief that a continuous full employment policy would undermine the power of business leaders to control the workers. The higher stage of reforms would mean '*full employment capitalism*' and for this to become a reality – I quote Kalecki's words – 'a fundamental reform will have been incorporated in it' which would develop new social and political institutions to reflect a substantial participation of the working class.[4] At that time Kalecki thought that without such a fundamental reform capitalism would be scrapped as an outmoded system. Fascism or socialism was to be the alternative outcome. This was the meaning of the last sentence of his 1943 paper: 'The fight of the progressive forces for full employment was at the same time a way of preventing the recurrence of fascism'.

Let us take up now the situation of the Western World in the 1960s. Kalecki wrote several times about the radically changed situation, particularly, that capitalism evidently did not face the danger of being scrapped as an outmoded system. Not only did he not expect any socialist revolution, but he felt that even 'full employment capitalism', as defined in his 1943 essay, was behind the horizon. He would not repeat his much earlier statement that 'what the masses now ask for is not the mitigation of slumps but their total abolition'. This perspective belonged either to the remote past or to the distant future. If there was a change of view, it was the result of a changed situation. Now, to use his own words, the masses seemed to demand not the abolition of the system, but the mitigation of slumps. This became the crucial assumption of his new article.

In the 1943 article he assumed that government intervention in this regime of the political business cycle would be limited to public investment ruling out subsidies to consumption. He then postulated, clearly as a part of the concept of 'full employment capitalism', the application of such measures as family allowances, old age pensions, reduction in indirect taxation, subsidizing prices of necessities. But at the end of an exceptional decade as were the 1960s Kalecki could have thought that, under strong pressure of the masses, these postulates were more or less fulfilled. In this sense capitalist reforms went further than to a simple 'stop and go' policy. Even the consequences of such a policy mean that cycles became milder simply because the anti-recession policy led to a strengthening of the so-called automatic stabilizers. For example, Kennedy and Johnson are praised for reducing poverty almost by half. This means that a part of budget expenditures became inflexible, less prone to fluctuations. Let us recall the controversy between Kennedy and the Council of Economic Advisers, which shows that Kennedy's team went further than a conventional 'stop and go' policy, promoting investment even in a period of economic revival.

The Kennedy and Johnson presidential years belonged to triumphant economists as true creators of economic policy, or perhaps more than that, creators of the threshold of a new economic system.[5] Walter Heller, at that time chairman of the Council of Economic Advisers, reports about a meeting with Kennedy at the Economic Club of New York (the big business community): after his speech on cutting taxes Kennedy said to him: 'I gave them straight Keynes and Heller and they (the business community) loved it' (Heller 1966: 35).

What was new in their policy? The novelty was that Kennedy came to the parliament and the business community with the proposal to cut taxes not during a recession but at a time when recovery was already on. And this happened after a long battle of Heller and other advisers for an economic policy designed not only to fight recessions, but also to promote growth. It was the time of the second conflict over Berlin. Initially Kennedy proposed a tax increase (of US$3 billion) to finance Berlin defence. Moreover, he wanted to balance the state budget already in the fiscal year 1963. In opposition to this, the economic advisers were arguing for the continuation of tax-cutting policy, and have finally won. Early in 1963 Kennedy launched a massive tax cut and the economy started to boom. In Heller's words it was to be 'a new era in American economic policy'.

I have a feeling that there was no such new era in the motherland of Keynesianism, the United Kingdom. To give an example: in 1965 I visited England endowed with introductory letters from Oskar Lange to several leaders of the then ruling Labour Party. I went there with the naive belief that the Labour Party was the embodiment of full employment policy. I said something to that effect to Thomas Balogh, one of the close advisers to

Prime Minister Harold Wilson, but he disillusioned me furiously. It seems that the Keynesian recipe was being implemented no more than half-heartedly. Thus, there was no such time in England as an era of economists deciding on the directions of economic policy. That is why Kalecki addressed his new concept to the United States and Germany without mentioning Britain.

Of course, looking back at the development of the world economy during the last quarter of the century, one may say that in 1969–70 Kalecki tended to be over-optimistic. After all, the concept of a 'crucial reform' in his intention was to be not only a summary of what has already happened, but also a forecast. True, at the end of his considerations Kalecki admitted that some signs of future destabilization could be seen, but they were rather weak. He wrote:

> The relative stability of reformed capitalism depends on a high degree of social conformity. One can express the cautious opinion that recent student movements seem to be an omen of the declining ability of the bourgeois power apparatus to manipulate new generations entering the historical scene. This phenomenon is all the more serious since, with the rapid progress in science and technology, intellectuals are beginning to play an ever greater role as a social group.
>
> (Kalecki 1991: 476)

Needless to say, further development did not confirm even this cautiously optimistic prognosis. After all, the year of publishing this chapter (1971) marked a turning point: it was in a sense the year of ending the era of Bretton Woods Accords and the two decades of remarkably successful Keynesian policy of welfare state. This was a period often termed as The Golden Age of capitalism. Since the beginning of the 1970s, the regime of crucially reformed capitalism became obsolete. Obsolete became also every idea of a socialist revolution. In the light of social and economic developments during the third quarter of the last century, the criticism offered by Antonio Pesenti sounds as totally belonging to the remote past. The following will suffice: 'Let us take the class struggle, for instance. At least in Italy the Communist party . . . has been able to set the goals of the struggle for a socialist transformation of society'.

The long downturn

My second question is whether Kalecki's concepts of the regime of political business cycle and of crucial reform may be helpful in explaining what happened in the world economy in the next quarter of century, termed by Robert Brenner (1998) as 'the long downturn', and in the present time to which he gave the label of 'global turbulence'.

I think that we do not find in Kalecki's writings any answer to the crises caused by the world turbulences in financial markets. In this respect the contribution of Keynes (particularly the idea of 'casino capitalism') is much more stimulating than that of Kalecki.

But the Kaleckian explanation of the long downturn seems to be very simple and fully symmetrical to the explanation of the long upturn: Kalecki would most probably say, that the essence of 'crucial reform' was the successful governance of overall demand. Withdrawal of this type of state intervention or its radical reduction must have caused a return of strong business fluctuations and hence a decline in the rate of economic growth. I would like to mention some evidence showing that political rulers indeed acted in this direction and were prepared to pay the recession price for reducing inflation and disciplining the workers.

First, the empirical research done by Sharon J. Erenburg (1984) and David Alan Aschauer (1998) shows a strong dependence of overall economic performance in the United States on investment in public capital (material and human infrastructure). These two authors have, I think, convincingly argued, that the relative decline of government investment in public capital which was started already in the late 1960s went on *pari passu* with – and has caused – a decline in the rate of growth of GDP and employment.

This refers to action of the government. On the non-action side, there is strong evidence that there was a longing for recession among OECD member countries. The Swedish economist Gosta Rehn, who spent several years as an expert at the OECD Headquarters and developed a critical attitude to this organization, noticed as highly probable that 'the sudden increase in unemployment after that first oil price jump in 1973 was not planned by governments. But when it occurred, they were pleased to see that unemployment was not as dangerous politically as many had thought' (Rehn 1987). Indeed, if we assume that OECD officials expressed the opinion of at least the majority of member governments, they did not leave any doubt about the priority given by the latter to price stability over employment and growth and hence about their acceptance of desirability of recession. Some remarkable quotations follow.

In the 1970 Report by the Secretary General of OECD we read: 'the problem of inflation arises in part from the very success of post-war economic policies in other directions – notably in achieving high levels of employment'. By now, however, there is an 'urgent need to give priority to price stability'. The author of the Report was fully conscious of the implications:

> 'Giving higher priority to price stability means giving lower priority to something else, and in a number of countries this may temporarily have to be growth and employment' (OECD 1970: 8–10; quoted after Korpi 1991: 335). The recommendation was very clear: 'Excess demand should be eliminated and governments should be prepared, where necessary, to accept a temporary reduction in the rate of activity until there are signs that better price stability has been achieved' (ibid.).

There remained, however, a serious problem of how to overcome the mentality of societies shaped by the 'crucially reformed capitalism'. The report continues:

> Today a serious recession would be clearly recognized to be the result of a deliberate policy being followed by the government while in the 1930s it could be thought that this was the result of a natural disaster. Therefore, the fundamental problem is how to get people to exercise the moderation that they would do if they believed that a major recession was possible, without actually having to administer the lesson.
>
> (ibid.: 35)

Seven years later, after the OPEC crisis, OECD recommended to the governments a passive attitude to unemployment in the following words: 'A less rapid reduction of unemployment now, in order to achieve lower level of unemployment later on' (OECD 1977: 26).

Conclusions

In summing up I come back to the comparative economic systems approach. Contrarily to a widely held conviction that Kalecki limited his interest to a general theory of capitalism, and at a later time also to a theory of the 'really existing socialism', we find in his writings concepts of a variety of capitalist economies: fully fledged capitalism; the regime of political business cycle; capitalism of full employment; and, finally, the crucially reformed capitalism, or neo-capitalism. In his other works, not mentioned here, we also find references to intermediate systems and mixed economies. We may also trace a variety of socialist economies, or 'socialisms' (centrally planned; planned and self-managed; crucially reformed, etc.), but this exceeds my present interest. What is important, is that in all these cases the key to his classifications lies in broadly understood socio-economic policies, in the role of the state and the scope and strength of participation of main social classes. One could write a textbook of comparative economic systems based only on Kaleckian terminology. In his seminal work 'The great transformation' Karl Polanyi (1944, 1962: 76) presented the concept of a double movement. In 'soldier's words' it means: marketization and privatization of the economy, if left to themselves, become socially destructive. Society, social movements and the state have to counteract these destructive tendencies as a means of self-protection. One could say that Michal Kalecki made a step further, distinguishing between various economic systems according to the degree of the society's capacity of self-defence.[6]

Notes

1 I co-authored this article. My role was limited, however, to the historical part of the essay (I wrote about the old controversy between Bernstein, Hilferding and Rosa Luxemburg). The article arose from our several discussions mainly about the need for a crucial reform of the 'really existing socialism'. Kalecki's idea was to show first that even capitalism had undergone the necessary reforms, and then he would have come to the most important task: outlining a 'crucial reform' of

socialism. He repeated several times that during the debate of the fifties he has underestimated the role of the market, employees' participation and decentralization. Unfortunately, he died a couple of months later.

2 These were remarks on the Janusz Gorski's paper 'On the development of the supply-and-demand models of economic growth in bourgeois economics', in *Zeszyty Naukowe Uniwersytetu Lodzkiego*, No. 10/1965.

3 I myself remember that when Kalecki was sending to the *Economic Journal* his last purely theoretical article on 'Trend and business cycles reconsidered' (1968), he told me this: 'my criticism of capitalism goes even further than that of Karl Marx. Marx took an expansion of capitalism for granted, whereas I think that you have to explain this by some exogenous factors'.

4 The closest historical example of the full employment capitalism would be the Scandinavian system which existed at least until the beginning of the 1990s.

5 Prior to that only the Swedish economists have in the 1930s already experienced their age of this type.

6 'Social history in the nineteenth century was thus the result of a double movement: the extension of the market organization in respect to genuine commodities was accompanied by its restriction in respect to ficticious ones. . . . Society protected itself against the perils inherent in a self-regulatory market system' (Polanyi 1944, 1962: 76).

Part II

The model

5 Money and finance in Kalecki's analysis

Malcolm Sawyer

Introduction[1]

This chapter argues that Kalecki's writings contain many significant insights on money and finance, and that his macroeconomic analysis had a greater appreciation of the role of the monetary sector than has been generally recognized. Dymski (1996: 116) notes that

> scholars are in broad agreement that Kalecki's monetary approach is underdeveloped. . . . We might add that monetary concepts seldom appear in Kalecki's mature writings; when they do, the author treats them sparingly. For example, in the various permutation of Kalecki's dynamic investment model, financial elements are incorporated only partially, and the banking system plays a passive role

and that 'Kalecki *purposely* set financial factors into the background of his model of the business cycle' (ibid.: 133: emphasis added).

However, it is argued here that Kalecki presented a number of ideas which now appear in the structuralist post-Keynesian analysis of endogenous money and in the circuitist approach, and that he did develop a substantial analysis of the workings of the monetary system. It has though to be acknowledged that Kalecki's writings on money were laconic (even by Kalecki's own standards) and he did not ever present a systematic analysis of the complete monetary and financial system.

Kalecki (like Keynes) viewed the rate of interest as in some sense a monetary phenomenon, and specifically not as a mechanism for bringing about the equality between savings and investment. Kalecki wrote that 'the rate of interest cannot be determined by the demand for and supply of capital because investment automatically brings into existence an equal amount of savings. Thus, investment "finances itself" whatever the level of the rate of interest. The rate of interest is, therefore, the result of the interplay of other factors' (CW II: 262). Thus an important aspect of any Kaleckian analysis of interest rates must be the influence of monetary and financial factors on interest rates, rather than any notion of the demand for and supply of loanable funds determining interest rates.

Kalecki can be seen to have used at least two modes of analysis (which are by no means unique to him). The first mode was in the nature of a thought experiment in which the effects of some specified change is tracked through, holding a range of other variables constant. This mode does not imply that the variables held constant are unimportant or do not actually change, but rather are held constant to facilitate the analysis and to illustrate some key points. Kalecki (CW I: 201–19) provides an example of this mode of reasoning in which he compares the operation of 'three systems'. The second mode was to seek to track changes in the economy through time, and this is evident in Kalecki's analysis of the trade cycle. Since the trade cycle is seen as a continuous process through time with no beginning and no end, it is impossible to talk of causation in the sense of an initial cause. It is also the case that the analysis of the trade cycle could be viewed as firmly based in historical time (in the sense of recognizing that time is irreversible).

The analysis of monetary factors in Kalecki can be seen as an uneasy mixture of these two modes of analysis. The operation of the trade cycle draws on the second mode and the upswing of the trade cycle requires credit creation (and the downswing may well involve some credit destruction). The creation and destruction of money and credit is intimately involved with the operation of the trade cycle. But the analysis of the ramifications of the creation of money is undertaken using the first mode of analysis (which is, in effect, a comparative static one).[2]

In one of his earliest papers, Kalecki acknowledged the link between the cycle and money creation. He asked:

> how can capitalists invest more than remains from their current profits after spending part of them for personal consumption? This is made possible by the banking system in various forms of credit inflation. Hence . . . without credit inflation there would be no fluctuations in investment activity. *Business fluctuations are strictly connected with credit inflation*. . . . A similar type of inflation is the financing of investments from bank deposits, a process usually not classified as inflation but one which perhaps has the greatest importance in the inflationary financing of investments during an upswing in the business cycle.
>
> (CW I: 148, 149; emphasis in original)[3]

Dymski argues that

> Kalecki's framework cannot be encompassed in a real analysis: his theoretical building blocks can be *consistently* combined only in a monetary analysis. Kalecki assumes a disequilibrium world; this implies a monetary analysis irrespective of any conditions imposed on preferences and technology. Further, a disequilibrium analysis like Kalecki's is inherently 'monetary' because agents seeking to carry value forward must rely on nominal assets whose real value is not predetermined within the system.
>
> (Dymski 1996: 122)

However, as Dymski goes on to note, Kalecki developed a real, rather than a monetary, model. The neglect of monetary factors is even more evident in models which have attracted the label of Kaleckian or with the name of Kalecki linked with that of Steindl have been analyses of 'reals' without money or finance involved in any essential way. Further, Kalecki's 'writings treat monetary and financial dimensions of economic fluctuations in a bifurcated way: in describing aggregate dynamics, Kalecki does not consistently draw out the implications of the monetary factors he introduces at the microeconomic level' (ibid.: 133).

Kalecki's writings on money were undertaken in the 1930s and early 1940s and hence refer to his interpretation of the prevailing monetary arrangements at that time, and some of his writings refer to Poland in the early 1930s and others to the UK in the late 1930s and early 1940s. This is reflected in his treatment of gold as part of the stock of money when writing in 1932 (reprinted as CW I: 147–55), as cash as the main medium of exchange for wage-earners (see below) and the Central Bank as a direct lender to the private sector.

Credit money and investment

In his writings in the 1930s, in which Kalecki advanced the crucial role of investment in the expansion of the level of economic activity, he clearly saw the key role of the extension of credit in the financing of that expansion. But the main focus of that analysis was on investment decisions, and not on the extension of credit, which was viewed as generally granted permissively enabling investment to occur. He used the working assumption that 'the financing of additional investment is effected by the so-called creation of purchasing power. The demand for bank credit increases, and these are granted by the banks' (CW I: 190). However he argued that credit was generally available at the relevant prevailing rate of interest, though noting that banks could respond to an increased demand for loans by raising the corresponding rate of interest:

> [T]he possibility of stimulating the business upswing is based on the assumption that the banking system, especially the central bank, will be able to expand credits without such a considerable increase in the rate of interest. If the banking system reacted so inflexibly to every increase in the demand for credit, then no boom would be possible on account of a new invention, nor any automatic upswing in the business cycle. . . . Investments would cease to be the channel through which additional purchasing power, unquestionably the *primus movens* of the business upswing, flows into the economy.
>
> (CW I: 489)

In a similar vein, he argued that

> if this rate [of interest] were to increase sufficiently fast for the influence of the increase in gross profitability to be fully offset, an upswing would prove impossible. There is thus a close connection between the phenomenon of the business cycle and the response of the banking system to the increase in demand for money in circulation, at a rate of interest which is not prohibitive to the rise in investment.
>
> (CW I: 473)

Kalecki made six further significant points to which little attention has been paid, even in commentaries on Kalecki's work. First, there is reflux (though Kalecki did not use that terminology) whereby the initial expansion of loans circulates as deposits, and then some, if not all, of those deposits are used to repay loans.

> Disregarding the technical side of the money market, e.g. the variable demand for means of payment, we may say that these outlays are 'financing themselves'. Imagine, for instance, that some capitalists withdraw during a year a certain amount from their savings deposits, or borrow the amount at the central bank, in order to invest it in the construction of some additional equipment. In the course of the same year that amount will be received by other capitalists in the form of profits (since according to our assumptions, workers do not save), and again put into a bank as a savings deposit or used to pay off a debt to the central bank. Thus the circle will close itself.
>
> (CW I: 472)

Second, on the financing of demand, Kalecki began by analysing the case where balance sheet value of assets and liabilities remains constant during business cycle. He divided the liabilities of the consolidated balance sheet of banks[4] into: '(i) "unattached" deposits, i.e. deposits without a specific designation; (ii) investment reserves, i.e. funds used for the immediate financing of the production of capital goods; and (iii) money in circulation, i.e. cash balances and banknotes in circulation' (CW I: 93).[5]

When enterprises plan to increase investment, they shift funds from the 'unattached' deposits to the investment reserves. When I (investment orders) are greater than A (production of investment goods) then there is a net flow from (i) to (ii), which is taken to be typical of a cyclical upswing. When I is less than A, typical of the downswing, then the net flow would be in the reverse direction.

Kalecki then dropped the assumption of constant balance sheet value.

> In reality, the increased demand for investment reserves and money in circulation is met not only by a change of unattached deposits to deposits

> of specific designation but also by an expansion of the credit operations of banks, i.e. by credit inflation in the strict sense, when the assets and liabilities of banks increase. In other words, the increase of credits is matched on the side of assets by an increase in investment reserves, and on the side of liabilities by an increase of money in circulation.
>
> (CW I: 95)

Third, the reflux may not be complete and there can be some lasting expansion in the stock of money following an expansion of loan because of an increased transactions demand for money. Kalecki noted that there is 'an increased demand for money in circulation [in the upswing of the business cycle] in connection with the rise in production and prices' (Kalecki CW I: 93). Hence, the transactions demand to hold money increases. However, the transactions demand for money is influenced by relevant rates of interest:

> Fluctuations in the demand for investment reserves and money in circulation are tightly linked with changes in the rate of interest. For a partial conversion of unattached deposits into 'attached' accounts to take place, the spread between the 'credit' rate (the discount rate, interest on stocks and bonds, etc.) and the bank rate on deposits must increase. Only then will it pay owners of unattached deposits to invest in stocks and bonds, thereby providing funds for conversion to attached accounts. This greater spread between the credit rate and the bank rate on deposits is also required to stimulate the expansion of banks' credit operations, i.e. for credit inflation in the strict sense.
>
> (CW I: 96–7)

Kalecki envisaged that the relationship between the different rates of interest could change, and in particular that there is not a constant mark-up by banks as between, for example, the interest rate on loans and that on deposits.

Fourth, Kalecki considered an expansion of the banks' balance sheets driven by an increase in loans. He argued that the volume of bank deposits would be determined by the volume of bank loans, provided that interest rates adjusted so that the public were willing to hold that volume of bank deposits:

> It has been frequently maintained that bank deposits are fully determined by bank credits; and, in particular, that the movement of deposits in wartime depends on the amount of government borrowing from the banks. The statement is correct, but subject to the condition that the short-term rate of interest is allowed to vary. If, for instance, banks buy more bills while the total volume of business transactions is unchanged, bank deposits will rise but the short-term rate of interest must fall. If the short-term rate of interest is unchanged . . . current accounts will increase more or less proportionately with the volume of transactions.
>
> (CW VII: 159)

A footnote adds the caveat that 'provided there is no change in the habits of cash holding and there is no considerable shift between accounts of high and low velocity'. A significant aspect of this analysis is that the structure of interest rates is seen to change as the balance sheets change.

Fifth, an increase in investment and subsequent increase in output brings about a greater transactions demand and loans tend to increase (cf. CW I: 293–4).[6] Then 'banks are obliged to sell bills and bonds in order to expand their credits' (CW I: 294). The sale of bills increases the discount rate: Kalecki envisaged the central bank supplying cash by buying bills and bonds on the market (CW I: 293). He indicated that the interest rate on deposit accounts (corresponding to what we label M2/1 below) usually rose in line with the discount rate, and hence there would be little incentive for the time deposit holders to switch to bills. Current accounts (roughly now M1) bore a zero rate of interest at the time Kalecki was writing, and the holders of such accounts would then have an incentive to switch into bills: the transactions demand for that money declines. For the sale of bonds, Kalecki thought the effect on the interest rate on bonds would be rather less than the effect on the discount rate. However, he then argued that 'it is plausible that a deposit-owner . . . may be induced to buy bonds even though the rate on deposits has increased much more than the yield of bonds' (CW I: 296).

The particular significance of this discussion is that both relative and absolute interest rates change in respond to an increased demand for loans. It can also be noted that Kalecki viewed the central bank discount rate as market determined and varying in response to the demand for bills by the banks.

Sixth, credit expansion by a single bank is constrained by the activities of other banks:

> An individual bank cannot carry out such operations without restraint, but must moderate the rate of its credit inflation in line with the rate of this inflation in other banks, for otherwise its settlements with other banks, to which its cheques go, will be unfavourable for it, and balancing processes will set in. Its rate of credit inflation will be checked, and that of other banks will be raised. The effects of credit inflation of private banks are exactly the same as the inflationary effects of the central bank.
>
> (CW I: 150–1)

Kalecki's analysis of money largely concerned money as a medium of exchange rather than as a store of wealth. Kalecki distinguished between narrow money and broad money (other than narrow money), with most discussion concerning the former and the demand for the latter being related to wealth and a spectrum of interest rates. Money is credit money, and the creation of credit money is generally required if the economy is to expand. But the amount of money which remains in existence depends upon the demand to hold that money.

On Pigou and Keynes effects

In the debates following the publication of *The General Theory* (Keynes 1936), two particular routes were put forward through which lower prices and wages could eventually generate a move to full employment, namely the real balance or 'Pigou effect' and the 'Keynes effect'. With the first effect, lower prices generate higher real value of money, which stimulates consumption and reduces savings, and in the second higher real value of money supply generates lower interest rates, which stimulates spending, particularly investment. Kalecki rejected both of these routes as ways by which full employment could be achieved.

It is well known that credit money does not constitute net worth since while a deposit is an asset for the individual, it constitutes a liability for the bank. Further, the banks' balance sheets are composed of assets and liabilities generally denominated in nominal terms, and hence the wealth of the banks is not changed through variations in the price level.

A paper by Kalecki in 1944 (reprinted as CW I: 342–3) is an early, if brief, statement of this in his attack on the real balance (Pigou) effect on the level of effective demand. He argued that an

> increase in the real value of the stock of money does not mean a rise in the total real value of possession if all the money (cash and deposits) is 'backed' by credits to persons and firms, i.e. if all the assets of the banking system consist of such credits. For in this case, to the gain for money-holders there corresponds an equal loss for the bank debtors. The total real value of possessions increases only to the extent to which money is backed by gold.

A footnote adds 'Or government securities. The classics and Prof. Pigou do not, however, postulate the existence of national debt as an essential feature of capitalist economy'. It could have been added that government securities involve assets (the prospect of future income) and liabilities (the prospect of future taxes to pay the interest on bonds) and to that degree do not constitute net worth for the private sector.

Kalecki also pointed out that when gold forms a small part of national wealth, the fall in wage rates and prices necessary to restore aggregate demand to the full employment level would be enormous. Further, falls in the general level of prices would increase the real value of debts and 'would consequently lead to wholesale bankruptcy and a confidence crisis' (CW I: 343).

This paper by Kalecki shows the importance of some outside money (to use the terminology of Gurley and Shaw 1960) for the operation of the 'Pigou effect', and drew upon the equality of deposits and loans in the balance sheet of banks. He also hints at the role of declining prices (rather than lower prices) in generating bankruptcies and undermining confidence.

Kalecki doubted the strength of the 'Keynes effect' as a means by which aggregate demand could be stimulated through lower prices. He argued that if wages and prices decline, then

> the value of output must diminish and the demand for cash for transactions fall (sic) off. Thus the rate of interest tends to decline, and this encourages investment so that we have yet another possible way for a wage cut to raise employment. This argument, though theoretically quite correct is, however, without practical importance. The increase in the demand for cash in general affects only slightly the long-term rate of interest, which is the most important rate in the determination of the level of investment. Thus it seems quite justifiable to neglect this channel through which a wage reduction could influence the level of employment.
>
> (CW I: 283)

In a similar vein, in a book review published in 1937 (re-printed as CW VII: 314–15), Kalecki considered a case where there was a very substantial reduction in all prices and wages. He then argued that

> the demand for cash for transactions declines, the rate of interest falls off, and this may encourage investment activity, and thus increase effective demand. This is, however, a complicated process not at all equivalent to an increase in 'the purchasing power of money' proportionate to the fall in costs and prices. And its result may be slight indeed, for the fall in the long-term rate of interest is likely to be small.
>
> (CW VII: 314)

Principle of increasing risk

Kalecki in effect summarized the conditions governing the borrowing by enterprises, whether in the form of loans, bonds or equity, in the phrase the 'principle of increasing risk'. The 'principle of increasing risk' can be simply stated. The more a company wishes to borrow (relative to its profits and to its own wealth) the greater is the perceived risk (on the part of the potential lender and of the borrower) that the company will not be able to repay the loan (interest and principal). The lender will charge a risk premium to cover the greater risk exposure, and hence the cost of borrowing will rise with the volume of borrowing. But the higher cost would raise the risk of default and at some point the cost of borrowing may become prohibitive. Kalecki (CW I: 285–93) in his paper, first published in 1937, on the principle of increasing risk does not explicitly mention banks and their lending but rather is concerned with the cost of finance facing the individual firm where 'the entrepreneur is not cautious enough in his investment activity, it is the creditor who imposes on his calculation the burden of increasing risk, charging the successive portions of credits above a certain amount with a rising rate of interest' (CW I: 288).[7] In a book first published in 1954 and containing a chapter which was in effect a version of Kalecki's paper of 1937, Kalecki stated that 'a firm considering expansion must face the fact that, given the amount of entrepreneurial capital, the risk increases with the amount invested' (CW II: 278). However, in this version of 1954 he did not translate that increased risk into increased loan charges (Kalecki CW II: 277–81).

There appears to be a conflict between the principle of increasing risk (as applied to bank loans) and the working assumption which Kalecki made as indicated above to the effect that when 'the demand for bank credits increases . . . these are granted by the banks' (Kalecki CW I: 190). However, in Kalecki's approach, the granting of loans at the prevailing rate of interest is a condition for the full expansion of planned investment to take place and, as other quotes given above indicate, the banks could abort any expansion if they raised interest rates on loans substantially rather than meeting the increased demand for loans.

A number of comments on the relationship between the principle of increasing risk and the shape and slope of the supply of loans curve can be made. First, Kalecki viewed the 'principle of increasing risk' and the rising cost of finance as a significant factor limiting the expansion of the individual firm. He dismissed the significance of diseconomies of large scale and the limitations of the size of the market as constraints on the expansion of the firm (CW II: 277). He continued by arguing that there is a factor

> of decisive importance in limiting the size of the firm: the amount of entrepreneurial capital, i.e. the amount of capital owned by the firm. The access of a firm to the capital market, or in other words the amount of rentier capital it may hope to obtain, is determined to a large extent by the amount of its entrepreneurial capital. . . . It follows . . . that the expansion of the firm depends on its accumulation of capital out of current profits. This will enable the firm to undertake new investment without encountering the obstacles of the limited capital market or 'increasing risk'. Not only can savings out of current profits be directly invested in the business, but this increase in the firm's capital will make it possible to contract new loans.
>
> (CW II: 277–8)

It may then be concluded that Kalecki saw the operation of the 'principle of increasing risk' as a significant feature of a capitalist economy, and not a peripheral one. This would suggest that an analysis of a market capitalist economy that draws on the work of Kalecki should retain the 'principle of increasing risk' as a component.

Second, most enterprises (the more 'cautious' ones following the terminology in the quote from Kalecki given above) may be far below the borrowing levels at which the 'principle of increasing risk' would have a major effect on the cost and availability of borrowing. In such a case, most enterprises may be observed to face approximately constant costs of borrowing since they would find it too costly to stray into the scale of borrowing, relative to profits and own wealth, where the costs rise sharply. 'Many firms will not use to the full the potentialities of the capital market because of the "increasing risk" involved in expansion' (CW II: 278), though it should be noted that this arises from firms' own perceptions of the risks faced.

Kalecki argued that 'it would be impossible for a firm to borrow capital above a certain level determined by the amount of its entrepreneurial capital' (CW II: 277). Further, 'that firms below a certain size have no access whatever to the capital market' (CW II: 278). Hence the loans schedule facing many enterprises will have a final vertical section, and for other enterprises the loan schedule may in effect be non-existent.

Third, over the course of the business cycle, an enterprise's ability to borrow from banks can be seen to depend on two sets of factors. On the one hand, there is the balance between loan repayment commitments and its flow of profits. The loan repayment commitments would depend, *inter alia*, on its past borrowing and the extent to which it has been able to repay loans based on borrowing from households in the form of bonds, equity etc. On the other hand, the banks' willingness to lend may vary as their 'liquidity preference' and general optimism and pessimism varies. It is then a complex matter to say how the volume of borrowing in the form of loans and the relationship between loans and interest rates will vary during the course of the business cycle. There is no general prediction which can be given as to the co-movements of loans, the stock of money and interest rates over the course of the cycle.

The 'principle of increasing risk' applies at the level of the firm, and it is seen as operating to limit the growth of the firm. For the firm, its own stream of profits is a significant influence on its ability to borrow. It is well known that in the Kaleckian approach aggregate profits are determined by aggregate investment. Thus it is not possible to proceed immediately to the aggregate level by the summation of the individual level since the borrowing of a firm depends on its investment plans, and the collective realization of those investment plans determines profits which in turn influence the ability of enterprises to borrow.

Lavoie has argued that it must be concluded that 'neither Kalecki's principle of increasing risk nor Minsky's financial fragility hypothesis, whatever their virtues within their domain of validity, can sustain the hypothetic construction of an upward sloping credit-money supply curve' (Lavoie 1996: 287). It is argued here that the 'principle of increasing risk' would support the construction of an upward sloping supply of credit (loans) by the banks' schedule facing an individual firm. It has, though, already been suggested that firms may seek to ensure that they typically do not borrow so much as to put them into the region where the cost of borrowing which they face rises rapidly. But it is also argued that this tells us nothing about the supply of money (bank deposits) schedule. Nor does it tell us anything about the co-movement of interest rates and loans (or the stock of money) over the business cycle, and it is the latter which Lavoie seems to have in mind when he talks of an upward-sloping credit-money supply curve.

Interest rate determination

Kalecki introduced the notion of the degree of monopoly in the context of pricing behaviour and also for the determination of the distribution of income, but it appears that he did not apply the degree of monopoly (or any related notions on mark-up pricing or even constant mark-ups) to the determination of the structure of interest rates (e.g. as between rate of interest on loans and the discount rate). Indeed, some interest rates were treated more like flex prices than fix prices (to use Hicks' terminology) and more like demand determined prices than cost determined prices (to use Kalecki's own terminology). There does not appear to be any suggestion in Kalecki's writings that the loan rate of interest is a mark-up on the Central Bank discount rate (with the mark-up set by the degree of monopoly) nor of the deposit rate of interest as a mark-down on the Central Bank discount rate. This contrasts with the treatment by Moore (1988: e.g. 61) who appeals to mark up pricing (though viewed as consistent with profit maximization) for the setting of interest rates on loans and deposits, and Rousseas who argues that 'the best way of doing so [shifting the emphasis from liquidity preference theory to credit money] is to apply Michal Kalecki's theory of mark-up pricing to the loan rates charged by banks for bank credit' (Rousseas 1992: 54). Kalecki did though indicate that 'the [interest] rate paid on deposits . . . usually moves parallel to the discount rate' (Kalecki CW I: 295).

As indicated in the Introduction, Kalecki did not envisage that the interest rate was determined by the interaction of savings and investment (equivalently the loanable funds approach). Instead, he argued

> that the short-term rate is determined by the value of transactions and the supply of money by banks; and that the long-term rate is determined by anticipations of the short-term rate based on past experience, and estimates of the risk involved in the possible depreciation of long-term assets.
>
> (CW II: 262)

The determination of the short-term rate of interest was seen by Kalecki as arising from the transactions demand for money interacting with the stock of money. The notation used is that M is the stock of money, which consists of current bank accounts and notes (i.e. close to M1 in present parlance), and T is total turnover. The short-term interest rate 'is the remuneration for forgoing the convenience of holding cash in its pure form' (though money would be a better term here than cash). It should be noted that Kalecki implicitly assumed that the rate of interest on holding money was zero, which would be an assumption in line with the prevailing practice at the time Kalecki was writing (and for many years after) that banks did not pay interest on current accounts:[8]

> When holding money is compared with holding short bills, the only difference is that the bill is not directly usable for settling transactions and that it yields interest. When holding money and holding a bond is compared, however, the risk of a fall in the price of the bond has also to be taken into consideration.
>
> (CW II: 263)

He concluded

> that the velocity of circulation V is an increasing function of the short-term rate of interest ρ or: $\frac{T}{M} = V(\rho)$. It follows directly from this equation that given the function V the short-term rate of interest, ρ, is determined by the [nominal] value of transactions, T, and the supply of money, M, which, in turn, is determined by banking policy.

Kalecki's discussion of the equality of transactions demand for money and the stock of money is characteristically laconic, but can be elaborated as follows. The banks can vary their portfolios of assets and liabilities and in doing so would influence the structure and general level of interest rates and the stock of money. However, the level of interest rates and the (nominal) level of economic activity also influence the non-bank sector's willingness to hold money. Further, 'banking policy' will influence the supply of money where I would argue banking policy should be read to include the lending policies of commercial banks as well as the setting of the discount rate by the Central Bank. Indeed, Kalecki's later discussion in the paper from which the quote above was taken implies the former rather than the latter.

Kalecki described the determination of the stock of money in the following way:

> The process by which banks increase the supply of money deserves to be considered in some detail. For the sake of simplicity, let us assume that bank deposits consist only of current accounts. Imagine that banks decide to reduce their cash ratio (i.e. the ratio of the amount of notes and accounts in the central bank to deposits) and buy bills. The price of bills will rise, and thus the short-term rate of interest will fall to that level at which the public will be prepared to add to their current accounts the amount which the banks expend on bills.
>
> (CW II: 267)

The stock of money and the short-term interest rate (on bills) are thus viewed as determined by the interaction of the willingness of banks to supply money and of the public to hold (demand) money.

The long-term rate of interest (on bonds) is linked with the short-term rate of interest (on bills) based on substitution between the corresponding financial assets. The precise mechanism is not of central importance here but it can be readily summarized by the following. 'In order to establish a connection between the short-term and the long-term rate of interest, we shall examine the problem of substitution between a representative short-term asset, say a bill of exchange, and a representative long-term asset, say a consol' (CW II: 268). Kalechi derived the following relationship:

$$r = \frac{\rho_e}{1 + \frac{g}{r_{\max}}} + \frac{g - \varepsilon}{1 + \frac{g}{r_{\max}}}$$

where r is long-term interest rate, ρ_e is expected rate of interest on bills (averaged over the holding period of bonds), r_{max} the yield corresponding to the minimum 'plausible' price that bonds could reach at the end of the expected holding period, g is a parameter relating the expected gain on bonds to the minimum 'plausible' price and ε reflects the uncertainties in the rate of return on bills and the recurrent purchase costs.

It is readily apparent that Kalecki's approach to the determination of the short-term and long-term rates of interest is one based on monetary factors. There is no mention of loanable funds or of the equality between savings and investment, which is much as expected given the quotes with which we began the chapter. There is also the general notion that relative interest rates are influenced by substitution between different financial assets.

Different types of money

In the Keynesian framework, the distinction is drawn between the various motives for holding money, transactions, precautionary and speculative along with (generally forgotten) finance motive. The transactions and precautionary motives are related to the level of nominal income and the speculative motive to the level of wealth. However, the resulting demands for money fuse into a single demand function which is then often estimated with the demand for money as a function of income, rates of interest etc. This has been summarized in the following term:

> The distinction between the demand for transactions and precautionary balances, determined chiefly by the level of income and that for speculative balances, determined by the rate of interest is often referred to as the distinction between the demand for *active* and *idle* balances. Since all money is at each moment being held by someone, this terminology is not too helpful empirically, and we do not use it in this book.
>
> (Laidler 1985: 51)

The approach of Kalecki is similar to that of Keynes in that there is a recognition of a transactions related demand and a portfolio (wealth-related) demand for money, but there is the crucial difference that each of the demands is related to a different definition of money. The transactions demand for money is a demand for money used as a medium of exchange, which is satisfied by a narrow definition of money.[9] The portfolio demand for money is a demand for money as a store of wealth which is generally linked with a broader definition of money and excluding those forms of money which yield a zero or negligible rate of interest. The notation used here is that M0 refers to base money (coins, notes and reserves with Central Bank), M1 refers to those liabilities of the banking system the transfer of which is a generally accepted medium of exchange (but not here notes and coins), M2/1 refers to broad money M2 minus M1 and is those liabilities of the banking system which have a fixed nominal value but which are not directly transferable. Banks are defined here as those institutions some of whose liabilities are generally accepted as medium of exchange. Other financial institutions may accept deposits with a fixed nominal value and could be counted part of a broad money stock, but here we confine M2 to the liabilities of the banks.

In Kalecki's approach, the demand for M0 is linked to wages as a transaction demand, but this reflects the situation in the 1940s when most workers did not have access to a bank account. In 'Wage bill and cash circulation' (CW VII: 38–44), Kalecki correlates wage bill with the circulation of coins and notes. 'This correlation may then be used as the basis of an extrapolated estimate of the current wage bill' (ibid.: 38). The demand for M0 by the public is clearly seen as a transactions demand.

The demand for M1 is also a transactions demand, as discussed above. In particular, Kalecki argued that 'if the short-term rate of interest is unchanged . . . current accounts [i.e. M1] will increase more or less proportionately with the volume of transactions' (Kalecki CW VII: 159), which can be read as saying that the demand for M1 is the transactions demand. Hence (and in light of the discussion in the previous section), the demand for M1 can be taken as a function of the volume of transactions and of the short-term rate of interest.

There is little discussion by Kalecki of the nature of the demand for broad money. He did though remark that

> the rise in deposit accounts [i.e. M2/1] depends on the rate of accumulation of liquid reserves of the public and the relative attractiveness of deposit accounts as compared with other relevant assets. The 'lending power' of the banks is then limited by these determinants of the movement of deposits [in current accounts and in deposit accounts].
>
> (CW VII: 159)

In a similar vein, he argued that

> savings are 'invested' in deposits either because more of them are needed as cash balances for transactions, or because this type of reserves seems for various reasons more attractive than the holding of bonds. In the first case deposits accumulating on current accounts are 'tied up' in settling transactions (chiefly by firms) and are not available for spending on consumption. The second case, the accumulation of deposits mainly on deposit account, does not differ fundamentally from investment in long-term securities. It is sometimes said that it is easier to liquidate deposits than bonds and to use the proceeds for consumption. This, however, is relevant only when actual dissaving takes place: as long as consumption is below current income the form in which past savings are held is of no importance. And even in the case of dissavings the obstacles in parting with a bond as compared with withdrawing a deposit seem to have been rather exaggerated
>
> (CW VII: 84–5)

though he doesn't indicate why or how there is this exaggeration.

In the specific context of the UK in the period 1938–42, Kalecki reported that current account deposits (M1) rose rapidly (almost doubling in four years) while deposit accounts (M2/1) were almost static. He then remarked that

> there is no reason to expect a similar pace in the movement of current and deposit accounts, for ... with a given short-term rate of interest current accounts increase more or less proportionately with the volume of transactions while the rise in deposit accounts depends on the rate of accumulation of liquid reserves and the attractiveness of deposit accounts as compared with other relevant assets.
>
> (CW VII: 162)

Thus it can be concluded that the demand for M2/1 is a portfolio demand related to the wealth of the public and to the spectrum of interest rates including the rate on deposit accounts (and it would be expected that the demand for M2/1 would be positively related to the deposit account rate of interest, though the demand for M1 would be negatively related to that interest rate).

It can first be noted that if the identification of M1 with a transactions demand and M2/1 with a portfolio demand is correct, then it follows that if there is concern over the relationship between the demand for money and the level of nominal income, then M1 is the relevant definition of money. It is not a matter of saying that the relevant definition of money for the purposes of monetary policy and demand management is that for which there is a stable demand, but rather that which is the generally accepted medium of exchange. But in the approach of Kalecki, the view is that the nominal volume of transactions determines the demand for money, rather than the stock of money determining the nominal volume of transactions.

Second, in so far as the stocks of M1 and M2/1 are demand driven, then they can readily evolve in quite different ways over time, simply because the former is transactions driven whilst the latter is wealth (portfolio) driven. If the income to wealth ratio is stable, then it could be that the evolution of M1 and M2/1 follow similar paths as the demand for each of them evolves in similar ways.

Third, the linkage between M1 and M2/1 arises because of the ready transferability by individuals from M2/1 deposits to M1 deposits, in part because those different types of deposits are held with the same financial institution and in part because the relative price of the two types of deposits is fixed at 1 since both have a nominal price of unity. There are some costs (monetary, time etc.) of making the transfer between current accounts and deposit accounts as there are with other transfers between financial assets, though no price uncertainty. In the event that a bank was indifferent between M1 deposits and M2/1 deposits (and hence, e.g. held the same reserve ratio for M1 and for M2/1), then it could be argued that the potential purchasing power in the economy at a particular time was measured by M2 (including M1), a point discussed further below.

When the stock of money is viewed as essentially demand determined, then it is immediately apparent that the time paths of different definitions of money will typically diverge in so far as the factors influencing the demand for the different definitions of money are also different.

Fourth, Kalecki noted, albeit in a footnote in one of his early papers, that the shift between different types of money would have implications for the reserves of the banking system. 'This increase in circulation contains, *inter alia*, an increase in the cash reserves of banks in connection with the shift of certain sums from time to demand deposits . . . which also takes place on account of an increase in turnover' (CW I: 150, n2).

Monetary policy

Kalecki said very little on monetary policy and, in so far as he did, he saw monetary policy in terms of open market operations and variation in the interest rate. However, his discussions suggested severe doubts on the effectiveness of monetary policy as a means of stimulating the level of aggregate demand. The doubts stem from the view that long-term interest rates were seen as relevant for many decisions but there being rather small movements in such long-term rates. 'The relative stability of the long-term rate of interest is generally known. . . . It seems unlikely that changes in the long-term rate of interest of the order of those noticed . . . can influence investment activity' (CW I: 296–7). This leads him to dismiss those theories of the business cycle which suggest that the end of a boom derives from an increase in the rate of interest. 'For the rate of interest can stop the boom only by hampering investment, and it is chiefly the long-term rate which matters in investment activity' (CW I: 298). It would also be that a substantial fall in the rate of interest would be necessary to have a significant effect on investment (cf. CW I: 403).

Kalecki also argued that it has 'long been indicated that it is not at all certain whether consumption is really encouraged or discouraged by a higher rate of interest' (Kalecki CW I: 262). Further, increases in wealth (notably stock market values), generated by declines in the level of interest rates, would have little effect on consumer expenditure by capitalists. 'The effect would be significant, most probably, only if the fall in the rate of interest were considerable, which would require open-market operations on a very large scale' (CW I: 403).

Two significant points which arise from Kalecki's brief comments on monetary policy. First, monetary policy has relatively little impact on the level of aggregate demand, and in part this arises from the notion that long-term interest rates may influence spending decisions but themselves vary little. Second, insofar as monetary policy can influence spending, it does so through effects on investment. It could then be added, though Kalecki himself did not, that monetary policy would then influence the real side of the economy (through investment and thereby capacity) and the classical dichotomy is thereby undermined.

Conclusions

The preceding discussion suggests that there are six key features in Kalecki's monetary analysis. These are:

- i loans have to be provided by the banking system to enterprises if their planned investment decisions are to come to fruition, thereby generating an immediate increase in the stock of money;
- ii the stock of money depends on the willingness of the non-bank public to hold (demand) money;
- iii the stock of money also depends on the decisions and actions of the banking system;
- iv loans are provided subject to the principle of increasing risk;
- v a change in the demand for loans generates a change in the balance sheet of banks with consequent effects on the structure of interest rates;
- vi a distinction be drawn between money as a medium of exchange and money as a store of value, with different moneys serving those purposes.

With the exception of the last point, these features have been incorporated into the structuralist post-Keynesian analysis of money (cf. Pollin 1991, for example).

It has been argued that 'Kalecki's early writings on capitalist economies demonstrate his appreciation of monetary issues, and suggest that the paucity of monetary elements in his formal model(s) reflects a strategic choice'

(Dymski 1996: 116). We do not dissent from that view but rather suggest that there is a substantial analysis of monetary elements contained in the writings of Kalecki even though his writings focus more on the real than on the monetary.

Notes

1 This chapter is an amended and shortened version of 'Kalecki on money and finance' published in *European Journal of the History of Economic Thought* [8(4): 487–508] published by Taylor & Francis and appears with the kind permission of the publishers. I am grateful to: two anonymous referees; P. Arestis; G. Dymski; G. Fontana; W. Godley; P. Howells; M. Lavoie; J. López; T. Palley; N. Shapiro and J. Toporowski for comments and general discussion on earlier drafts.
2 I am indebted to J. Toporowski for alerting me to this point.
3 Kalecki defined inflation in terms of 'the creation of purchasing power not based on a contribution to current social income' (CW I: 148).
4 J. Toporowski has pointed out that Kalecki included 'banks of issue' (CW I: 93), which would now correspond to central banks, in the consolidated balance sheet of banks.
5 According to Toporowski the original Polish of item (i) is better translated as '"free" or "untied" deposits, that is deposits that are not ear-marked for any specific purpose', where for 'any specific purpose' Kalecki had in mind items (ii) and (iii).
6 In the discussion to which reference is made in the text, Kalecki used the term advances for what we have termed loans, and 'a loan' to signify bonds when he wrote about the floatation of loans (cf. CW I: 293).
7 Chilosi (1982: 83) views Breit's approach as concentrating on the risk of the lender, whereas Kalecki concentrated on the risk of the borrower, and notes that Kalecki acknowledged in a footnote to the quote given in the text the work of Breit.
8 British terminology is followed here, hence current accounts equate with demand deposits and deposit accounts with time deposits.
9 The general tone of Kalecki's discussion would suggest that he was concerned with money as a medium of exchange rather than as a means of final payment, though the distinction is not one to which Kalecki gave any attention.

6 Kalecki's theory of income determination and modern macroeconomics

A reconstruction and an assessment[1]

Alberto Chilosi

Introduction

Kalecki's theory of income determination is notable for having been built, unlike Keynes', on imperfectly competitive foundations. This constitutes a clear advantage both under the profile of realism as well as of interpretative power. An imperfectly competitive framework most naturally leads to the issue of the incomplete exploitation of productive capacity, since an imperfect competitor is typically constrained in what he perceives to be able to trade. At the price he sets he would obviously like to trade more and, if he is a producer, only partially exploits his productive capacity. In the real world an imperfect competitor feels his sales, and his opportunities for profit, to be intrinsically constrained by insufficient demand, and tends naturally to believe that a policy increasing demand should improve the results of his business. This can contribute to form social support for expansionary policies.[2]

In the early post-war years the theory of income determination was usually formulated, following Keynes' lead, under the assumption of perfect competition.[3] This approach found its consecration in the so-called neo-classical synthesis that dominated the 1950s and 1960s. With the quest for the microfoundations of macroeconomics, which started at the end of the 1960s, the appropriateness of building macroeconomic theory on imperfectly competitive foundations, with price-maker agents, was eventually rediscovered. According to Benassy's account of the evolution of macroeconomic theory, 'after a slow start in the mid 1970s, the macroeconomics of imperfect competition has become an established and rapidly expanding field of research' (Benassy 1995: xi). It is remarkable that this quote completely ignores Kalecki's pioneering contributions of the 1930s. As a matter of fact, in Benassy's extensive anthology of the macroeconomics of imperfect competition (Benassy 1995) Kalecki's name is mentioned only once (in Oliver Hart's path-breaking article of 1982). In the Dixon and Rankin 'Imperfect Competition and Macroeconomics' Kalecki is not even mentioned. In this chapter we will address two questions: (i) why was Kalecki's lead not followed and why did the imperfectly competitive foundations of macroeconomic theory become an established area of mainstream economic research only more than 40 years after his first contributions in the area were published in the international arena?; and (ii) what kind of relationship do the more recent macroeconomic models based on imperfectly competitive foundations have with Kalecki's theoretical framework, and in what do the assumptions and conclusions of more recent models differ from Kalecki's?

Why Kalecki's lead in building a macroeconomic theory based on imperfectly competitive foundations was not followed for so long

It is rather puzzling that for more than 40 years after Kalecki had adopted a more realistic imperfectly competitive approach his lead was not followed, and the mainstream[4] macroeconomic theory of income determination continued to be based, somewhat incongruously, on the hypothesis of perfect competition. What were the reasons? The most trivial one is that modelling imperfect competition is in general more complicated than modelling perfect competition. Another is that, if an underemployment equilibrium exists in the case of perfect competition, it could be presumed that it would exist even more under imperfectly competitive conditions, that is much further away from the Walrasian model.[5] But this is not the end of the story. There are a few more specific reasons, which may be conjectured:

i Kalecki's theory of income determination is intrinsically embedded in his theory of the trade cycle. This may have misled the readers who would not immediately perceive that Kalecki had an alternative income determination theory that could be considered separately from his trade cycle theory. While the Keynesian trade cycle theory appeared after the *General Theory* (in the case of Harrod 1936 immediately after), Kalecki's appeared before the latter, and this obscured his achievement as far as the theory of income determination is concerned. Paradoxically, one may maintain that on this account Kalecki was belittled because he went further too soon.

ii Some of Kalecki's most relevant contributions of the 1930s were not later republished in the parts where their imperfectly competitive foundations are expounded. In particular, his original presentation of the theory of income determination based on imperfectly competitive foundations, contained in his review article of the *General Theory*, remained unknown and untranslated in the West until 1979.[6] Its basic framework was incorporated in his 1937 version of trade cycle theory, but not highlighted as an autonomous contribution (Kalecki 1937c). Moreover Kalecki later repudiated all the parts of his theory that were explicitly based on maximizing behaviour, albeit in an imperfectly competitive framework, and which, because of this, could better appeal to 'mainstream' macroeconomic theorists. Those parts were never included in the re-editions of his selected works that took place in his lifetime.[7] Thus, the development of Kalecki's non-competitive framework did not provide a suitable background for the more modern mainstream macroeconomic theorists building on imperfectly competitive foundations.

iii The strict dichotomy between workers, who consume everything they earn, and capitalists, who save a constant part of their incomes, while complicating the model of income determination does not really appeal to our times, since it hardly corresponds to the complex social structure of modern industrial societies. Manual workers, to the determination of whose share in national income (in conformity with Bowley's law) the 1938–9 theory of distribution factors was geared, are more and more a smaller and decreasing share of the labour force. Unlike the supply curve, the theory of profits, which was an essential part of his theory of income determination to which Kalecki gave particular emphasis, is unrelated to the competitive structure of the economy.

iv The introduction of imperfect competition in macroeconomic theory follows as a theoretical development from the initial quest for the microeconomic foundations of macroeconomic theory that started at the end of the 1960s, and focused during the 1970s on the so-called non-Walrasian models. Thus the genesis of imperfectly competitive based macroeconomic models seems to follow the intrinsic logic of development of the theory rather than being inspired by suggestions from the past. Moreover the more recent development of imperfectly competitive founded macroeconomic models is highly dependent on the analytical framework provided by Dixit and Stiglitz in 1977, with the use of the two-tier utility function, which snugly leads to the formalization of the imperfectly competitive structure of an economy with isoelastic demand functions. This certainly constitutes a more powerful theoretical instrument for rigorously pursuing Kalecki's search for the determination of the equilibrium of an industry and of an economy under imperfectly competitive conditions, than the tools available to Kalecki in the 1930s.[8] In the next section we will compare the overall theoretical results.

The imperfectly competitive New-Keynesian macroeconomic models and Kalecki's macroeconomic theory

Even if the new imperfectly competitive macroeconomic models are based on more complex analytical foundations, they present considerable similarity – albeit usually not acknowledged – with specific aspects of Kalecki's theoretical framework, which have by now become so ingrained in the toolkit of modern economics to lose the original Kaleckian connotations. This applies in particular to the use in a macroeconomic context of Lerner's notion of the degree of monopoly and the constancy of the latter as resulting from isoelastic and isoelastically shifting demand curves.

Without going into technical details let us see what the main conclusions of those models are and what relations they bear with Kalecki's. The various contributions differ in assumptions and in model construction, but the basic conclusions are the following:[9]

i Imperfect competition in the goods market leads *per se* to various degrees of underutilization of resources (in particular labour). This is hardly surprising: it is a simple generalization in a general equilibrium framework of what could be very simply shown in a representative firm context (Dixon and Rankin 1994: 194; Ardeni *et al.* 1996: 61–2). But, unless there are some rigidities, there is no involuntary unemployment. In case of imperfect competition in the labour market there is involuntary unemployment, however (and this is a also straightforward generalization of what could be argued in partial equilibrium). In Kalecki the emphasis is on underutilization of resources and unemployment, not because of imperfection of competition, but because of insufficiency of effective demand.

ii Monetary policy aimed at increasing effective demand may or may not lead to an increase in income and employment depending on the existence or absence of some kind of rigidities. Imperfect competition per se does not lead to Keynesian (Kaleckian) results, but rigidities that do not lead to Keynesian results in the perfectly competitive framework (such as those arising from menu costs), lead to Keynesian conclusions under imperfect competition. This seems puzzling since one would expect that monetary expansion would in any case raise the demand curve for the representative producer, bringing about an increase in production. But this does not happen unless, because of some sort of nominal rigidity, the cost curves are not shifted upward in the same proportion. This would happen, in particular, if workers are 'fooled' by unanticipated monetary expansion (Dixon and Rankin 1994: 178). (One can reason in this respect on the basis of the graphical presentation of the representative imperfectly competitive producer equilibrium, as in the model of the 1936 Kalecki review article on the *General Theory*.)

iii Expansionary fiscal policy may or may not lead to an increase in employment and effective demand, depending on the concrete specifications of the model.[10] Despite some differences, the role of nominal rigidities in generating unemployment equilibria does not seem to differ much in case of presence or absence of imperfect competition. In the fix-price traditional Keynesian models of the Keynesian cross and of the Hicksian IS–LM framework the rigidities were nominal. The fix-price assumption certainly corresponds better to the Kaleckian framework of the horizontal aggregate supply curve, with constant variable unit cost and constant markup, than to the perfectly competitive framework of the *General Theory*. In the latter an increase in employment was accompanied by an increase in price level and a decrease in the real wage. In the *General Theory* the relevant rigidity was that of the *nominal* wage rate (even if it has been much debated whether this was really the essential point). In other terms, employment could increase only as long as workers were victims of money illusion. In Kalecki the relevant rigidities leading to involuntary unemployment equilibria are rather of a real nature and can be found in the theory of profits, in the exogeneity of *real* short-run investment and in the constancy of the degree of monopoly, which is supposed to be given by the conditions of competition only, which are unaffected by, or do not systematically respond to, monetary shocks.[11] Indeed, monetary shocks cannot affect either real capitalist consumption (which depends on real profits only and is independent of private wealth) or investment, which depends on past decisions, unaffected in any case by monetary factors. A decrease in wages, given a constant degree of monopoly, results in a corresponding decrease in prices. If the level of investment is given in real terms this leads to a reduction in nominal profits and constancy in the level of real profits. Thus, national income and employment remain unchanged. On the other hand, the same considerations lead to a different result than that mentioned above in the framework of the imperfectly competitive New-Keynesian models, as far as fiscal policy is concerned: in Kalecki there is no crowding out by assumption (since monetary factors do not matter) and public expenditure adds to private expenditure, arbitrarily increasing national income up to the assumed full employment level, provided at least that it is not financed through wage income or wage goods taxation.[12]

Conclusion: an assessment of Kalecki's contribution to modern macroeconomics

Kalecki's theory of income determination is notable for linking the theory of distribution, on the one side, and the theory of income determination, on the other. The theory of income distribution is based, notwithstanding the sometimes heroic simplifications on which it rests, on the basic idea that the structure of distribution in a market economy depends on the structure of market imperfections and of market power. This is an important idea which leads to a deep understanding of the way the capitalist economy actually works and which constitutes a lasting contribution to modern economics. Another important idea which can be derived in Kalecki's theoretical framework is that by reducing the extent of market power and market imperfections it is possible to increase, *ceteris paribus*, the level of national income and of employment. Indeed, in his theoretical framework, for any given level of profits, determined by the exogenously given (in the short-run) level of investment, the lower the degree of monopoly, the greater the level of employment and national income, and the greater the share of wages in national income. This contributes to the rationale for keeping market power in check with anti-trust legislation and easing the restrictions on access to markets, while increasing the extent of the latter.[13]

Important pieces of his theoretical construction, such as the basic idea of building the theory of income determination on imperfectly competitive foundations, the implicit assumption of the isoelastic transposition of demand curves and his use of the notion of the degree of monopoly have been a lasting legacy to the toolkit of modern economics in general and modern macroeconomics in particular.

However, the idea that by increasing demand real income can increase up to full employment without adverse inflationary consequences may have corresponded to the conditions of the 1930s, but certainly not to those of more recent times. There seems to be a wide consensus today (apparently not shared by the more extreme rational expectation monetarists only) as to the fact that with expansionary policies there is in general a tendency in the short run both for inflation and national income and employment to rise, but the subsequent costs of the process in raising inflationary expectations *may* not be worth the short-run increase in employment. At the same time, the rise in inflation may not occur if on the supply side there are forces such as increasing returns, fast technical progress, ongoing market liberalization and increasing international competition ('globalization') that lead to elasticity of supply.[14] Moreover, because of hysteresis, greater short-run price stability may bring about increased long-run unemployment (possibly the European case), and this choice may similarly be considered as objectionable. Policy makers and the public cannot be content to be concerned with the consequences of their actions in the short run only, since in the long run, and especially in the middle run, 'we are *not* all dead', even if policy-makers themselves, though alive, could by then have been voted out of office.

These same considerations point to some practical futility of what seems to be the basic theoretical mover in the construction of imperfectly competitive new-Keynesian models, namely the issue of whether the introduction of imperfect competition *per se* brings about the existence of involuntary unemployment, even under rational expectations. The answer to this question is negative, but turns out to be positive if some kinds of monetary rigidities (such as menu costs) are considered. This seems of interest if seen in the framework of the ongoing theoretical debate of Keynesians (New- or otherwise) against Monetarists but of little relevance for understanding the issues of macroeconomic policy in a real world, inevitably full of rigidities and imperfections, especially of an informational nature, where the existence of involuntary unemployment is a simple fact of life, but where the simple existence of unemployment cannot be considered *per se* a justification for Keynesian (Kaleckian) policies.

By contrast, Kalecki was always much concerned, in his theoretical constructions, with burning real world policy issues. Yet his basic message, that demand creation by governments could provide the solution to the unemployment issue, a solution which in capitalist economies would remain unimplemented in practice for the political difficulties it implies (Kalecki 1943b), has proved of non-lasting value, aside from its continuing ideological impact. Moreover, the idea that inflation pertains only to the realm of distribution and that it is in any case associated with the full utilization of productive capacity and full employment, as conveyed in particular by his 1955 treatment of hyperinflation (Kalecki 1955, 1962),[15] gives a potentially dangerous message. (This is especially borne out by his conclusion that hyperinflation would eventually be stopped merely because of the impossibility of further squeezing the incomes of the rentiers, and not because of its disruptive consequences on all aspects of the functioning of a market economy.) There are plenty of examples where inflation has been accompanied by heavy unemployment and low utilization of productive capacity, even by negative growth rates. Kalecki was writing well ahead of the stagflationary experiences of the 1970s, which have contributed to deeply changing our appraisal of inflationary phenomena, but he should have witnessed the disruptive consequences of the hyperinflationary experiences of the 1920s. However he was deeply affected by the deflationary experience of the 1930s, and this was the challenge his intellectual power was addressing. One cannot really blame Kalecki for having been a man of his times.

Notes

1 Revised version of a paper originally written for the Kalecki Memorial Conference. In the preparation of the present version I have taken advantage of useful remarks by Giuseppe Ciccarone.

2 On the other hand expansionary policies in context of 'monopolistic markets' may simply lead to inflation rather than increased employment, as already expounded in the early 1930s by Gunnar Myrdal, in the theoretical context of Wicksellian cumulative processes. (Cf. Myrdal 1933: 444–54, and especially 450–2, corresponding respectively to 143–58 and 153–4 of the 1939 English version.)

3 In the 1930s imperfect competition played some role, besides Kalecki's macroeconomics, in Harrod's macroecoeconomic theoretical framework of his *Trade Cycle* (1936), where it was instrumental in deriving the 'Law of the Decreasing Elasticity of Demand' (cf. in particular pp. 16–22).

4 I am not considering here post-Keynesian theorizing, which has been heavily influenced, in particular, by Kalecki's theory of profits.

5 I am indebted to Gabriele Pastrello for this remark.

6 It was translated and commented for the first time in Chilosi (1979).

7 It is also notable that in those re-editions Kalecki carefully suppressed all occurrences of the term 'equilibrium' and all the references to Keynes. On this point see Chilosi (1989: 118).

8 Needless to say, the use of utility functions to derive demand functions would have been most un-Kaleckian in any case.

9 It must be stressed that these conclusions refer specifically to those new macroeconomic models that are based on imperfectly competitive foundations, such as, for instance, Blanchard and Kiyotaki (1987).

10 A model where the use of fiscal policy is not empowered to bring about higher employment and effective demand is for instance that of Snower (1983).

11 According to Mott (1998: 264), the real rigidity that matters in Kalecki is the 'price-cost mark-up rigidity'.

12 For fiscal policy in Kalecki the primary reference is to his 'Theory of Commodity, Income and Capital Taxation', *Economic Journal*, Vol. 47, n. 3, 1937,

pp. 444–50; reprinted in the slightly modified 1971 version in CW I: 319–25. The article is rather muddled as to the treatment of profit taxation (see Asimakopolous' remarks reported in CW I: 562). In particular, to prove the expansionary impact of expenditure financed by profit taxation some kind of balanced budget multiplier argument would have been required. Instead Kalecki assumes, rather incongruously given his hypotheses, the independence of capitalist consumption expenditure from profit taxation in the short run, with the effect of making capitalist consumption a function of gross and not of net profits, and therefore unaffected by taxation.

13 For instance, in a Kaleckian perspective one should have favoured the European Monetary Union, if this were eventually to lead to greater competition and lower degree of monopoly. The abdication of autonomous monetary policies by the single European states would not matter, since in his theoretical framework monetary factors are of no importance. A different consideration would obviously apply to the limitations on budget deficits envisaged by the Maastricht criteria.

14 A good case in point may be the expansion of the American economy under the Clinton presidency. An enlightening non-technical discussion of related arguments can be found in Solow and Taylor (1998).

15 It is interesting to note that a similar remark could be addressed to the usual textbook presentation of the natural rate of income and unemployment. If the Phillips curve is depicted in a monetarist perspective as a vertical line corresponding to the natural unemployment level, and money is considered a simple veil, inflation, being perfectly expected, has no real consequences. In order to graphically convey the idea that high inflation has negative real consequences, even if it is perfectly expected as an average (so that there are no systematic errors of forecast, conforming to the rational expectations paradigm), the vertical Phillips curve should be made to bend rightwards after a certain level, because of the increasing natural rate of unemployment corresponding to decreasing (possibly negative) productivity growth.

7 Kalecki's principle of increasing risk, the distribution of income, and consequences for macroeconomic performance

Tracy Mott

The significance of Michal Kalecki's 'principle of increasing risk' to illuminating macroeconomic performance is that it relates macroeconomic performance to income distribution by limiting the ability of economic actors to increase income or wealth to a magnitude related to their current income and wealth. Kalecki's (1937a) article entitled 'The Principle of Increasing Risk' was written to answer the question of what determines the limit to the size of the capital investment of a particular entrepreneur in any particular period. As this is a worthwhile query in itself, let's first look at what Kalecki said about this and then at how it relates to macroeconomic matters.

The principle of increasing risk

Kalecki rejected the conventional answer of diseconomies of scale as furnishing a limit to the expansion of a firm. Any particular unit or type of capital may have its own optimal size, but replication at this optimal size rules out any potential diseconomies arising from such.

As a firm grows in size relative to its product markets, as explained in the theory of imperfect competition, Kalecki allowed that limits to investment would arise from limitations on demand for the firm's output. He said that this, however, cannot be the only limit on expansion because, for example, we see larger and smaller enterprises started at the same time in the same industry.

This other limit comes from the size of the firm's entrepreneurial capital, Kalecki argued. The more of a firm's or entrepreneur's own wealth that is tied up in a particular fixed investment, the more danger will arise to this wealth position in the event of failure and the more difficulty will be faced in case of a sudden need for liquidity. Borrowing will add to the level of this risk, and so access to external funds will also be limited by the availability of own capital.

Kalecki pointed out that such increasing marginal risk with the amount invested requires modification of John Maynard Keynes' theory of the determination of aggregate investment spending. Keynes argued that investment should be undertaken up to the point where the 'marginal efficiency of investment', or the prospective rate of return on investment, equals the rate of interest. Kalecki noted that we must add the marginal risk premium to the interest rate. Keynes' *General Theory* (1964 [1936]: 144–5) notions of 'borrower's' and 'lender's' risk are getting after a similar idea, but Keynes did not fully identify or spell out the determinants of the type of risk Kalecki's article is recognizing.

Following from the above reasoning, the level of the marginal risk premium is given by the size of the own capital of the enterprise. In investment studies this idea of Kalecki's led to the use of current profits or cash flow, debt levels or ratios, and other measures of firms' access to liquidity as explanatory variables in empirical estimations. Important theoretical and empirical work on investment influenced by these considerations was performed by James Duesenberry, John Meyer, Edwin Kuh, and others in the 1950s and early 1960s (e.g. Meyer and Kuh 1957; Duesenberry 1958; Kuh 1963; and Meyer and Glauber 1964).

By the mid-1960s, however, the influence of Franco Modigliani and Merton Miller's (1958) article arguing that the degree of debt-leverage should not affect the value of a firm and of Dale Jorgenson's (1963, 1967, 1971) empirical investment studies supporting his 'neoclassical' investment model led to decreased support for the idea that 'financial' factors affect investment spending. All the while, though, Hyman Minsky was developing his 'financial instability hypothesis' as an interpretation of and addition to Keynes' theory, which came to the implications of Kalecki's principle of increasing risk by way of analysing the cyclical and secular patterns and effects of investment finance (Minsky 1957, 1963, 1975, 1986). Independently, Joseph Stiglitz and his co-authors have derived limitations on an enterprise's access to credit on the basis of informational imperfections (Stiglitz and Weiss 1981; Greenwald *et al.* 1984; Greenwald and Stiglitz 1988, 1993). Finally, Steve Fazzari and his co-authors have undertaken a number of empirical studies which reveal evidence restoring the importance of financial factors to investment spending (Fazzari and Mott 1986–7; Fazzari and Athey 1987; Fazzari *et al.* 1988; Carpenter *et al.* 1994).

I would argue that an even greater significance of Kalecki's principle of increasing risk is that it offers us an important, and I would even say, necessary, interpretation of the central conclusions of Keynes' *General Theory*. Keynes' ideas about investment, consumption, liquidity preference, and the like, which seem to be based on perhaps plausible but nevertheless 'ad hoc' insights from the point of view of neoclassical economics can through the principle of increasing risk become grounded in some fundamental principles of the income distribution and capital accumulation processes of a capitalist economic system. Relations which Keynes presented as dependent upon 'psychological' considerations can now be seen to be determined by income categories and their role in determining consumption and accumulation. The dependence of consumption on income, e.g. is due to the role of wages as payments for labouring rather than selling or renting property. Those who are dependent on labouring for their livelihood have no other collateral than their wage-income from which to finance consumption and so the correlation between consumption and wages, the major distributive share of national income, must be close.

The 'Keynesian' idea that fluctuations in investment spending are responsible for fluctuations in output and employment should be related to Karl Marx's notion of the circuit of capital, M–C–M'. The willingness and ability to sink profits into productive capital in the hope of making more profits also determines what profits will be there next period. So, across firms the amount of profits determines what is available both in terms of own funds and ability to borrow, and in the aggregate the willingness to sink these funds into illiquid investments determines the level of profits then realized, which are now available to support next period's investments.

Similarly, a drop in effective demand because investment is not considered sufficiently profitable in several or all industries cannot be overcome by liquidating unprofitable businesses or by an easy money policy. Neither lenders will want to provide nor borrowers be willing to commit to the repayment of finance with poor security. Wealth must be in the hands of those who will spend to prevent an economic downturn or to start a revival of economic activity (Mott 1982, 1985–6).

The importance of monetary magnitudes in 'Keynesian' macroeconomics, which has often been reduced to and criticized as 'money illusion', now also becomes justified. The importance of money in the economy is not that the right quantity of money has to be available to facilitate transactions at the existing price level. It is rather that value must be expected to be realized and actually realized in money for the circuit of capital with its alternating poles of liquidity and illiquidity to continue smoothly.

A Kaleckian macroeconomic model

To relate all this more precisely to the distribution of income and to relate both to macroeconomic performance, I will use a slight modification of a model constructed by Donald Harris in 1974 (see also Asimakopulos 1975 and Harcourt 1972: 210–14 for similar models):

$$pY = W + \Pi \tag{1}$$

$$W = wL \tag{2}$$

$$L = bY \tag{3}$$

$$pI + pA = s_{\Pi}\Pi + pT \tag{4}$$

$$p = \phi wb \tag{5}$$

Equation (1) provides that the aggregate price level, p, multiplied by real national income, Y, equals the aggregate wage bill, W, plus aggregate money profits, Π. Equation (2) separates the wage bill into the money wage, w, multiplied by the level of employment, L. L in turn is determined in equation (3) by b, the ratio of employment to national income or output, multiplied by Y. Equation (4) gives the Kaleckian macroeconomic equilibrium of injections equal to leakages by changes in the level and distribution of national income. Thus we have the price level multiplied by the level of real investment spending, I, plus p multiplied by autonomous spending, A, which here is export surplus plus real government spending, equal to the propensity to save out of profits, s_Π, multiplied by money profits plus p multiplied by real taxes, T. We are assuming zero saving out of wages. This simplifies the analysis and should not make a difference to the results unless we were to assume that the propensity to save out of wages is implausibly high relative to s_Π. Equation (5) tells us that the price level is determined by the mark-up, ϕ (>1), multiplied by the index of labour costs, b, as we are assuming a fully integrated economy, so that labour is the only non-produced input.

At this point the endogenous variables are p, Y, W, Π, and L. Equilibrium conditions from this model are:

$$Y^* = \frac{\phi(I + A - T)}{s_\Pi(\phi - 1)} \text{ and} \tag{6}$$

$$\left(\frac{\Pi}{p}\right)^* = \frac{I + A - T}{s_\Pi} \tag{7}$$

Equation (6) provides the Keynesian 'multiplier' relation of one over the propensity to save multiplied by investment plus government deficit plus export surplus, where since saving is only out of profits, the mark-up, which determines distribution between wages and profits, has to be included. Equation (7) shows Kalecki's determination of profits by spending out of profits plus government deficit and export surplus, or Keynes' 'widow's cruise' theory of profits in his *Treatise on Money* (1930/1971; see also Levy (1943) and Boulding (1950)).

The following investment function, which captures the influences on investment from profits and output relative to productive capacity already in place, provides the proper depiction of the influence of the principle of increasing risk on the determinants of investment. That is:

$$\frac{I}{Z} = \frac{I_0}{Z} + \alpha\frac{\Pi/p}{Z} + \beta\frac{Y}{Z} + \gamma - \delta\frac{i}{Z}, \text{ or} \tag{8}$$

$$I = I_0 + \alpha\frac{\Pi}{p} + \beta Y + \gamma Z - \delta i$$

where Z = productive capacity measured in terms of how much output it can produce, or full capacity output, I_0 = autonomous investment spending, and i = the relevant representative of the complex of interest rates. Strictly speaking, the logic of Kalecki's principle of increasing risk should have, rather than real profits, real business saving, which equals retained earnings plus depreciation allowances. We might also take the level of debt or the ratio of debt to equity or to total capital into account on the grounds of increasing risk, but that would complicate our mathematics without adding any insight to our basic question at this point (for permutations see Kalecki 1971a and Steindl 1952/1976).

The inclusion of an interest rate here requires some discussion. The effect of interest rates on business investment has been shown to be rather slight. Interest rates do, however, show a significant influence on residential investment and on consumer durables spending. The division of national income into the categories of consumption and investment by which all durable consumer goods are included in consumption expenditure except housing, which is counted as investment, is somewhat arbitrary. For the purposes of this chapter, we shall see, all that is needed is to show the effects of the parts of both consumption and investment which are influenced by total income and either profits or wages and those which are influenced by interest rates. This particular investment function will accomplish such.

Taking Z and i as given at any moment, we have six equations for our six unknowns, and we can solve the model for the equilibrium values of the endogenous variables of interest. Solving for Y and Π/p, we have

$$Y^* = \frac{\phi(A - T + I_0 + \gamma Z - \delta i)}{(s_\Pi - \alpha)(\phi - 1) - \beta\phi} \text{ and} \tag{9}$$

$$\left(\frac{\Pi}{p}\right)^* = \frac{(A - T + I_0 + \gamma Z - \delta i)(\phi - 1)}{(s_\Pi - \alpha)(\phi - 1) - \beta\phi} \tag{10}$$

Real wage income is given by

$$\left(\frac{W}{p}\right)^* = \frac{A - T + I_0 + \gamma Z - \delta i}{(s_\Pi - \alpha)(\phi - 1) - \beta\phi} \tag{11}$$

If we now start to examine changes in income distribution and their effects on macroeconomic performance, we see the following. The only parameter which might be thought to change distribution between wages and profits is the mark-up, ϕ. Obviously an increase in ϕ will lower wage income. If we look at the effect of a rise in ϕ on profits by differentiating $(\Pi/p)^*$ with respect to ϕ, we see:

$$\frac{\partial(\Pi/p)^*}{\partial\phi} = \frac{-\beta(A - T + I_0 + \gamma Z)}{[(s_\Pi - \alpha)(\phi - 1) - \beta\phi]^2} \tag{12}$$

This shows that, e.g. an increase in the mark-up will actually decrease profits. The economics behind this is as follows. The effect of a rise in the mark-up, or profits per unit, on total profits is given both by the change in profits per unit and the resultant change in the number of units sold. The change in the number of units sold attendant upon a change in the mark-up is given by differentiating Y^* with respect to ϕ, which yields:

$$\frac{\partial Y^*}{\partial \phi} = \frac{-(A - T - I_0 + \gamma Z)(s_\Pi - \alpha)}{[(s_\Pi - \alpha)(\phi - 1) - \beta\phi]^2} \tag{13}$$

Since we know that $s_\Pi > \alpha$, or national income would be negative, it must be that $\partial Y/\partial\phi < 0$. This will be true even if investment spending were taken to be unaffected by the change in the mark-up because a rise in the mark-up will redistribute income from wages, which here are all spent on consumption to profits, part of which are saved. The fact that investment should be further depressed by the fall in Y with a rise in ϕ makes the negative effect of a rise in the mark-up even stronger. The number of units sold thus drops so much that profits overall decrease despite the higher level of profits per unit.

If investment spending were not affected by the fall in Y (taking β in effect to be zero), $\partial(\Pi/p)/\partial\phi$ would equal zero. If we were to allow positive saving out of wage income, along with $\beta = 0$, as long as the propensity to save out of wages is less than the propensity to save out of profits, $\partial Y/\partial\phi$ would still be < 0, but $\partial(\Pi/p)/\partial\phi$ would now be positive. Still, the magnitude of saving out of wages is not likely to be high enough to make $\partial(\Pi/p)/\partial\phi$ large enough to be significant, and were we to re-introduce the likely effect on investment spending ($\beta > 0$), $\beta > s_W$, the propensity to save out of wages, would again make $\partial(\Pi/p)/\partial\phi < 0$ (see Mott and Slattery 1994 for the maths involved here). All this might lead us to think that an increase in mark-ups in order to gain finance for increased investment spending in accordance with the principle of increasing risk should only be warranted if the increase in investment spending had been decided on in advance and were to be maintained despite the decrease in sales attendant upon the rise in mark-ups and so decrease in real wages.

In the model as constituted so far, a fall in b, meaning a rise in productivity, will affect nothing because it will lower employment by as much as it increases real wages. A change in w will only affect the price level p as long as b and ϕ are unchanged. A rise in i will reduce national income, wages, profits, and employment. If we assume a positive correlation between Y and p, rising i should lower p as well, or its rate of change, if we posit the correlation to be between Y and the rate of change of p. Either of these correlations could give us a distributional conflict between the recipients of interest, or rentier income and those who receive either wage- or profit-income as rising prices decrease the real value of interest income.

Open economy considerations

To extend the analysis to more complex and perhaps more relevant situations, we can allow changes in prices also to have an effect on a national economy's trade balance. The simplest way to do this with the present model is to divide our parameter A into a term G for the level of government spending and a term for the export surplus or deficit, which we will take to be determined by a parameter μ multiplied by p plus a parameter m (the marginal propensity to import) multiplied by Y. Substituting for the endogenous variable p its equal, the exogenous variables ϕwb, and including the effect of mY, we will now have:

$$Y^* = \frac{\phi(G - T - \mu\phi wb + I_0 + \gamma Z - \delta i)}{(s_{\Pi} - \alpha)(\phi - 1) - \beta\phi + m\phi} \text{ and} \tag{14}$$

$$\left(\frac{\Pi}{p}\right)^* = \frac{(\phi - 1)(G - T - \mu\phi wb + I_0 + \gamma Z - \delta i)}{(s_{\Pi} - \alpha)(\phi - 1) - \beta\phi + m\phi} \tag{15}$$

Now, though the sign of $\partial Y/\partial\phi$ will still be negative, the sign of $\partial(\Pi/p)/\partial\phi$ will depend upon the sign of $m - \beta$. That is, though the existence of a high marginal propensity to import relative to the influence of changes in national income on investment cannot cause a rise in mark-ups actually to increase national income, it can while decreasing national income actually increase profits. The more open the economy then, the more room there is for a conflict between wages and profits.[1]

Another new development with the opening of our model economy is that we now can see effects on national and share incomes from changes in the money wage. A rise in w, unless equally or more than offset by a fall in ϕ, will now reduce the real income of every class of income recipients.

This reminds us that the effect of increases in ϕ should now be affected by whether they come at the expense of money wages or prices. If higher markups come about due more to lower money wages than to higher prices, the magnitude of the harm to national output and employment will be less. Another matter that we need to take into account in the open economy case is that changes in interest rates will now have a stronger effect on output, employment, and prices because of their effects on foreign exchange rates.

Longer-run effects

If we alter our model further by taking into account the effects of investment spending on productivity and capacity, we will see some more important considerations for macroeconomic performance and policy choices. Obviously as investment spending increases productivity, we can decrease the positive correlation between output and price increases. The more open the economy, of course the greater the significance of this effect. If higher mark-ups do turn out to lead to higher profits and higher investment, here is where a tradeoff of present for future real wages can be a wise choice. Unlike the case of accepting lower money and real wages to keep the domestic price level down to please the rentier mentality or the 'gnomes of Zurich', a present sacrifice in this context can bring a significant future gain, provided that the productivity gains that are achieved do go to wages and not to profits, especially once an investment boom has created an amount of productive capacity that will not be utilized unless real wages and so consumption demand are high enough.[2]

If we haven't previously realized it, we surely by now must see that parts and certainly the whole of this story can only be told by entering the realm of dynamics. The relations among incomes, employment, prices, mark-ups, money wages, interest rates, investment, and consumption that we have examined require a deeper analysis of their timing than I have presented here. To the extent that they involve policy decisions as well as the consequences of firm and household economic behaviour under the limits given by the principle of increasing risk, such phenomena are not mechanical in the ways they develop over time.

As a start that may point us a good bit along the way, hopefully in this chapter we see many of the implications of Kalecki's analysis and we have set out the major issues helpfully. As a conclusion at this stage of the work, I suggest that we remember that, as Kalecki (1939a: 318) insightfully wrote, 'The tragedy of investment is that it causes crisis because it is useful'. He also noted the baleful consequences to employment and incomes arising because of the maintenance of price-cost margins at a time when investment spending is not considered to be profitable (Kalecki 1954a: 254–5).

What we can perhaps hope for when attempting to use and to build on his analytical framework is to be able to identify some likely consequences of various policy choices and ways in which forethought and social cooperation can prevent at least the worst of the unnecessary suffering into which we can fall. Ideally, we will learn to do even more.

Notes

1 Philip Arestis has suggested dividing the import propensity into a propensity to spend on imports out of wages vs. out of profits. This would not only enrich the analysis as it is, but it would also facilitate consideration of choices in tax policy.

2 Since our variable I stands for gross investment, in equation (8) the parameter γ must be >0 because gross investment can never be negative, and as we multiply through by Z, in the levels Z becomes a scale variable. We know, however that a lower Y/Z will depress I/Z, so growth in Z in excess of growth in Y will lead I to be lower than otherwise.

8 Is equality harmful to growth?

Henryk Flakierski

Introduction

In this chapter I analyse the influence of one factor only on growth in capitalism, namely of income distribution. One has to be aware of the fact that there are many other factors which affect growth independently of income distribution. Hence inferences and conclusions from our analysis must be taken with caution and cannot be considered as full proof.

However, income distribution is an important category in analysing growth in all major theoretical models. For example, for the classical school, the structure of income distribution is one of the major factors determining growth. In this model, assuming full utilization of capacities, any redistribution in favour of profits or in favour of the more affluent, given the propensities to save, will increase the size of savings and, with it, automatically, investment and growth. Considering that in this model savings determined investment, any increase in inequality of income distribution is growth enhancing.

In contradistinction with this approach, in Kalecki's theoretical system, assuming underutilization of capacities as the norm, a more egalitarian distribution of income is one of the more important factors of increasing effective demand, employment and growth.

Kalecki rejects the idea that an increase in inequality necessarily will increase savings and even if it does, it does not follow that it will necessarily increase investment. The classical model of a tradeoff between inequality and growth is based on unrealistic assumptions of full utilization of capacity and perfect competition.

Under realistic assumptions of under-utilization of capacities and monopolistic structures as the norm in capitalism, redistribution from wages to profits may have a negative effect on aggregate income, because as Kalecki argues, the decline of wages will reduce the profits in the sector of producing consumer goods for the workers. Therefore, it cannot be excluded that total profits and with it total savings in the economy will not increase (Kalecki 1971a). The same idea is expressed in the Keynesian language in the following way: every redistribution in favour of the high-income group will reduce the marginal propensity to consume and with it a decline of the multiplier will ensue. As a result, a higher propensity to save will not increase the amount of savings (Keynes 1964).

What is more, according both to Kalecki and Keynes, by redistributing income from the more to the less affluent the propensity to save is reduced. As a result, a better utilization of capacities is achieved and with it a larger aggregate income. Similarly, a shift in income distribution through taxation of capital to public expenditure on income support for the poor will result in higher levels of demand, investment and growth. High wages spur effective demand, whereas reducing them on a macro scale, claims Kalecki, will not increase profits under monopolistic market structures, and, therefore, will not be growth-enhancing. Kalecki's theory of effective demand as the major determining factor of the national income is *par excellence* egalitarian (Kalecki 1944a: 372–6).

A critique of the anti-egalitarian approach

By and large, anti-egalitarianists do not deny that redistribution of income in favour of wages will have a positive effect on effective demand. However, at the new stage of capitalist development (global competition and export-led growth) the positive effect of redistribution on aggregate effective demand is more than offset by the negative effect of increased cost of production, which undermines international competitiveness and with it the net export surplus (Bowles and Boyer 1995). In other words, the global integration of national economies has made the output more sensitive to the world demand conditions. As a result, the enhancing effect of high wages and social benefits on effective demand has become less important for growth than the negative effect of redistributive policies on the cost of production and investment. The above arguments for economic policy reorientation from the demand side to supply-side problems have led to promoting policies of greater inequalities, justified by a promise, in the long run, of a trickle-down effect. The analysis of supply-side problems is obviously useful, but the neo-classical supply-siders try to justify larger inequalities as a tool for enhancing performance.

The neo-classical supply-siders overlooked certain important aspects, which indicate that economic performance is positively correlated with smaller inequalities. To mention only a few:

i Investment in human capacities: redistribution of income will improve the material conditions of life of the less affluent part of society. Improvement in their health, education, self-esteem will inevitably have a positive effect on their economic performance, whereas an increase in inequalities will have a minimal effect on economic performance, especially as far as the top income groups are concerned.

ii Conflictual relations are costly: monitoring employees in a conflictual atmosphere (created by large differentials) is costly and very often inefficient. A lack of identification with the firm is as well conducive to difficulties in promoting employees' performance. In other words, a high degree of inequality exacerbates conflictual relations and with it agency problems. Institutional structures supporting high levels of inequality are very often costly to maintain. Private corporations especially face serious costs in enforcing inequalities like expenditures on work supervision, and labour discipline to implement requires many monitoring resources. Co-operation and trust are essential to economic performance, particularly where information is incomplete and unequally distributed in the work-force. More equal societies are better able to develop trust and co-operation than societies more economically divided.

iii Some economists of the new left (Gordon 1995) strongly emphasized that conflicts and co-ordination problems are conducive to low productivity growth and investment, even when other elements of the macro-economic structure are positively affecting effective demand or squeezing out more work effort. Egalitarian distribution can play a positive role in solving agency and co-ordination problems and with it enhance productivity growth, independently of their effect on effective demand. Solving these problems through a more egalitarian structure is '. . . a better form of supply side economics than the conservative policy of repressive redistribution and deregulation' (Epstein and Gintis 1995). However, to reduce agency and co-ordination problems in capitalism, strong egalitarian policies would require systemic changes in the relations between owners and workers. This would likely require changes in the enterprise property rights, which naturally is a tall order to implement in the framework of the capitalist system.

iv The argument that redistribution of income, in view of globalization, will have a negative effect on investment is strongly exaggerated. The process of investment is still mainly national; the vast majority of investment in the developed countries is of domestic origin. On top of it international movement of direct investment takes place mainly between high wage countries and not from the high wage countries to the low wage countries.[1] Hence, the argument that high wages are an impediment to investment is not very convincing. What is more, globalization of the world economy has even now serious obstacles to unrestrained international capital flows. As a result in the long run, profit rates, costs, prices, are not equalized, as the neo-classical theory claims. One of the weaknesses of the neo-classical approach is the assumption that transaction enforcement by a third party is costless. In reality many domestic and virtually all international transactions lack such a third party enforcement. Because of that internal lenders will lend or invest only as much capital as their enforcement capabilities will allow (Epstein and Gintis 1992).

What is the empirical evidence about the correlation of income distribution and growth? Although statistical methods used in this matter are far from perfect, divergent methodologies often give very different results. However, recent research had badly shaken the notion of an efficiency-equity tradeoff, or in other words has badly shaken the equality pessimism, which asserts that egalitarian objectives negatively affect economic performance. For instance, Persson and Tabellini (1994) find that inequality and growth are negatively correlated in a cross section of 67 countries as well as in long-time series for nine developed capitalist countries. This study finds as well a positive correlation between equality and investment. The same conclusions we find in some studies of the World Bank for the 16 OECD countries: slower growth in labour productivity is associated with higher inequalities in those countries (OECD 1991; Glynn 1995). What is more, countries experiencing rapid growth in productivity between the 1960s and 1990s, including Japan and South Korea, have less inequality than the more *laissez-faire* industrialized countries, which have experienced at the same time weak productivity growth and higher inequalities (Bowles *et al.* 1990). The positive correlation between equality and growth is undisputed as far as the 'golden age' in the developed countries is concerned after World War II, i.e. in the years 1947–73. In this period, inequality was modestly reduced in the western world (Sawyer 1982). It is a fact that developed countries as a whole in this period had grown faster under a welfare regime than in any other period in the history of these countries. The reversal of egalitarian policies since the mid-1970s and the gradual erosion of the welfare state have not been accompanied by high productivity growth.

Irrespective of how equality affects productivity, egalitarianism is a value in itself. It is not just and not only a means to unrelated goals. 'Severe inequalities degrade those on the bottom. This degradation violates the duty to show equal respect. It damages self-respect. It destroys fraternity. . . . Equality is of intrinsic moral importance because of its link to fairness, self-respect, equal respect and fraternity' (Husman 1998: 83).

The bargaining power in Kalecki's theory and its critics

In his theory of distribution Kalecki considered the bargaining power of organized labour as one of the factors which determine the share of wages and profits in the national income. The more powerful the trade unions, under conditions of oligopolistic markets and underutilization of capacities as the norm in capitalism, the more the mark-ups will decrease and with them the redistribution of income in favour of wages will take place (Kalecki 1971a). However, taking into account the fact that the balance of forces in the class struggle in capitalism is not favourable for the workers in most cases, the possibility of changing the income distribution in favour of wages via pressure by organized labour, can take place only seldom and under special circumstances. Some economists are questioning Kalecki's idea that organized labour can, through the class struggle, change in the long run the distribution of income in capitalism at all.

Robert Brenner argues that under capitalism, profits and wages are not entirely the outcome of the interaction between capital and labour (Brenner 1998: 229). Although the class struggle is not without importance in the distributional process, it is rather production, employment and distribution which depend upon autonomous decision to invest, which are entirely under the control of capital. A satisfactory rate of return is a *sine qua non* for the viability of the firm. The capitalists can achieve a reversal in the distribution back in their favour without confronting their workers directly. They are able to respond to profit-reducing increases in labour costs just by reducing the rate of growth of capital and with it the demand for labour, which will moderate the labour demand for wage increases. Hence, according to Brenner, a profit squeeze linked with labour demands is possible only in the short run. It seems to me that Brenner's criticism of Kalecki's view on the role of class struggle in changing income distribution is not justified. Kalecki has made it very clear that the bargaining power of the workers can change the income distribution only 'in fairly narrow limits' (Kalecki 1971a: 163). Kalecki is very clear about the possible scope of changes in the distribution of income under the pressure of organized labour. He was aware that squeezing profits has its political limits, which eventually will undermine business confidence, a confidence so important for the functioning of the capitalist economy, and that sooner or later the captains of industry will say 'enough is enough' to make concessions to the workers and by reducing investment and government spending, the capitalists will put the workers in their place. Even tight labour markets, even strong labour unions, cannot, in the long run, change the distribution of income to the detriment of profits. The system, in the long run, has an internal servomechanism to defend the profit rate against labour encroachment.

Kalecki in his seminal article 'Political aspects of full employment' (Kalecki 1943), gives a systemic insight why full employment, and with it high wages, are incompatible with the capitalist mode of production. Although he assumed that formally it is possible to achieve full employment by redistributing income in favour of wages, in order to stimulate effective demand, however, such redistribution will be opposed successfully by the capitalists as measures contradicting the logic of private capitalist enterprise. The pioneering nature of the 'Political aspects of full employment' article as well as the author's foresight with regard to the future development of capitalism justify a lengthy quotation:

> under a regime of permanent full employment, the 'sack' would cease to play its role as a disciplinary measure. The social position of the boss would be undermined, and the self-assurance and class-consciousness of the working class would grow. Strikes for wage increases and improvements in conditions of work would create political tension. It is true that profits would be higher under a regime of full employment than they are on the average under *laissez-faire*, and even the rise in wage rates resulting

> from the stronger bargaining power of the workers is less likely to reduce profits than to increase prices, and thus adversely affects only the rentier interests. But 'discipline in the factories' and 'political stability' are more appreciated than profits by business leaders. Their class instinct tells them that lasting full employment is unsound from their point of view, and that unemployment is an integral part of the 'normal' capitalist system.
>
> (Kalecki 1943b)

The new macroeconomics of the Left

Kalecki's idea that capitalism is not able to create institutions for disciplining workers without unemployment, has inspired a new type of macroeconomics by the New Left. On this theoretical basis, they have analysed in the 1980s and 1990s the causes of the demise of the 'golden age', especially the analysis of the contradictory nature of the accumulation process in capitalism (Marglin and Bhaduri 1990; Epstein and Gintis 1995: 3–8; Bowles and Boyer 1990).

These economists have posed the question: 'Why has the "golden age", with its high growth rate, increases in real wages (very often faster than labour productivity), and a rich developed welfare system, collapsed in the 1970s?'. They make it clear that this cannot be explained by some external shock like the increase in prices due to the oil crisis. The reason for the collapse has deep structural causes. The mere success of the 'golden age' contains the seed of its distraction. The key element during the 'golden age' was state management of aggregate demand through fiscal and monetary policies. The state, in order to manage aggregate demand at a high level of employment (in some cases full employment), has introduced the institution of bargaining and labour law, favourable for the employees, as a part of a social contract to reduce class conflict through an equitable distribution of income. The achievements of this period created an 'illusion that a new era of co-operative capitalism has replaced the antagonistic class relations of an earlier period . . .' (Marglin and Bhaduri 1990). But, as Kalecki has predicted, when the regime of high employment persists for a certain prolonged period of time, the working class becomes more assertive and militant, better organized and more cohesive as a class. Under conditions of high employment the cost of losing a job declines and with it pressures of the employers on the workers to increase labour productivity become less effective. Under the regime of high employment levels it becomes difficult to maintain labour discipline. Such a situation obviously is not in the interest of the capitalist class, and a retreat from high levels of employment will take place.

Although Kalecki found redistribution of income in favour of wages desirable for full employment and growth, he never had any illusions that such policies could be sustained in the long run under capitalism because it is against the interests of the capitalist class. Hence his prediction of a political business cycle, from increased to reduced interventionism. The prediction of the Left, based on Kalecki's theory of distribution of the non-egalitarian trend, has been vindicated.

Already in the second half of the 1970s, and later in the 1980s and 1990s, in most OECD countries, there was a visible increase in inequalities of earnings (wages and salaries). But this experience is not uniform across all countries. There was a big variety of change in this field. The USA, UK and Canada were the leaders in this anti-egalitarian trend. It is interesting to note that those were already countries with the highest level of inequalities in the developed world. Although even in the most egalitarian Nordic countries we observe some modest increases in inequality of earnings, but those increases have taken place in countries with low levels of inequality; nevertheless, this was a reversal of the previous trend of egalitarianism.[2]

A similar conclusion in this matter is made by A.B. Atkinson (1999). However, the scope of his income concept is wider; apart from earnings, he takes into account other incomes linked to market activities, like income of the self-employed, dividends, interest, rent, etc., but the outcome of his analysis of changes in inequality are not very different from P. Gottschalk and T.M. Smeeding, because earnings have a predominant influence on the distribution of the total market-related incomes, because they constitute the majority 70 per cent of market income for most households.

It is therefore not an exaggeration to conclude that we observed, in the 1980s and 1990s, an indisputable decline in labour power in all major capitalist countries, especially in the USA, UK and Canada. What is more, in the above mentioned countries, labour was not able, even in prosperous years of fast growth in productivity, to change the distribution of income in labour's favour. The stagnation of real wages in the above-mentioned countries in the 1990s, in spite of high growth in productivity, is a good case in point.

A question arises whether or not the increases in inequality of earnings and other market-related incomes, have been mitigated by fiscal policies of the state via taxation and money transfers and other social benefits (Atkinson 2000). Although there are differences between countries in this respect, in most developed countries fiscal policies of the state have partially or entirely offset the increase in inequality of market-related incomes. As a result, the final distribution, measured by the disposable income (equal to market incomes plus all kinds of transfers, minus taxes), was rather stable, especially in the Nordic countries, or shows only modest increases in inequality.

This picture is quite different in the US and UK – countries of the highest level of inequalities in the industrialized world. We observe in the 1980s and 1990s an increase in inequality not only in market related incomes, but also in disposable incomes.[3] Although there are many factors which have contributed to the increase in inequality of the final distribution, like the composition of the families, and other demographic aspects, the deliberate state policies have played an important role. Direct taxation has become less progressive, and transfers and other social benefits have become less favourable for the recipients. As a result, the income policies of the state not only have not offset the increase in inequalities of earnings and other related market incomes, but have actually increased the inequalitarian trend of the overall final distribution.

Can this trend be reversed and a return to more egalitarian policies of the 'golden age' be effected? This is not very likely. This would require the state to reconcile the interests of the major classes. The state must become a neutral broker between their interests. However, 'the capitalist state which acts to the mutual benefit of all the major classes can only be the product of special and passing historical circumstances' (Bhaduri 1986: 286). Besides, to implement egalitarian measures to overcome co-ordination and agency problems in order to enhance labour productivity growth, will require systemic changes incompatible with the capitalist mode of production.

It cannot be denied that active demand management by the state has played an important role in the success of the 'golden age'. However, it should not be overlooked that the success of this era took place under special favourable circumstances, which existed in the developed countries at that time. It is unlikely that those circumstances will repeat themselves. There were other autonomous factors apart from the active role of the state in demand management, which have contributed to the success of this post-war period. A strong push in the release of pent-up wartime consumer demand and post-war reconstruction. Fear of communism especially in the 1950s and the 1960s created strong political pressure to make concessions to employees as far as social welfare is concerned. Another aspect of fear of communism was the cold war with its tremendous build-up of armaments, which was conducive to maintaining high levels of effective demand.

Notes

1 Although capital flows to underdeveloped and post-communist countries are not negligible, they still comprise a much smaller part of capital investment.

2 See more in detail in Gottschalk and Smeeding (1997: 633–87). Statistical data computed by the above authors indicate that the decile ratio for male employees is in the US nearly twice as high as in Sweden (7.2, 3.9), and for female employees more than twice as high (11.6, 5.1). See table on p. 643. As far as the Gini coefficient – a summary measure of inequality – is concerned, the level of this indicator is 1.53 times larger in the US than in Sweden. See p. 661.

3 The decile ratio in the period of 1979–93 in the US has increased by more than 30 per cent and the Gini coefficient in this period by 16 per cent. See more in detail in Gottschalk and Smeeding (1997: Fig. 4, 664, table 3, 665. The situation in the UK was even worse – the increase in the Gini coefficient for disposable income in the period 1977–90 was 42 per cent. See Atkinson (1999: Fig. 1, 4).

Part III

The policies

9 A Kaleckian policy framework

Peter Reynolds

Introduction

The aim of this chapter is to draw together the various components of a policy agenda, deriving from the work of Kalecki that is appropriate for developed economies in the contemporary world. The proposed agenda is Kaleckian in the sense that it draws on and derives from the work of Kalecki.

Any proposals for economic policy need to be based on a particular view of how economies work and thus a clear theoretical framework for any alternative economic policy requires articulating. My own leaning is towards the type of framework that is partly explicit and partly implicit in the writings of Michal Kalecki.

One of the most notable features of Kalecki's work was that he contributed significantly to the economics of capitalist economies, socialist economies and developing economies. This reflected recognition that neither economic theory nor economic policy could be developed in isolation from the institutional context. Hence, in the early twenty-first century, there is little point in articulating a framework that does not translate into a highly internationalized (global) and highly technological (information-based) economy and furthermore, into a world where countering inflation is high on the policy agenda. The 'stylized economy' which I propose to consider is one where unemployment, in a significant and meaningful sense, not only exists but persists and has persisted for many years. Hence, the economy we are examining bears a close resemblance to OECD Europe and I leave it to others to decide how far the ideas translate to other economies.

Following a few words on conventional economic policy in the next section outline the bare bones of a theoretical framework, deriving largely from Kalecki but with many similarities to the work of Kaldor and Keynes. In section four, which is the main part of the chapter, I examine some implications for economic policy, focusing mainly on the topics of employment and inflation. Section five concludes the chapter.

The state of conventional economic policy

So as to be clear about the difference between the policy proposals to be outlined below and both conventional and so-called 'Keynesian' predecessors, we will take a very brief 'Cook's tour' of the main approaches to policy that have been adopted post-1945. The 1950s and 1960s perhaps represented the golden age of macroeconomics, where for all significant First World economies 'Keynesian' policies successfully ensured the concurrent maintenance of low unemployment and low inflation. The predictions of this type of 'hydraulic Keynesianism', to use the expression coined by Coddington (1983) are captured in the simple Phillips curve, whereby policy-makers face a trade off between unemployment and inflation. The popular identification of Keynesian economics with demand management meant that the simultaneous occurrence of both high unemployment and high inflation signalled the demise of 'Keynesianism'. The first modern phase of monetarism, which Tobin (1981) and others, including Arestis and Sawyer (1999a) refer to as Monetarism Mark I, gained the upper hand. Friedman (1968) and others revamped the Phillips curve in terms of an expectations-augmented approach and managed to tell a bizarre but apparently convincing story that Keynesian employment policies only worked because they were able to fool people in to working, under the misapprehension that they were receiving higher real wages than was really the case. Furthermore, as soon as people realized that their real wages were not as high as they had previously believed, they quit their jobs! Hence, when the concept of rational expectations was added to this analysis, along with various additional assumptions about the extent to which people have access to information and can process that information, we have the New Classical Macroeconomics, or Monetarism Mark II, where the only role for demand management in affecting employment is a very short-lived one, whereby if people can be taken by surprise they can be fooled in to taking a job – which, of course, they will subsequently quit when they realize that they are not being paid as much, in real terms, as they thought.

In the world just described, the only lasting effects of changes in aggregate demand are on prices. Furthermore, following a belief in Ricardian Equivalence, the only way for governments to influence aggregate demand is via monetary policy, so that, in this version of Monetarism, changes in the money supply are the main macroeconomic policy instrument and they are directed at the objective of price stability. The most extreme manifestation of this approach to macroeconomic policy was the early 1980s, which was characterized by Monetary Authorities independently targeting National Monetary Aggregates. The economic policies pursued by President Reagan in the US and Prime Minister Margaret Thatcher in the UK were among the most extreme examples. Now we come to the version of monetarism operating in the late 1990s and early twenty-first century which, following Arestis and Sawyer (1999a), we refer to as Monetarism Mark III. There is a subtle change in emphasis in that now interest rates are explicitly the policy instrument and inflation is explicitly targeted. The policy algorithm is essentially: 'When economies are thought to be "overheating" interest rates are increased.' There is now an extensive literature on 'inflation targeting', including discussion of the indicators used to signal overheating, although this is generally taken to mean either that inflation is increasing or that it is expected to increase.[1] Appreciation of the formation of economic agents' expectations remains an important underpinning of this approach to policy. Hence, there is also a fashion to favour Central Bank Independence, to improve the credibility of the Monetary Authority in a world where economic agents are assumed to be forward looking. Despite declared beliefs that there is no role for 'demand management' to reduce unemployment; whenever the threat of inflation arises the Pavlovian response is to raise interest rates, with the declared intention of reducing consumer demand (never mind investment for the moment) to reduce inflationary pressures.

In a publication produced by the Monetary Policy Committee of the Bank of England, the Bank of England's view of the transmission mechanism is set out.

> First, official interest rate decisions affect market interest rates. . . . At the same time, policy actions and announcements affect expectations about the future course of the economy and the confidence with which these expectations are held, as well as affecting asset prices and the exchange rate.
>
> Second, these changes in turn affect the spending, saving and investment behaviour of individuals and firms in the economy. . . . So changes in the official interest rate affect the demand for goods and services produced.
>
> Third, the level of demand relative to domestic supply capacity . . . is a key influence on domestic inflationary pressure.
>
> Fourth, exchange rate movements have a direct effect . . . and an indirect effect . . . on the component of overall inflation that is imported.
>
> (Bank of England Monetary Policy Committee 1999: 3)[2]

Thus, it is acknowledged that monetary policy works through aggregate demand and hence that it affects short-term output as well as long-term inflation. In fact the Bank of England attempts to quantify the relative effects. Econometric simulations with the Bank of England's own model, 'suggests that temporarily raising rates relative to a base case by 1 percentage point for one year might be expected to lower output by something of the order of 0.2 to 0.35 per cent after about a year, and to reduce inflation by around 0.2 percentage points to 0.4 percentage points a year or so after that, all relative to the base case' (ibid.).

Following a brief review of the Kaleckian theoretical framework, I shall argue that such an approach to policy is inappropriate and condemns approximately 13 million citizens of the EU, or 33 million citizens of the OECD to long-term unemployment.[3]

The theoretical framework

The model that I propose to sketch is essentially that contained in *Theory of Economic Dynamics* (Kalecki 1954a). We assume a two-sector economy, comprising a 'manufacturing' sector where price changes are largely cost-determined and a 'raw materials' sector, where price changes are largely determined by demand. As Kalecki noted, 'these two types of price formation arise out of different conditions of supply' (Kalecki 1954a: 11). In the primary sector there tends to be inelastic supply, particularly in the short period. In the manufacturing sector prices are determined by a mark-up on costs, where the mark-up reflects the degree of monopoly.

This dichotomy is an analytical convenience. Following Kalecki, we acknowledge that in the manufacturing sector there may be some change in the mark-up over the trade cycle and we can also be flexible about the exact composition of the two sectors. For example, in most economies, the housing and construction sector exhibits characteristics more in common with the primary goods sector than the manufacturing sector and there is much scope to argue about where we place the service sector, though at least a large part of it does exhibit characteristics more in common with the manufacturing sector.

In passing, we note that by determining the mark-up, which we define here as profits plus overheads plus prime costs relative to prime costs, the distribution of the product of the manufacturing sector is thereby determined. To make this point most forcibly, if we momentarily abstract from materials inputs and overheads, then the mark-up is simply the reciprocal of the real product wage. We define P, Q and L as aggregate price level, gross output and labour input respectively and let k and w represent the mark-up and the money wage rate. Thus, $PQ = kwL$. Rearrangement then shows the real wage, $w/P = Q/kL = (1/k)(Q/L)$. The real wage is the reciprocal of the mark-up multiplied by output per person. From this, very simplified, perspective, the real wage is determined not in the labour market but in the product market. We return to this below.

Kalecki's microeconomic analysis of prices is juxtaposed with his macroeconomic analysis of profits and investment so that output is determined in a way very similar to Keynes' *General Theory*. In *Theory of Economic Dynamics*, profits are determined by past investment and a 'Kaleckian multiplier' which (for a closed economy with no taxation) is the inverse of the capitalists' propensity to save. '[T]he gross income . . . is pushed up to a point at which profits out of it, as determined by the "distribution factors" correspond to the level of investment . . .' (Kalecki 1954a: 61).

An important feature of the Kaleckian approach is that it permits us to highlight the interaction between the manufacturing and primary goods sectors. As demand for manufactured goods expands, the demand for inputs from the primary sector increases and their prices rise. These price rises become cost increases for the manufacturing sector and via the mark-up these are translated into price rises.

The link between changes in industrial output and commodity prices is not conjecture. From a variety of sources, samples, estimation procedures and precise measures of the variables concerned, the evidence very strongly substantiates the existence of a strong and statistically significant relationship between changes in the level of world industrial production and changes in the prices of primary commodities. (See, for example, Sylos-Labini 1982; Kaldor 1983b; van Wijnbergen 1985; Gilbert 1990; Bloch and Sapsford 1991–2, 1996, 2000; Reynolds 1992; Borensztein and Reinhart 1994; Hua 1988.) The relationship appears to be more pronounced after about 1970, since when, for every 1 per cent rise in industrial sector output, above trend, commodity prices increase by approximately 1.5–2.5 per cent.

The Kaleckian framework and economic policy

Output and employment

Clearly, it is in the theory determining the levels of output and employment that there is significant similarity in the works of Keynes and Kalecki. Although Kalecki wrote extensively on effective demand, there are just three aspects to the problem of effective demand that we consider here. These are (i) unemployment persistence and the problem of effective demand in the long run and the short run; (ii) the potential sources of demand; and (iii) contemporary constraints on demand management.

Unemployment persistence, the long run and the short run

As already indicated, in the European OECD economies, not only are there high levels of unemployment but these levels have persisted for many years. With the exception of a three-year period between 1989 and 1991 in Germany and a similar period since 1999 in the UK, none of the major European Union economies have had unemployment below 6 per cent since 1982 and double-digit figures have been common – or even typical.[4] For two decades there have been more than 11 million people unemployed. There are currently 13 million people unemployed in the European Union alone. Whether or not one believes in the monopoly capitalism or stagnationist theses of Baran and Sweezy (1968), Steindl (1952/1976) and other 'Kaleckians'; as Bharadwaj (1983) observed, once it is clear that the economy does not tend towards full employment even in the long run; then it follows that effective demand is a problem in the long run too. Furthermore, as is clear from Kalecki's (1968) reference to the long run as a succession of short periods, it is futile to seek a different theory of effective demand for the long run.

In Kalecki's (1950) 'note on long-run unemployment', he argued that although cyclical unemployment is usually explained in terms of fluctuations in aggregate demand, if productive capacity is sufficient to maintain full employment and there is no shortage of labour during booms; then, 'the unemployment arising during depressions is tantamount to a deficiency of effective demand on the average over the period of the cycle' (Kalecki 1951: 63). Unfortunately, where unemployment has persisted for many years, the existence of sufficient capacity to maintain full employment cannot be assured and consequently the question of capacity in the manufacturing sector, along with other constraints to the use of demand management policies must be considered. These problems are returned to below.

Recognizing that there is a long-term deficiency of demand takes us only a little way further towards understanding the nature of the problem. Even if the proximate cause of the high unemployment is a reduction in demand, the appropriate solution may not simply be to increase aggregate demand. One way to perceive the problem is that we need to find a way of moving from the current steady state of high unemployment to a steady state that has acceptably low levels of unemployment and acceptably low rates of inflation. Recognizing that such a steady state exists is one thing. Finding a way to get there is another.

Kalecki (1951) argued that if there is a long-term problem of a deficiency of demand then one appropriate policy might be to switch effective demand from those with a relatively low propensity to spend to those with a relatively high propensity to spend. Since the current monetary policy regime is predicated on the assumption that high interest rates are associated with lower levels of consumers' spending, largely due to the redistributive effects from high spending debtors to low spending creditors, it follows that one way to address the long-run deficiency of demand is via a long-term strategy of permanently low interest rates. However, even if low interest rates are one of the features of our preferred, high employment steady state, it does not follow that reducing interest rates will necessarily lead to increased employment at least not with inflation rates that are politically acceptable. The dynamics of transition need to be addressed.

Potential sources of demand

In maintaining a level of demand high enough to sustain full employment, Kalecki acknowledges the importance of markets external to capitalism. Effectively, Kaldor (1983a) made the same point. He reminded us of the argument made by Keynes that endogenous demand may not be sufficient to match full-employment aggregate supply and so a source of demand exogenous to private capitalism may be necessary. However, in the contemporary world it is difficult to identify a sufficiently powerful source.

Issues concerning the composition of demand can most readily be examined using a simple flow of funds framework of the form:

$$(G - T) + (PX - PY) + (X - M) = 0$$

where terms are as conventionally defined.

The stimulus can come from the left-hand side of any of the three bracketed terms but almost certainly all five other terms will evolve subsequently. There may be constraints associated with any of these terms, though at the moment there is a strong political constraint attached to the budget deficit, so that there is a *prime facie* case for focusing policy on either the private or foreign sector. However, since the crisis in economic policy is manifest at a global level, it seems that least resistance is likely for any policies that are directed at the private sector. To be sustained, a high-employment steady state will require a permanently high level of private sector demand.

Contemporary constraints to demand management

The constraints to demand management in a contemporary setting include:

- i political considerations;
- ii the international dimension;
- iii the perceived government budget constraint and
- iv inflationary impact.

We deal only briefly with the first three of these.

Political considerations

Political constraints to the adoption of full employment policies were well articulated in the famous 1943 paper, 'Political aspects of full employment'. They are also further discussed by Kaldor (1983a). Apart from the dislike of government intervention in the economy *per se*, the bottom line appears to be that if full employment is sustained then workers will have the upper hand; the threat of the sack will cease to be an effective disciplinary measure and worker productivity will be reduced. This is clearly an important matter and other contributors to this volume address it.

The international dimension

One of the constraints to the use of demand management policy that was voiced particularly during the 1970s was concern that if an individual country expanded alone then it would have to endure an increase in imports, leading to balance of payments difficulties if the exchange rate were pegged or to a depreciation in the currency if the exchange rate was left to market forces.

One response, which was associated with the term 'international Keynesianism', was to suggest that this problem could be avoided if the major industrial economies were to expand together. Although a global demand expansion may go some way towards addressing individual countries' balance of payments constraints, the experience following the Bonn summit of 1978, where the then G5 economies pursued just such a policy, was a renewed bout of inflation. Within the Kaleckian model outlined above, this is exactly what we would expect. If all countries seek to expand together then the pressures on the world's commodity markets will be severe, due to supply inelasticities. Inflation is the natural consequence. Paradoxically, inflation is likely to be less of a problem for individual countries that choose to 'go it alone'.

The perceived government budget constraint

The problem of the government's budget constraint may be more political than economic but nevertheless it needs to be addressed. Despite an apparent consensus that the 3 per cent limit imposed under the Maastricht Treaty was arbitrary, its continuation under the Growth and Stability Pact seems to be assured. However, as Arestis and Sawyer (1999a) point out, to the extent that the constraint is based on concerns of long-term stability, the sustainable deficit is determined by the difference between the country's growth rate and interest rate. The higher the growth rate and the lower the interest rate, the larger the sustainable deficit. It is worth making two observations on this condition, both of which were made by Kalecki (1943b). First, not all interest payments are a burden since interest paid to domestic residents will be subject to tax, so that the net interest burden will be slightly lower. Second, a policy of low interest rates can reduce the effect of this particular constraint on fiscal expansion.

To the extent that the deficit is a problem, then following Allsopp (1993) and Allsopp and Vines (1998), this is most helpfully analysed within a Flow of Funds framework, as set out above. The government sector's deficit is then seen, at least in part, as an endogenous response to a collection of private sector decisions which in aggregate imply a private sector surplus. This points to the need to encourage private sector spending and as I shall argue below, there is particularly the need, at least in the transition phase, to encourage investment until capacity is restored.[5]

Inflation

Although the problem of avoiding inflation may be examined simply as one of the constraints to achieving full employment, its dominant position in the policy agenda of most governments leads us to treat price stability also as an objective in its own right.

In a series of papers in *The Bulletin of the Oxford University Institute of*

Statistics in the early 1940s (subsequently reproduced in *Studies in War Economics*) Kalecki commented on the government's response, particularly its budgets, to the pressures resulting from financing the war economy. Indeed, in Kalecki (1941) he commented that, '(T)he fundamental problem of war finance is how to avoid inflation . . .'. The main thrust of these papers was to argue in favour of rationing and against indirect taxes, which he saw as merely a form of government-controlled inflation. He also acknowledged that stocks are an important way whereby demand fluctuations can be met without prices needing to change. This implies that larger stock levels are to be preferred and encouraged, which again suggests the need for policies to reduce the cost of stock holding. Thus, an interesting theme that is beginning to emerge is that the potential inflationary consequences of a high level of demand are countered by policies that focus on quantities, rather than on the prices themselves. Before taking this any further, I wish to draw more extensively on Kalecki's writings, particularly his theory of costs and prices.

In 1943 Kalecki wrote the paper on 'Costs and Prices', which was subsequently to appear in *Theory of Economic Dynamics*, in which he introduced the dichotomy between cost-determined and demand-determined price changes, referred to above. Within this framework, in the short run, changes in demand can influence prices:

i by any direct effect in the sector where price changes are demand determined and indirectly, resulting from the impact of increased industrial output on demand-led prices;
ii indirectly, resulting from the impact of increased industrial output on wage rises demanded and achieved; and
iii directly in the manufacturing sector, where full capacity is reached.

Before we address each of these in turn, we should note that this approach to understanding the causes of inflation need not conflict with the work of those who choose to focus on conflict over relative income shares as the root cause of inflation. What it highlights is that the pressures leading to conflict are not independent of demand (a point made in Rowthorn 1977) so that policy measures to address the inflationary consequences are a necessary complement to any measures aimed at sustaining a higher level of demand, irrespective of any other considerations.

Addressing demand-led price fluctuations directly

In the context of a two-sector world model, much attention was once focused on world commodity prices and there is an extensive literature on world commodity-price stabilization schemes – which both Kaldor and Keynes contributed to significantly. There is little point in reviewing such schemes here, except to note that there is a strong case for keeping them on the policy agenda. It is also worth noting that most schemes involve the use of buffer stocks to absorb short-term fluctuations in demand and thereby mitigate the effect on prices. Whether such buffer stocks are held explicitly as part of a stabilization programme or as private sector measures to reduce the disruptive effects of demand fluctuations on production, there is a clear case for reducing the costs of stock holding, which means maintaining a policy of low interest rates.

There is a clear pointer from Kalecki's price dichotomy – which to my knowledge has not been taken up elsewhere – and which does require addressing – and that is the behaviour of demand-determined prices other than those of primary commodities. One sector of particular significance is the construction sector, especially domestic housing. House prices are extremely volatile, far more so than the prices of manufactured goods, and paradoxically the behaviour of house prices seems to be one of the key indicators of whether the sector is 'moving'. Yet, housing costs do feed into most Consumer Price Indices and although there seems to be a popular perception that a small degree of price rises in the housing sector is a good thing, house-price inflation plays a key role in the inflationary process.

Furthermore, interaction between the domestic housing sector and the manufacturing sector plays a key role in the output–inflation dynamics of the private sector. Indeed, this interaction has much in common with the interaction between the world industrial and agricultural sectors, analysed for example by Kaldor (1976, 1983b). For countries with a large privately owned domestic housing stock, houses form the most significant asset for many people. Periods of house-price inflation consequently lead to significant increases in wealth, in turn leading to increases in consumers' spending. In fact, Allsopp (1993) effectively articulates the case that the budget surpluses experienced by the UK government in the early 1980s can be seen as an endogenous response to an increase in private sector spending, fuelled by the 'feel-good factor', of those who had recently experienced an appreciation in their main asset, resulting from the inflation of the late 1970s, and at least partly financed by loans secured on the increased equity. Unfortunately, the unfettered dynamics of this interaction is that the increase in consumer demand is met by the usual government response of monetary tightening to dampen inflationary pressures.

A real problem is that variations in interest rates are the main policy-weapon used to tackle inflation and yet their impact on major sectors of the economy is perverse. First, they raise mortgage costs directly, thereby increasing housing costs and any sensible measure of the rate of inflation, though, in the UK case, this perversity is to some extent obscured since the Bank of England's inflation target is defined in terms of RPIX, which excludes mortgage interest payments. Second, as already mentioned, since interest payments form a part of the costs of stockholding, interest rate hikes increase firms' costs and by reducing the levels of stockholding they remove one of the economy's automatic price-stabilizers.

Thus, it follows that:

i world commodity price stabilization must be more actively promoted;
ii a policy of long-term low interest rates needs to be maintained;
iii policies need to be devised for the domestic housing market to improve the speed of output response and reduce the extent of price response to fluctuations in demand.

Instead of seeing highly flexible – which often means volatile – prices as an indicator of a successful market economy in operation, it needs to be understood that volatile prices are a symptom of the failure of output to adjust and thus reflect a failure of market economies.

Wage rises demanded and achieved

In the papers that Kalecki wrote in the early 1940s, referred to above, he was very negative about any attempts to deal with war finance via taxes. He saw the problem of war finance as one of removing the inflationary pressures by reducing consumption in an equitable way. As already indicated, he favoured measures directed at output. One reason for a distaste of fiscal measures is that they lead to a reduction in workers' real disposable income. One consequence of such measures – which one might expect to be even more pronounced in a peacetime economy – is that the pressures towards conflict are thereby enhanced. However, in the context of a situation where we are starting with a significant pool of unemployed workers, most of whom receive some form of welfare support, an expansion of aggregate demand and employment can reduce the pressures leading to conflict by causing a net increase in the real income of everybody.

Every person that is newly employed will simultaneously receive a new wage and stop receiving unemployment benefit. It is a matter of simple arithmetic – and does not rely on neo-classical economics – to realize that the net additional output produced by the new worker must be greater than or equal to the wage paid. Yet the additional net income of that worker will equal the wage paid, minus direct taxes on that wage, minus the welfare benefits no longer received, minus any indirect taxes paid as a result of any increase in consumption spending deriving from whatever the final net increase in income turns out to be. There is therefore a significant net increase in output, equal to direct taxes on the new wage, plus the welfare benefits no longer received, plus any indirect taxes paid as a result of any increase in consumption spending by the newly employed. This represents a net increase in output available for distribution. Every reduction in unemployment necessarily increases the size of the cake to be shared between existing income recipients. If aggregate demand increases, there is no logical reason for inflation to originate from additional wage rises demanded and achieved. However, it is acknowledged that if inflation is permitted to take hold via another route, such as through the prices of imported goods and services increasing as a result of a depreciation in the exchange rate, then, of course, the usual wage-price spiral may ensue.

The topic of money wage increases was addressed by Kalecki in the famous 'class struggle . . .' paper, published posthumously (Kalecki 1971b). However, in that paper the focus was very much on the effect of money wage increases on income distribution, rather than on money wage inflation. The main message of this chapter was that workers would increase their real income not by money-wage increases *per se*, but by any effect of 'money wage increases demanded and achieved' on firms' ability to maintain their mark-ups. As already explained, since the real wage is the inverse of the mark-up, the way for workers to increase their real wage is by constraining the mark-up.

This leads to an interesting issue, not directly addressed by Kalecki, concerning the case for the use of incomes policies to constrain money-wage increases and thereby contain what in many quarters is perceived to be one of the main inflationary pressures. If money-wage increases have no effect on workers' real incomes, one of the main objections to the implementation of incomes policies is removed. Unfortunately, it is not that simple. As I have discussed elsewhere, whether real wages are determined mainly in the product or in the labour market depends on the relative speeds with which prices and money wages are adjusted, on whether prices are adjusted fully to reflect cost increases, and whether money-wages are adjusted fully to reflect price increases (Reynolds 1996: 83).

The capacity constraint

In that sector where price changes are largely cost-determined, Kalecki was explicit that, 'The production of finished goods is elastic as a result of existing reserves of productive capacity' (Kalecki 1954a: 11) However, following a period of sustained high unemployment, there is no reason to expect an economy to have capacity sufficient to employ the entire workforce at levels of efficiency which would be competitive. Investment in both physical and human capital is therefore essential. Acknowledging the importance of encouraging investment is probably one of the few things that most economists would agree on and so we do not pursue this further, other than to look at one particular aspect. As Kalecki (1933a, 1954, 1971b) repeatedly emphasized, and Joan Robinson (1962, 1969) elaborated, there is a two-sided relationship between investment and profitability. In a private sector or mixed economy, investment is stimulated by expected profitability and profitability is enhanced by investment. In a capitalist or mixed economy, if investment in capacity is to be increased, it may be necessary to devise and adopt measures to encourage profitability, especially in those sectors where investment is needed to relieve supply constraints.

The role of monetary policy

The role of monetary policy, particularly in relation to investment, is a topic where again Kalecki's work offers valuable insights:

> It must be noted that the precondition of successful government intervention – and of the natural upswing as well – is the possibility of meeting the increased demand for credits by the banking system without increasing the rate of interest too much.
>
> (Kalecki 1935a)

This was in the context of Kalecki recognizing the danger of government spending crowding out private spending via the mechanism of interest rate rises. Keynes also, of course, acknowledged the importance of finance in his interchange with Ohlin, following publication of the *General Theory*. The importance of finance is now well understood in the literature on post-Keynesian economics (see e.g. Davidson 1978). It was also understood by the early post-war Chancellors of the Exchequer in the UK, Hugh Dalton and Stafford Cripps and by the UK government-appointed Radcliff Committee.[6]

The messages are clear:

i A degree of endogenous credit (and monetary) expansion is necessary if unemployment is to be reduced to socially acceptable levels.
ii Interest rates must not be allowed to rise to become too high. High interest rates discourage investment. Furthermore, as argued above, they also enter into costs of production and can contribute to price increases. They are also important as a cost associated with stock holding. Yet stocks fulfil a vital role in ensuring that demand fluctuations are not translated into price fluctuations, more specifically, in helping economies to run at higher levels of demand and employment before pressures are put on the prices of essential commodity inputs.

Increasing interest rates to prevent economies from overheating only works at the expense of output and employment. While such policies continue to be adopted, economies will continue to operate with this long-term deficiency of demand and we will never move to a steady state of higher employment.

Conclusion

For the last two decades the world appears to have settled around a sort of steady state where unemployment rates in Europe are two to three times higher than in the two decades previously. Governments, much of the economics profession and others treat this as a 'supply-side problem' and appear resigned to the fact that once inflation starts to increase, the 'natural rate of unemployment' must have been reached and it is time to depress demand.

Kalecki's insights into the working of the world economy, particularly his dichotomy into sectors where price changes are largely cost- and demand-determined helps us to understand that continuation of this gloomy scenario is not inevitable. However, if the world is to move to permanently higher levels of employment then certain problems need to be addressed directly.

There is a necessity to address the capacity problem and the problem of price fluctuations in the primary sector. This means addressing the supply conditions in those industries and sectors where because of short-run supply inelasticities, output cannot be increased without price inflation and devising and adopting effective ways to stabilize such prices. Much could be done in terms of devising an agenda for successful intervention in those specific markets where the burden of adjustment tends to be borne too heavily by prices rather than by outputs.

Further, it may now be necessary to permit demand to increase, albeit at a modest pace, temporarily beyond the point of acceptably low levels of inflation. As prices rise in a demand-led way, profitability will increase and this will provide the incentive for investment. Such a policy could be enhanced temporarily by additional measures to stimulate investment (such as tax incentives) and by measures which discourage consumption relative to investment, although clearly not to the extent that the incentive to invest is significantly weakened.

Put bluntly, in the 1980s we witnessed governments deliberately permitting a rise in unemployment in order to beat inflation. This was usually accompanied by a promise that the rise in unemployment was only to be temporary. That promise has not been fulfilled: 13 million citizens of the EU – and the rest of us – are still paying the price. It may now be time to endure modest rates of inflation in order to encourage sufficient investment in capacity to return the world to a level of activity where more socially acceptable employment levels can be maintained.

Notes

1 For a review of inflation targeting, see Bernanke *et al.* 1999.
2 We note in passing that on page 12 of the same publication, the Bank of England acknowledges that the model used to generate the simulations is approximately linear, 'so rises and falls in the official rate of equal size would have effects of similar magnitude but opposite sign'.
3 Figures refer to unemployed, 2001 (OECD 2002: 222).
4 Standardized unemployment rates (OECD 2002: 221).
5 Kalecki (1945) was sceptical of the possibility of maintaining full employment by permanently increasing the level of investment since this would require cumulative, rather than one-off changes in the policy instruments.
6 Committee on the Working of the Monetary System (1953).

10 Three ways to . . . high unemployment[1]

Kazimierz Laski

Introduction

As a matter of definitions private investment plus budget deficit plus export surplus, which can be called together net injections into the aggregate demand, are *ex definitione* equal to private savings. A major economic problem is the question what determines what: do net injections determine private savings or vice versa? This very question seemed to be definitely resolved at the time when *The Economics of Full Employment* (1944) was published, and for many years thereafter the theory of effective demand giving priority to net injections seemed to be well established. But since the oil crisis and the surge of inflation in the 1970s a new paradigm in economic theory has prevailed. This new paradigm was not quite new. Mainstream economics returned gradually to the old *laissez-faire* competition theory which the theory of effective demand had seemed to substitute for good. According to the new–old theory, the spontaneous action of market forces is an optimal solution for all economic problems. As far as unemployment is concerned, the new–old theory has returned to the view that it is mainly caused by real wages being too high and by lacking flexibility of the labour force and has nothing to do with aggregate demand. The policy conclusions derived from the new-old paradigm were contrary to the recommendations of the theory of effective demand given in the famous paper of Michal Kalecki (1944a), 'Three ways to full employment'. Those very conclusions have been, in the opinion of the present author, mostly responsible for the high unemployment in Germany and the EU in the last decades.

In the first part of the chapter we sketch the theoretical background on which Kalecki's 'Three ways to full employment' was based. The role of investment as the driving force of a capitalist economy is stressed. Special attention is devoted to those factors which determine the degree of utilization of capacity and of the labour force. This part of the chapter has been written for those readers who are not closely familiar with Kalecki's theory.

The second part of the chapter is devoted to an empirical investigation. The author tries to imagine how Kalecki would investigate some reasons for high unemployment in Germany and follows this imaginary approach. Our main interest is not Germany but the relevance of Kalecki's remedies for fighting unemployment.

Growth and unemployment

In developed economies – as opposed to the underdeveloped ones – the existing capital stock offers enough jobs for the available labour force. Hence GDP*, denoting potential output at full capacity utilization, implies full employment in the sense that at this output level there exists no other than frictional unemployment, being a small fraction of the total labour force. Actual output GDP ≤ GDP* depends, however, on aggregate demand and is smaller than potential output if aggregate demand is too low. In this case capacity is not fully utilized, and the lower the degree of capacity utilization, the higher unemployment. Both the capacity and the degree of its utilization depend first of all on investment.

Kalecki introduced the very important distinction between investment decisions *ID* and investment realized *I*. Investment decisions belong to the most complicated economic events because they involve risk. Indeed their rentability in the future depends on factors that cannot be foreseen with any precision. It is therefore that *ID* are mostly preceded by long considerations which take into account not only economic but also such factors like confidence in the political stability. Investment decisions require some time to be completed; indeed they are produced as a rule on order while typical consumer goods are produced for unknown buyers.

Assuming that the time lag has been chosen as a time unit we arrive at $I(t) = ID(t-1)$; hence investment decisions from yesterday become today's realized investment. Assume now a closed economy without a government. In such an economy we have *ex definitione* $S(t) = I(t)$ because we get saving and investment by deducing simply from GDP(t) consumption $C(t)$. This equality is a tautology but as different agents stand behind $I(t)$ and $S(t)$ the real question is: how this equality comes into existence? According to the theory of effective demand saving is determined by (but does not determine) investment. Indeed as $I(t)$ depends on $ID(t-1)$ and $S(t)$ depends mostly on incomes created in period t, the causal relation can go only from investment to savings not vice versa. Savings of the present period would have to influence investment decisions of the past period if they were to determine investment of the present period. On the other hand, the assumption that investment of a given period determines savings of the same period does not lead to any logical difficulty. The mechanism by which investment determines savings is rather simple. While investment goods are produced economic agents involved directly and indirectly in their production get incomes. When these incomes are being spent demand for consumer goods comes into existence and the rest is being saved. This process lasts as long as new savings achieve the level of initial investment. Thus the process by which investment determines savings is linked with the income effect of investment and with the investment multiplier.

Investment creates an injection into the aggregate demand without creating a parallel supply. The same applies to two other factors which may arise in an economy with a government and foreign trade: the excess of government spending over its current revenues and the excess of exports to rest of the world over imports from the rest of the world.

More formally we have:

$$C + I + G + X = Y(\text{disp}) + T + M \quad (1)$$

where the left side enumerates all kinds of final goods produced in a given year while the right side shows value added created in the same year plus imports. The terms C, I, G and X stand for private consumption, private investment, government expenditure (for goods and services) and exports (of goods and services), respectively. On the other hand the terms $Y(\text{disp})$, T and M denote the disposable income of private households and firms, net revenues of the government (mostly taxes plus social security payments minus all kinds of money transfers, including transfers *in natura* free of charge, supplied to private households, such as e.g. education, health care etc.) and imports (of goods and services). By deducting from both sides of (1) the term C we get:

$$I + G + X = S + T + M$$

where private savings $S = Y(\text{disp}) - C$. Now we have on the right side three items which can be expressed as mostly functions of GDP and namely $S = s\text{GDP}$, $T = t\text{GDP}$ and $M = m\text{GDP}$ where the coefficients s, t and m represent the private savings ratio, the net tax ratio and the import intensity ratio, respectively. Hence we can write:

$$I + G + X = (s + t + m)\text{GDP}$$

and

$$\text{GDP} = (I + G + X)/(s + t + m) \quad (2)$$

According to (2) GDP is an increasing function of injections and a decreasing function of withdrawal coefficients. From (2) we can calculate the 'direct multipliers' I/s, G/t and X/m (Godley 1999). The term I/s, e.g. denotes the value of GDP which would have materialized if the terms G, t, X and m were zero. Similarly the term G/t denotes the value of GDP if all other terms I, s, X and m were zero, and X/m corresponds to GDP when I, G, s and t were zero. By calculating the time profiles of direct multipliers and comparing them with the actual GDP (the latter being simply nothing but the sum of all direct multipliers) we can find out what multiplier has most – and in what direction – influenced the growth process. If, e.g. in some period $I/s >$ GDP (and the difference between both terms increases) economic expansion is driven (and with growing intensity) by the private investment multiplier; to the contrary the same multiplier slows down (with increasing intensity) the economic expansion when $I/s < \text{GDP}$ (and the difference between both terms increases). A similar interpretation is possible when other direct multipliers are compared with actual GDP.

From (1) we can get also:

$$S = I + D + E \tag{3}$$

where $D = G - T$ and $E = X - M$ denote budget deficit and net exports respectively. We shall call the sum $I + D + E$ net injections into aggregate demand and denote by INJ(net). On the other hand using s which is the average (and marginal) private savings ratio we get:

$$S = \text{INJ(net)} \tag{3'}$$

and

$$\text{GDP} = (1/s)\text{INJ(net)} \tag{4}$$

According to (4) GDP is an increasing function of INJ(net) and a decreasing function of the private savings ratio. By taking the logarithmic derivatives after time of the variables in (3) we get:

$$g(\text{GDP}) = g[\text{INJ(net)}] - g(s) \tag{4'}$$

where g denotes the growth rates of GDP, INJ(net), (s). The most important item of INJ(net) is private investment, thus with some simplification we can say that the GDP growth rate is determined mostly by the difference between the growth rates of I and s.

Let us present this problem graphically: in Figure 10.1, starting from the origin, we draw a line S with the slope s, the average and marginal private saving ratio. This slope depends mainly on the distribution of income and the propensity to save from wages and profits. The distance $0B$ is full capacity utilization GDP* which is also the full employment output level. Investment I needed to provoke an aggregate demand equal to GDP* is the distance BE, which measures full employment saving S^*. If, however, actual investment is BD, it provokes saving equal to AC and aggregate demand equal to $\text{GDP} = 0A < \text{GDP}^*$. Hence, utilization of capacity is low and equal to $0A/0B$. In order to get as close as possible to GDP*, the distance DE must be filled by stimulating I, and if this does not work (or does not work in a satisfactory way) by engineering deficit spending D or by trying the 'beggar my neighbour' policy $E > 0$. The nearer $\text{INJ(net)} = I + D + E$ to the distance BE, the nearer GDP to GDP*. There exists also the possibility to reduce the slope of the S line by influencing s. This would shorten the distance BE and facilitate in this way the policy of full employment.

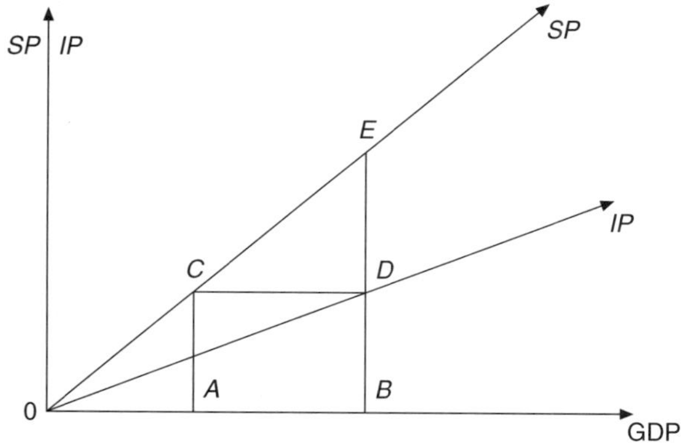

Figure 10.1 GDP according to aggregate demand

We have thus four major ways for keeping the degree of capacity utilization relatively high and unemployment relatively low. These are: (1) stimulating private investment; (2) increasing deficit spending; (3) supporting the trade balance; and (4) reducing the private saving ratio.

It may be emphasized that the inequality GDP < GDP* creates conditions for a policy that helps all participants of the economic process hence for a 'free lunch' in contradiction to a famous saying. Indeed, by increasing *IP*, *D* or *E* it is possible to increase incomes of workers and capitalists at the same time. This is the economic basis for co-operative capitalism in the above sense of the word. However, the redistribution of incomes implied by the turning of the *SP* ray is laden with social conflicts.

From the point of view of short-run full employment, there is no basic difference between the four methods presented above, but if we take future growth into account, the role of private investment is unique because it creates future jobs. Therefore stimulation of private investment should be the main instrument for full employment policy, and other methods should be taken into consideration only when this main way does not yield satisfactory results.

Unemployment in Germany and aggregate demand

There are two distinct periods of economic development in OECD–Europe in the second half of the last century: until and after the oil crises. Inflation that exploded in the 1970s to about 11 per cent was cut in following decades to 4.5 and 2.2 per cent against 4.3 per cent in the 'Golden age' period. On the other hand, the average unemployment rate in the 1970s was 6 per cent and moved in the following decades to over 9 and over 10 per cent: the last figure was higher than in the depressed years of the 1930s and four times the level in the 'Golden age' 1950–73 (2.6 per cent). Comparing the 1990s with the 'Golden age' we get a tradeoff: 2 percentage points less of inflation for 8 percentage points more of unemployment. The figures quoted above are taken from Maddison (2001: 132) who comments on them in the following way:

> The major reason for this rise was a change in macropolicy objectives. Initially, it was dictated by events but its continuance reflected a basic ideological shift. . . . The Keynesians were pushed to the periphery. . . . Friedman, Hayek and the neo-Austrians regarded unemployment as a useful corrective. . . . They argued that if simple rules were followed long enough, the economy would be self regulating. Responsibility for economic policy action should move from ministers of finance to central bankers.
>
> (ibid.: 131)

A similar development could be observed in Germany: the average unemployment rates for the years 1961–79, 1979–90 and 1992–2001 were 1.4, 5.6 and 8.4 per cent, respectively.

The period after 1979 has been subdivided, because of the German unification, into the 1979–90 segment covering only Western Germany and the 1992–2001 segment covering unified Germany.

Many economists, especially in Germany, argue that unemployment increased because labour productivity was rising too strongly in relation to GDP growth, substituting capital for labour because of wages being too expensive in relation to capital costs. This argument leaves completely aside the results of the discussion on the theory of capital which has proved that the inverse, monotonic relation between changes in capital intensity and

Figure 10.2 Unemployment rate (in % of labour force)

changes in the production factor prices simply does not exist (Pasinetti 1977: 172; Schulmeister 1998: 1–4) has criticized this approach using empirical data. 'Not even the explosive increase in the cost of capital relative to labour towards the end of the 1970s' – Schulmeister says – 'effected a slowdown in the growth of capital intensity' (ibid.: 4). He as well as Flassbeck (1998) come to the conclusion that the main cause of high unemployment in Germany was not high labour productivity, but the slowing down of GDP growth, the topic we are going to investigate now.

Indeed labour productivity grew in the period 1980–2002 by an average 1.47 per cent and GDP – by an average 1.91 per cent, hence employment grew by an average 0.43 per cent, too slow to absorb the existing labour force. In 1992–2002 labour productivity and GDP has grown almost *pari passu* (1.37 versus 1.41 per cent, respectively), leaving employment in this time practically stagnant.

Growth of GDP is caused by multiple factors, many of which are independent of the economic policies pursued. In particular, there are no spontaneous forces that in a market economy would assure – disregarding even cyclical fluctuations – an adjustment of GDP growth, and the derived demand for labour, to labour supply in such a way that the resulting unemployment remains constant. Given these conditions, the kind of policies pursued may, however, strengthen or weaken a spontaneous economic process. We shall try to show that these policies were in many cases responsible for the slowing down of growth and the surge in unemployment in Germany. In many instances they were in contrast to those advocated by Kalecki both in the sense of not doing what was required as well as of doing what should have been avoided.

We start by presenting the growth data for Germany in 1960–2001. In Figure 10.3 'direct multipliers' are confronted with actual GDP.

The X/m multiplier curve runs almost always above actual GDP proving that with different intensity the factor X *cum* m was a driving force of German growth. The G/t multiplier curve progress almost always below GDP until the middle of the 1970s and above GDP thereafter. Hence since the middle of the 1970s both multipliers X/m and G/t were higher than actual GDP. Because at least one multiplier must be lower than the actual GDP it follows that the most important multiplier I/s has run after 1974 always below actual GDP proving the braking (and in some periods with increasing intensity) role of I *cum* s in German growth. Figure 10.4 shows the time profile of I and s between 1961 and 2002.

Table 10.1 presents averages for chosen periods. The first five columns present the structure of final demand at the beginning and end of each period. We have calculated data for the beginning and the end of the period as a three-year average in most cases, in order to prevent random numbers in the border years. The further three columns present growth rates of GDP and its components for the considered three periods, while the last three show the direct multipliers of those components, which measure the contributions of

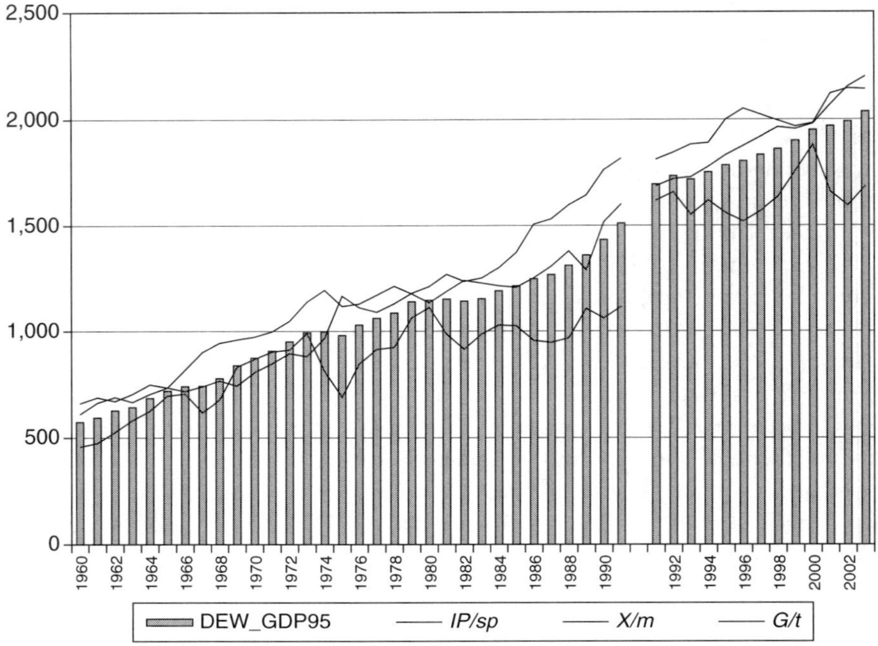

Figure 10.3 Direct multipliers and actual GDP (in 'conventional' constant prices 1995, in DM billion)[2]

growth of each of them in percentage points to the growth of the whole GDP in each period. This can be illustrated by the following example: private investment, *I*, increased in the period between 1960–2 aver. and 1978–80 aver. by a yearly average of 2.7 per cent. If all other parts of GDP were to remain at the initial level, then the resulting growth rate of GDP would amount to an average of 0.6 per cent. As has already been said the growth of GDP depends both on the growth of INJ(net) and *s*. In Table 10.1 the data for *s* are *ex definitione* identical with those for INJ(net) and can be found for each of the periods in the INJ(net) row. The data for *g*(*s*) are also presented.

The period 1961–79 (as presented in columns 1, 2, 6 and 9 of Table 10.1 as averages for 1960–2 and 1978–80 respectively) is our point of reference. The average growth rate of GDP in this period was 3.7 per cent. It was supported mostly by a 3.4 per cent growth rate of INJ(net) and a very small decline of 0.3 per cent in the private saving ratio *s* (not shown separately in Table 10.1). The internal structure of INJ(net) changed quite remarkably. In particular, the share of *I* declined and that of the budget deficit increased by approximately the same amount of percentage points. By far the greatest part of GDP is consumption *C*. Its share in GDP increased by 5.7 percentage points and correspondingly its rate of growth, 4.1 per cent, was clearly ahead

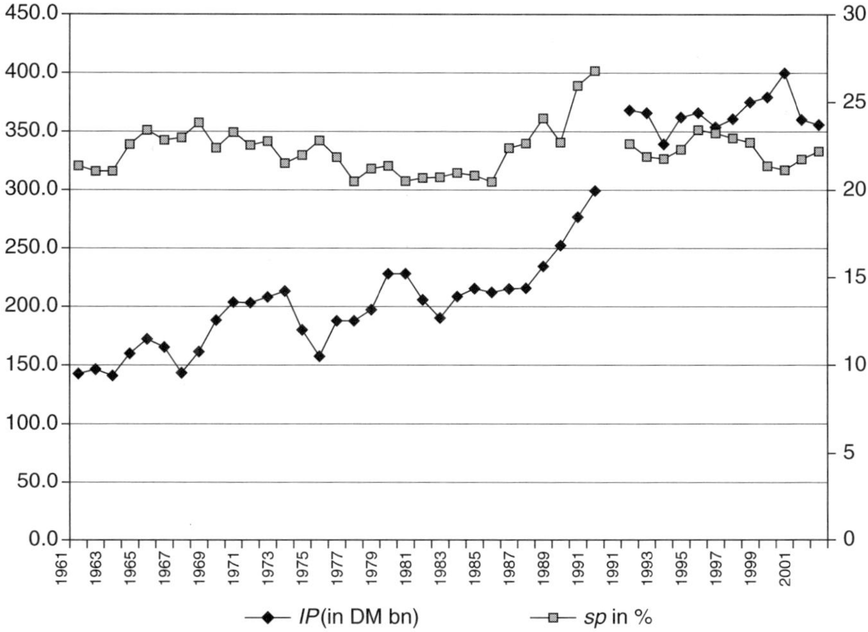

Figure 10.4 *IP* (DM billion at conventional constant prices 1995) and *sp* (in %)

of those for INJ(net) and GDP. This was possible at a more or less constant *s* because the share of government saving in GDP declined. Government saving is the difference between government revenue net of transfers, *T*, and government expenditure for collective consumption (and together with the budget deficit equals public investment). From the data in Table 10.1 it can be seen that the reduction of government saving was accompanied by a strong expansion of collective consumption. This increase has been a characteristic feature of the 'social market economy' (*soziale Marktwirtschaft*) in Germany. On the other hand, the relative share of private consumption, *C*, in GDP remained more or less stable (about 57 per cent), meaning that *C* and INJ(net) moved *pari passu* as expected by the almost stable private saving ratio.

The development in the period 1980–90 (see Table 10.1, columns 2, 3, 7 and 10) differed from that in the preceding period at least in three respects. First, the growth rate of INJ(net) accelerated from 3.4 to an average 4.2 per cent. Second, the most variable component of INJ(net) was the export surplus, which increased its relative share by 4.8 percentage points, while the other relative shares remained more or less constant. Third, and most importantly, the private propensity to save, *s* (corresponding to INJ(net)), which was relatively stable in the preceding period, increased now from 21.0 per cent to 25.1 per cent, that is by 4.2 percentage points. The combined acceleration of

Table 10.1 GDP: growth and structure, Germany, 1960–2002 (derived from conventional constant prices 1995, DM billion)

	GDP % structures					*GDP annual growth rates*			*Direct multipliers*		
	Western Germany			*United Germany*							
	aver. 1960–2	*aver. 1978–80*	*aver. 1989–91*	*aver. 1991–3*	*aver. 2000–2*	*/1/ to /2/*	*/2/ to /3/*	*/4/ to /5/*	*/1/ to /2/*	*/2/ to /3/*	*/4/ to /5/*
	/1/	/2/	/3/	/4/	/5/	/6/	/7/	/8/	/9/	/10/	/11/
Private investment	23.7	19.2	19.1	20.7	18.8	2.7	2.3	−0.4	0.6	0.4	−0.1
Exports (net)	2.0	0.9	5.7	−0.1	1.7	−3.3	22.5	–	−0.1	0.2	–
Budget deficit	−4.1	0.9	0.3	1.5	1.1	–	5.2	3.0	–	0.0	0.0
Injections (net)	21.7	21.0	25.1	22.1	21.7	3.4	4.2	1.2	0.7	0.9	0.3
Government saving	7.6	2.5	2.0	1.3	0.6	−1.8	−5.0	−22.5	−0.1	−0.1	−0.3
Consumption	70.7	76.5	72.9	76.6	77.7	4.1	1.9	1.6	2.9	1.5	1.2
Government	13.9	19.9	18.3	19.6	19.0	5.9	1.4	1.4	0.8	0.3	0.3
Private	56.8	56.6	54.7	57.0	58.7	3.7	2.1	1.7	2.1	1.2	1.0
GDP	100.0	100.0	100.0	100.0	100.0	3.7	2.4	1.4	–	–	–

INJ(net) growth and the rise of *s* resulted in a deceleration of the rate of growth in GDP from 3.7 to 2.4 per cent. A rise of *s* means *eo ipso* a fall of the private propensity to consume. Indeed, private consumption increased by an average 1.9 per cent compared with 4.1 per cent in the preceding period. The role of this factor can be seen from the last three columns of Table 10.1. The consumption growth alone was responsible for 2.9 per cent and 1.5 per cent of GDP growth in 1961–79 and 1980–90, respectively. The resulting difference of about 1.4 percentage points between the growth rates of consumption corresponds approximately to the difference in percentage points between the growth rates of GDP over the same time periods.

Between 1992 and 2001 (see Table 10.1, columns 4, 5, 8 and 11, covering unified Germany) the *s* ratio did not change appreciably as was the case between 1961 and 1979. At the same time yearly *g*[INJ(net)] diminished abruptly from 4.2 per cent in 1979–90 to 1.2 per cent (accompanied by a decline of 0.5 percentage points in its relative share in GDP). The combined result of these two factors was a further and rather dramatic slowdown of GDP growth to a yearly average of only 1.4 per cent. Even this meagre result was not due to private investment (which even decreased by an average 0.4 per cent) but to the expansion of the export surplus whose share in INJ(net) increased by 1.8 percentage points. Consumption growth with an average 1.2 per cent was much lower than in the preceding period.

Between 1961 and 1979 the GDP growth was caused mainly by the growth of INJ(net) (which in turn was based mainly on *I* growth and the decline of the budget surplus), slightly supported by a decrease of *s*. In the period 1979–90 the influence of INJ(net) growth (which was mainly supported by expansion of net exports) upon GDP growth was strongly weakened by an increase of *s*. In 1992–2001 the INJ(net) growth (based exclusively upon net exports expansion) was very poor and so was GDP growth in this period.

We can now try to formulate a hypothesis concerning some causes of unemployment in Germany following the Kaleckian approach. We will discuss the problem of private investment, of export surplus and of the distribution of income in this order. We start with private investment because it is by its very size (and also by its unique capacity effect) the most important part of INJ(net). Private investment expansion in Western Germany was strong until the end of the 1970s. In the 1980s the situation changed. In 1980–7 private investment stagnated and only in 1988–91 – probably provoked by the approaching unification with East Germany – it increased by an average 8 per cent per year. Due to this factor 1979–90 private investment '*I*' recorded still an average of 2.3 per cent. The development in the 1990s was even worse than that in the first part of the 1980s; the average annual *IP* rate of growth in 1990–2001 was negative at a depressing −0.4 per cent. One of the main reasons for slow growth of investment in Germany was the highly restrictive monetary policy of the Bundesbank oriented almost exclusively towards fighting inflation with complete neglect of its consequences for the employment situation. This topic has been vastly analysed and it is accepted in many studies that the decisive role has been played by the significant rise of the longer-term rate of interest in relation to the GDP growth rate (cf. DIW 1997: 489) and Flassbeck *et al.* 1997: 421–2).

The highly restrictive monetary policy was simply contrary to that advocated by Kalecki under similar conditions and requiring private investment stimulation, first of all by 'cheap' money. Another possible reason of the *I* slowdown has been the worsening financial position of the non-financial-enterprise sector. Its share in *S* diminished from about 57 per cent in the period before 1979 to about 53 per cent in the period thereafter, i.e. by almost 4 percentage points, while the share of other mainly rentier sectors increased. As the investment decisions depend very much on capital owned by investing firms, the shift of savings from those who make investment decisions towards those who save but do not invest could not but weaken the investment drive both by limiting the capital owned by the investors and by limiting their access to the capital market. Steindl (1990: 208) argues that business aims at keeping its indebtedness within certain limits, hence the proportion of borrowing in financing investment cannot grow continuously. If the degree of indebtedness of business goes beyond the limit considered safe by firms, investment of the non-financial sector may suffer.

Contrary to private investment foreign trade developed in Germany very well. With an average export surplus constituting 2 per cent of GDP over the whole period 1961–2001 Germany was together with Japan probably the largest net exporter in the world in the last quarter of the twentieth century. The greatest expansion of net exports has taken place between 1979 and 1990 and then between 1992 and 2001.

The exports achievements in Germany were mostly due to its almost constantly improving competitiveness. Indeed unit labour costs (ULC) increased in Germany in national currency units slower than those in EU15 and USA[3] and even in EURO although an appreciation of the DM took place almost all the time. However, real wages remaining strongly behind labour productivity and causing a competitive advantage for German exports in the form of slowly increasing ULC could not but restrict at the same time the demand for consumer goods on the home market.

Private consumption increased in 1979–90 by an average of 2.1 per cent annually and 1992–2001 by an average of 1.7 per cent compared to 3.7 per cent 1961–79. It is strange to assume that this drop was caused by supply difficulties in production for home goods but not for export goods. It is, however, easy to understand that exactly the same factors that provoked the export expansion limited internal consumption. The slow expansion of the internal market together with the restrictive monetary policy may have also influenced the low growth rate of investment in the period under consideration. The beggar-my-neighbour policy is often criticized by the losses it causes in countries with increasing import surpluses. It turns out that this policy while harming neighbours may bring losses also to the very country starting this policy. Kalecki stressed in his early writings that an export surplus achieved through lowering domestic wages and prices in relation to foreign wages and prices may at the same time limit growth of internal consumption (Kalecki [1939b] 1991, pp. 36–8). This seems to have happened in Germany in 1979–90 and also in the 1990s.

We have come to the last factor in our analysis of the causes of high unemployment in Germany, as seen from the toolbox of Kalecki. What we have in mind is the distribution of income between consumption and saving. In a situation in which INJ(net) do not reach the level necessary to achieve high employment at given *'s'*, Kalecki requires a redistribution of income from profits to wages in order to reduce the private propensity to save. However, as already stressed, mainstream economics explains unemployment by excessive real wages and requires their reduction in these circumstances. Hence a restrictive nominal and real wage policy has been advised and for quite a long time realized in Germany. This policy means a shift from wages to profits and may result in an increasing private propensity to save. The profits/GDP[4] ratio decreased between 1961 and 1979 from 38.4 per cent to 31.6 per cent; at the same time the coefficient *'s'* decreased from 21.7 per cent to 21 per cent. The profits/GDP ratio increased by 1990 to 35.1 per cent (i.e. by almost 4 percentage points) and the coefficient *'s'* increased to 25.1 per cent (i.e. by also 4 per cent). In the 1990s the profit/GDP ratio increased from 34.3 per cent in 1991 to 35.6 per cent in 2001 while the private saving ratio moved from 22.7 per cent to 21.7 per cent during the same period (oscillating in the range between 22 and 23 per cent).

The parallel movement of the profit and private saving shares in GDP is not accidental. But the combination of increasing and then stagnating at a relatively high level of shares in GDP of private profits and savings on the one hand, and stagnating and then falling private propensity to invest on the other, is a dangerous mixture as far as the employment situation in Germany is concerned. This is exactly the opposite of what Kalecki required in his 'third' way to full employment.

Conclusions

The 1997 victory of the Social Democrats in Germany had aroused hopes that at long last the aggregate demand approach would be taken seriously and Kalecki's recommendations would be late but in the end prevail. This hope has not materialized. Just before elections in Germany the number of unemployed persons exceeded 4 million. It seems that the red-green government elected 2002 would follow with even greater zeal the old policy of curing unemployment by thrift and by disregarding the difference between the rehabilitation of an individual firm and the recovery of a national economy, the biggest in the EU. Probably the time is not yet ripe for a change. The situation must obviously become still worse before – perhaps – it starts to get better.

In a speech held on the occasion of his 65th birthday, Kalecki told us that, with few exceptions, he avoided teaching all his life and saw his role rather as an economic adviser. With one exception his advice was simply ignored and found its lasting use in papers that have remained and constitute until today a rich source of inspiration for those who wish to learn. In only one case – Kalecki said – his advice was not ignored but taken account of. This happened in Israel at the very beginning of its independence. Instead of simply ignoring Kalecki's advice, the Israeli government did exactly the opposite. It is probably the fate of his remedies that we can repeat his sarcastic remark half a century later in the German context, and not only in that one.

Notes

1 This chapter could not have been written without the help of Roman Römisch, who was the best research assistant I have ever worked with. It is my duty and pleasure to express in this way my gratitude to him. All data used in this chapter have been taken from OECD National Accounts and Main Economic Indicators available in the WIFO Database.

2 Constant prices 1995 denote in this study current prices corrected by the GDP deflators. Thus in reality these are constant prices only for GDP; all elements of GDP expressed in these constant prices (such as e.g. consumption or investment) do not correspond to proper constant prices if they are calculated especially for those elements. Therefore we call them 'conventional' constant prices. They help us to preserve in our analysis the same price relations which prevail in the real economic process.

3 ULC in national currency increased in 1980–90 in Germany (West), the EU (15 countries) and USA by 1.9, 5.4 and 4 per cent per year respectively. The corresponding figures for 1991–2001 for Germany, EU and USA were 1.2, 1.6 and 1.7 per cent per year respectively.

4 Here we define profits simply as the operating surplus (gross).

11 Saving, investment and government deficits

A modern Kaleckian approach

Heiner Flassbeck

Introduction

The major puzzle of the world economy in the last 40 years is the growing discrepancy between the development of the world savings rate and the development of interest rates. While the rate of savings and investment had risen from the beginning of the 1960s to the middle of the 1970s, it fell, after the first oil price explosion, back to the level of the early 1960s and did not recover thereafter. World interest rates, short and long term, were low up until the middle of the 1970s but both rose sharply since the beginning of the 1980s and, up to our days, never returned to levels that had been regarded as 'normal' in the first decades after World War II.

These facts are outlined in a recent document of the International Monetary Fund (IMF 1995: 67–89, mainly chart 23 and chart 33). But the IMF's reading of the empirical evidence reveals a deep misunderstanding of the interdependent structure of a monetary economy. The IMF acknowledges that an exogenous upward shift in world investment demand is 'unlikely' to be the reason for the rise in long-term interest rates. The IMF supposes 'that the high degree of public dissaving over the 1980s and 1990s has been a key factor' (IMF 1995: 84). This is a surprising conclusion. The fact that the savings rate has been falling from 23 per cent (in the period 1960–72) and 25 per cent (1973–80) to 22.5 per cent from 1980–94 and even less in the last few years shows, if anything, that world investment demand has decreased as the overall growth rates of the world economy (the numerator of the savings ratio) definitely have been falling since the first oil shock. To break down the data for the major industrial countries 'into private and public saving' and to find that '*virtually all of the decline took place in public sector saving*' (italics in original) reveals nothing, given the fall in overall growth rates in company with rising unemployment (IMF 1995: 68).

Up to now we do not have a reliable method to identify the active or passive character of public budget deficits. But it is *a priori* a more than surprising thesis of the IMF to suppose that the switch to conservative governments in some big countries of the G-7 (United States, Germany, United Kingdom) at the beginning of the 1980s, with Japan being taken as 'conservative' in this respect too, can explain the shift towards an active role of public dissaving. Given these political circumstances it is obviously much more likely that public dissaving in this period was the result of the slowdown of growth and investment rather than its cause. In this as in other cases, the notion of 'public dissaving' is not helpful at all. It seems to be used only to hide the absence of a stringent theory.

The underlying theoretical constructs become even more confused if we take into account other facts. The most striking one is the rise of short-term interest rates over the same period. Whereas the increase in long rates could have been explained with the (unexplained) fall in the supply of long-term capital (savings), the rise in short rates (real as well as nominal) is hard to reconcile with the facts of a fall of the growth rates of real income, the fall of inflation rates and rising public deficits, given the traditional instruments of analysis. The IMF tries to explain *short* rates (1995: 84) with 'government budget policy' on the one hand. On the other hand they state that 'the relationship between monetary policy and real interest rates is not straightforward' (IMF 1995: 85) even without mentioning any differentiation of short and long rates. This is not only crude in theory but also obviously a result of the vested interest of an institution mainly governed by central banks.

Even more surprising than the role which is imposed to budget deficits in the discussion of savings and investment (see Ball and Mankiw 1995) is the fact that another phenomenon seems to be totally ignored. The capital output ratio, at least of some of the Western industrial countries (see Obstfeld and Rogoff 1996), is rising. Such a development was regarded to be of the utmost importance by many economists, including the one we are to honour at this conference, some decades ago (see Kalecki 1944b: 385). With falling productivity of capital, so their argument, only permanently falling interest rates could compensate investors for falling rates of return on fixed capital thereby preventing a secular fall in the savings and in the investment ratio. Rising interest rates and rising capital output ratios, as witnessed in the 1980s and 1990s had, according to this theory, to result in a fall in investment ratios and a fall of the growth rate of overall real income.

This chapter intends to illustrate that the analysis of the IMF and other recent publications on the topic are misleading and that the former writers like Kalecki were right. The relationship between savings and investment on the world level cannot be adequately handled with the simple instrument of supply and demand, assuming that the level of output or income or their growth rates are given. Any assertion, attributing movements of the real short and the real long interest rates to 'real' factors ('additional demand of developing or transforming countries, rising public deficits') alone, thereby neglecting the role of monetary policy and thus relying on a strict neutrality hypothesis, is not tenable.

The traditional approach

To illustrate the point of dissent between today's majority view and a Keynesian or Kaleckian theory let me first give a very simple example. At the beginning of 1994, nominal and real long interest rates all over the world started to rise. The proponents of the traditional approach explained this increase by the rising demand for capital from all over the world. It was, according to their view, only by chance that the Federal Reserve System of the United States had increased its short rates just before long rates began to climb. Robert Barro (1994) wrote in *The Wall Street Journal*:

> The recent rise in real rates is a symptom of an improving economic situation and has nothing to do with Fed policy. Basically, real rates are high when growth prospects are good and investment demand is correspondingly strong. . . . Mr. Greenspan could have told senators that the Federal Reserve lacks any strong influence over expected real interest rates, even in the short run. These rates are determined by the interplay between supply and demand of credit, determined by the willingness of people all over the world to save and their desire to invest. . . . The recent rise in long-term real rates is a good sign about the world economy. It suggests that long-run prospects for growth and investment are improved relative to those that prevailed last fall.
>
> (Barro 1994)

The IMF and Stanley Fischer argued that the increased demand for capital from the transforming countries of the East tended to increase real interest rates in 1994. This view should have been clearly falsified by the developments in the following year. The economies of the industrial countries slowed down remarkably after the expected lag in 1995 and nominal as well as real rates came down to the pre-slowdown levels first and to much lower levels later.

The budget deficit theory of interest rates is faced with insurmountable problems too if it is to be used to explain such a short run change in real interest rates as in 1994. All over Europe and in the United States budget deficits were reduced in the course of 1994 as governments benefited from a temporary acceleration of economic activity. But even in the 'long run' of the 1990s as a whole there is no correlation between government deficits and interest rates. Since the beginning of the 1990s long-term interest rates in the world, real as well as nominal, had been coming down. Budget deficits in Europe were quickly rising after the recession which started in 1989 and could be reduced for the first time, as mentioned, in 1994. The United States were able to reduce the public deficit at an earlier stage as economic policy, i.e. monetary policy there was able to initiate a private investment boom at a rather early phase of the cycle.

The most striking case in the 1990s is Germany. Due to the burden of unification the budget deficits, which had been virtually eliminated at the end of the 1980s, exploded in a very short period and reached 4.5 per cent (in relation to GDP) in 1993. Nevertheless, the nominal long rate fell from 8.5 per cent in the first quarter of 1990 to 6 per cent in the last quarter of 1993. The fall in the real rate in the same period was even steeper: from 5.7 to 2.25 per cent. All this despite the fact that there was a boom in West Germany with an unprecedented rise in the ratio of private investment to GDP. The riddle that the orthodox view faces today is of a similar quality. The United States have achieved surpluses in their government balances at the end of the 1990s but the long rate is much higher than in Europe where most of the governments are still struggling with high current deficits and high overall indebtedness of the government sector.

But a monetary explanation of interest rates is in a difficult situation too if it is used in a national geographical context. The short-term interest rate rose in Europe up to the autumn of 1992 whereas the long-term rate, as mentioned, fell since the end of 1990. In 1994, the short rates in most of the European countries did not rise although the long rate in Europe too jumped from 6.75 to 8.65 per cent from the first quarter of 1994 to the first quarter of 1995. It seems that most of the usually used theories to explain interest rates and their effect on savings and investment are not adequate, given the fact that there is a world market for capital and money, which, after the liberalization efforts of the 1980s and the convergence of inflation rates all over the industrialized world, seems to be much closer interrelated than it was before. To find satisfactory explanations for the worldwide increase in long- and short-term interest rates as well as for the fall in savings and investment to be observed in major regions of the industrialized world, at least since the end of the second oil price explosion, we will have to focus the investigation on events of a global dimension. Any kind of partial approach, be it sectoral or regional, is in danger of misinterpreting developments by putting artificial boundaries into a global economic framework.

Basics

The theory of saving and investment unfortunately is, up to our times, a rudimentary one. It consists mostly of the more or less sophisticated breakdown of an identity. Let Y be the gross domestic product of a closed economy (or the world), then the whole product obviously can be split into a part (C) that is consumed immediately (in the period of production) and a part (S) which is saved to be consumed later or to be invested (I) in order to increase the product Y (the national dividend) in a later period. We can write the product as:

$$Y = C + I \text{ or } Y = C + S$$

and we 'find' what was assumed, namely that:

$$S = I$$

To split up consumption and investment into the consumption or investment of certain groups of actors like 'the government' or 'foreign countries' in the case of an open economy does not add much information to the identity. It remains a simple definition. To make a theory of it, we have to identify the variables which determine the movements of *C* and *I* and in consequence the product of the world.

In face of numerous shocks in reality, the problem is highly complex as the *ex post* observed variables of saving and investment always fulfil the 'equilibrium condition' without indicating anything about the efficiency of the equilibrating mechanism. The fact that the gross domestic product of a closed economy (or the world) can always be split into one part that is consumed immediately (in the period of production) and another part which is invested immediately, leads to nowhere. The equation is just a simple definition.[1] Without identifying the variables determining the movements of consumption, investment and real income in the real world, the formula is of no use at all. If real income and overall output are not predetermined by 'long run variables', like the equipment with labour and capital or the education of labour and the availability of natural resources, an act of individual saving cannot be judged to be positive for *a priori* reasons.

If real income is not an exogenously given factor but a moving target, bombarded by unforeseeable shocks every day, it is *a priori* highly questionable to search for variables 'equating' saving and investment in a smooth way. The standard error of many authors is a notion of the kind that 'In equilibrium, however, the world interest rate equates global saving to global investment' (Obstfeld and Rogoff 1996: 31). As *S* and *I* are always identical *ex post*, the notion of 'equilibrium' as well as the assumed equilibrating role of the interest rate is without any informational content in a dynamic setting.[2] Applying strictly the idea of the interest rate as an equilibrating mechanism of saving and investment implies that real income (the product) of the economy under consideration is assumed to be either constant or to grow in the 'steady state' only with given constant rates. The explanation of cycles and depressions is, for logical reasons, outside the range of such an approach.

In a dynamic setting, two cases mark the continuum of the possible outcomes. First, if planned investment exceeds planned saving, demand on the capital market exceeds supply on this market forcing interest rates up to a point where investment plans are shaved and real income (growth) remains unchanged. This is the traditional neoclassical case. Second, if interest rates do not rise at all or not enough to equilibrate *S* and *I*, then real income (growth) may rise unexpectedly and induce the higher saving which is 'needed' to bring about the *ex post* equality of saving and investment. The additional saving may be the saving of companies due to higher profits, the saving of (private and/or public) households due to higher employment and wages, the saving of governments due to higher tax revenue and lower expenditure or the saving of the same actors in foreign countries.

Even if, at this stage, not much is known about the determinants of the system, the gulf separating the two extreme cases is easy to identify. If growth is not a given constant, and it would be particularly absurd to make such an assumption in a development framework, the second case is clearly superior to the first one. The IMF (1995), however, argues as if there is a rational choice between the two cases and favours the first one where interest rate flexibility 'replaces' flexibility of real income:

> In one view, saving is seen as resulting from a choice between present and future consumption. Individuals compare their rate of time preference to the interest rate, and smooth their consumption over time to maximize their utility. The interest rate is the key mechanism by which saving and investment are equilibrated. The other view sees a close link between current income and consumption, with the residual being saving. In this view saving and investment are equilibrated mainly by movements in income, with the interest rate having a smaller effect.
>
> (IMF 1995: 73)

Such a description reveals a highly mechanical interpretation of the process of development. It seems to suggest that movements in income are as good (or as bad) as the movements of the interest rate to equilibrate *S* and *I*. The movement (growth) of real income, however, is the main target of economic policy in all countries of the world. Hence, the 'instruments' of changes in income and changes in the interest rate can only be seen as alternatives if it is assumed that the growth rate of real income is given (exogenous) and cannot be influenced by any kind of macroeconomic (short-term) policies.

If exogenity of real income is not taken for granted, economic policy attempts to improve the growth performance are not in vain and the IMF approach is overly defensive. Beyond the neoclassical fiction, positive growth rates of real income and the creation of jobs are not automatically delivered by the market. If the expectation to gain temporary monopoly rents by pioneering investors is more important for the development of the system as a whole than the decision of consumers to 'smooth consumption over time', boom and bust cycles cannot be excluded and ask for the active commitment of economic policy.

In this view, the fact that saving and investment are equal *ex post* (not 'necessarily equilibrated by a market price'!) is not important at all for the dynamics of the system. With the movement of income being the main target of all the different agents in the economy investment plans exceeding saving plans should be the most normal constellation. In other words, even with the private incentive to 'thrift' unchanged, the economy as a whole may expand vigorously as the 'savings' corresponding to the increased investment are emerging in the form of increased (profits, mainly as temporary monopoly rents) saving of the company sector. In this view

> the departure of profits from zero is the mainspring of change in the . . . modern world. . . . It is by altering the rate of profits in particular directions that entrepreneurs can be induced to produce this rather than that, and it is by altering the rate of profits in general that they can be induced to modify the average of their offers of remunerations to the factors of production.
>
> (Keynes 1930/1971: 141)

A lot of related confusion surrounds the question 'what do budget deficits do?' (see as the most striking example Ball and Mankiw 1995). The source of the confusion here is mostly to be found in the uncritical mixture of judgements concerning the role of governments in questions of welfare and the efficient allocation of resources on the one hand and judgements concerning the role of governments as players on the macroeconomic field. One may argue that governments indeed are inefficient in many respects if compared with the private actors and that a withdrawal of government intervention may increase welfare in many cases. But this is a question quite independent of the one which deals with swings in macroeconomic balances of all the actors on the stage. And as on the stage the fact that one actor does not play his role adequately obviously does not mean that his character for the play as a whole is redundant.

The orthodoxy in economics, nevertheless, has fallen back to pre-Kaleckian and pre-Keynesian categories. Ball and Mankiw in their investigation of the effects of budget deficits start with a surprising hypothesis:

> Budget deficits have many effects. But they all follow from a single initial effect: deficits reduce national saving. National saving is the sum of private saving . . . and public saving. . . . When the government runs a budget deficit, public saving is negative, which reduces national saving below private saving.
>
> (Ball and Mankiw 1995: 96–7)

This is economic nonsense. Ball and Mankiw work with a model which must be based on the idea that there is something like a 'fund' of national saving which can be exhausted by the government. But a growing government deficit does not per se imply a reduction of national saving. The government may – this is the case Kalecki mainly focused on – with the new funds increase overall investment in the economy more than the private sector has done and could have done. Government deficits may rise because private investment falls and the government stabilizes demand in an effort to prevent a further fall of private investment and saving. In this case national savings will be higher with than without the budget deficit. Public budget deficits may rise because the government increases public investment which is needed to stimulate complementary private investment. Again national saving increases. Or budget deficits increase because a government stimulates private investment by tax cuts. Will national saving, the national investment ratio fall?[3] There is no fund of national savings and it is only a sad testimony of the regress in economic thinking that has taken place in many fields in the last few years that a paper like the one of Ball and Mankiw could have been published.

At this stage we have to mention other countries, i.e. the surpluses or deficits of regional conglomerations of private households, companies and a government sector. These are measured at geographical borders and are accounted as current balances. These balances are often called 'a country's savings' (Obstfeld and Rogoff 1996: 162). But such a terminology is extremely misleading. 'Countries' do not act economically at all. Countries, at least those at a similar stage of development, consist of the same groups of actors as other countries and the world as a whole. Each unit of these groups has, to survive in the market, to preserve its competitiveness in the whole free trade region, whatever the national borders may be. Given a more or less equal distribution of the groups inside the national borders will, as a rule, not lead to huge and sustained surpluses or deficits of the geographical conglomerations because that would imply a gain or loss of competitiveness or a permanent 'living beyond or below your means' of many units of the region. But this is prevented by sanctions of the financial system on the micro level (hard budget constraints) which are well known to everybody.

Thus, huge swings or persistent saving or dissaving of regions can only be due to discrepancies emerging between countries as a result of long-lasting divergent policy interventions (too expansionary or too restrictive policies and their effect on internal absorption) or as result of huge swings in the competitive position of a region (e.g. overshooting nominal exchange rates). The normal outcome, excluding policy interventions like interregional transfer systems, will be a more or less balanced 'budget' of any region in a free trade area. This is confirmed by many empirical investigations. Slope coefficients for industrial countries' national investment and saving rates are usually close to 1. That is to say that there seems to be not much of a contribution of 'foreign countries' to national saving.

This fact, which is, according to the above reasoning, the normal outcome has, after the publication of a paper by Horioka and Feldstein (1980), been the basis of many misleading speculations concerning international capital mobility. Feldstein and Horioka argued that the high slope coefficient is evidence for a rather small mobility of capital or restrictions for capital mobility even in the group of industrial countries as otherwise capital should be free to move and '. . . to seek out the most productive investment opportunities worldwide' (Obstfeld and Rogoff 1996: 162). This is a fundamental misunderstanding. It is just the other way round: the more similar in their structure and the more open the countries under consideration are, the smaller will be the net movements of capital (the balances) between them. Such a finding has no direct implications for gross movements. These can be extremely important and their movement may lead, without the 'contradiction' seen by Obstfeld and Rogoff, to '. . . the remarkable closeness of the interest rates that comparable assets offer despite being located in different industrial countries' (Obstfeld and Rogoff 1996: 162). The 'country' is usually no category of importance in the markets and for economics as well if we are not dealing with interferences into the market by national governments.

Profits and investment

To discuss the interdependent structure of the system which determines the behaviour of the actors more systematically, Keynes, Kaldor and Kalecki found, for good reasons, another identity useful. Given the identity used above, the profits of enterprises (*P*) always equal investment (including the consumption of entrepreneurial households) (*I*) plus the deficits of the other sectors (*DG*: deficit of government; *DF*: deficit of foreign countries or export surplus of domestic economy) diminished by the saving of the non-entrepreneurial private households (*S*):

$$P = I + DG + DF - S$$

An increase in government deficits or an increase in current account surpluses increases profits as well as a reduction of private saving increases profits. This irrefutable relationship given, the role of government deficits as well as private saving in the process of the determination of national or world saving appears in a different light. Additional expenditures of the government or private households leading to higher de-saving or reduced saving of these sectors do not imply a reduction of the national saving rate if these activities induce an increase of saving and investment in the company sector.

There has been a lot of discussion about the so-called Ricardian equivalence, i.e. the thesis that any fall of government saving (increase in government deficits) is fully compensated by a rise in private saving. The equation of distribution, however, sheds new light on this relationship. If the Ricardian equivalence perfectly holds for private households deficit spending of governments obviously cannot increase profits of enterprises and investment. But in reality there may be lags. If there is no full and immediate compensation by private households profits will increase and may induce additional investment. In this case the empirical evidence, which is anyway not convincing, has to be interpreted even more cautiously. Increased savings of the private sector as a whole may mean more investment in fixed capital plus higher private savings instead of a higher savings ratio of private households alone which is usually associated with the Ricardian equivalence. Government deficits may in this case bring about exactly the outcome a Keynesian or Kaleckian theory predicts but the evidence may seem to fit the Ricardian equivalence. The case demonstrates, the question how higher savings of a certain sector are transmitted into higher investment is still unsolved. It should be clear, however, that the existence of the Ricardian equivalence and an influence of government on interest rates is contradictory.

Even more convincing is the other way round. If the government saves more (reduces its deficits) it may be plausible to assume that private households save less even if there is no full compensation. But the company sector will react differently. With a first round cut in profits it is not plausible at all that firms will increase their investment in fixed capital. If they reduce investment and employment private households may reduce their savings rate in an attempt to stabilize their level of consumption. The outcome of this complex process in terms of national saving is not predictable. But whatever the outcome will be, it is more speculation than theory to interpret the result as being in conformity with the implied causality of the Ricardian equivalence. The normal causality should be the other way round: due to a certain exogenous shock private agents save and invest less than before. The public budget deficit increases automatically due to the effect of built-in-stabilizers, the empirical observation is a fall in overall saving (investment) and an increase in the deficit. To interpret this as evidence for the Ricardian equivalence is obviously nonsense. But again, the cases under consideration cannot be separated out by empirical methods.

Given these reservations it is hard to understand that the IMF comes to similar conclusions as Ball and Mankiw by stating that '. . . the empirical evidence suggests that there is less than a one-for-one increase in private saving when governments dissave, so overall national saving and world saving decline when governments run higher budget deficits' (IMF 1995: 85). But if this is right then the meagre statement that '. . . increased levels of government debt are generally associated with higher real interest rates' (IMF 1995: 85) definitively leads into the wrong direction. Why should the increase of a certain sectors' demand for capital lead to an increase of real interest rates if the overall saving declines? How can we conclude that interest rates rise before we know what has happened in the other sectors and thus for the demand for capital as a whole? Again, imagine the supply of capital falls for whatever reason. Higher interest rates may induce an increase in the saving ratio of private households. But the opportunity costs of investment have increased and the profit situation may have worsened due to falling demand. Is it serious to conclude that higher real interest rates will necessarily be associated with higher saving, given the fact that falling income is – necessarily – the 'equilibrator' in this case?

At this stage of the proceedings we have to introduce the monetary sphere of the economy. The equation of distribution deals only with the real side. Without money any change in I, DF, DG or S is accompanied by diminished or increased supply or demand on the capital market at least as far as the first round effects are concerned. If governments raise their deficits they demand more capital which may, without a perfect Ricardian compensation, increase the long-term interest rate and profits. If private households raise the amount they save out of a given income they provide the capital market with more supply lowering the long-term interest rate but diminishing profits. The counteracting forces on the capital and the goods market leave the question of the effects on investment unanswered, at least at the theoretical level. Thus, supply side policy without money is faced with a striking paradox. Assume the company sector 'decides' to increase investment (I) due to the government's decision to offer additional tax cuts or simply due to increased 'confidence'. This will bring about exactly the same repercussions from the capital market side as we usually impute to interventions of governments or an exogenous fall of private savings. Additional demand for capital by entrepreneurs will definitely improve the profit situation, but only at the expense of higher interest rates. If we are not able to discriminate quantitatively, that is to say by empirical investigations, the effects of the capital and the goods market, we will not even be able to decide, on a theoretical level, whether a market economy can ever leave the circular flow and create additional income or higher income growth.

Obviously, this is a very uncomfortable situation for economic theory, given the fact that the world economy grows. At a very early stage of economics as a science, however, this problem was addressed and a preliminary solution was found: the only way to finance additional investment and growth of the overall economy is the artificial creation of additional money. Additional money, so many early writers, including Schumpeter (1912) and von Hayek (1933), would allow to increase investment without negative repercussions from the capital market. This idea found its expression in the phrase of 'forced saving' which had occupied many economists in the 1930s.[4]

The importance of money had been clearly recognized at the beginning of this century by J.A. Schumpeter in his 'Theory of Economic Development' (1912). Hayek (1933) joined his view that only abundant money will allow high growth rates and a quick development of nations. For Schumpeter it is explicitly a *potentially* inflationary policy which spurs economic development. Monetary policy has to 'pre-finance' the process of development without knowing with certainty that the additional money will be used for real growth. This explains why catching-up processes are usually endangered by inflationary acceleration. The whole process is potentially inflationary without becoming inflationary in the least analysis.

Why is it that a thorough analysis of world saving and investment like the one of the IMF not even mentions the role of monetary policy? This shift in emphasis compared to former writers, obviously, is due to the fact that in the course of the rational expectations revolution of the 1980s it has become a general conviction that monetary policy overshooting a 'warranted' growth rate of money will induce inflationary expectations and inflation only. This idea says that the average economic agent has the expectation that the future inflation rate p^* will always be determined by the following equation:

$$p^* = mw - m^*$$

where *mw* is the warranted non-inflationary growth rate of (effective[5]) money (m) and m^* is the expected growth rate of m. The warranted growth rate of m equals the expected and warranted growth rate of real income or output. In a non-inflationary environment *mw* equals m^*. If money growth exceeds *mw* inflation is expected to accelerate to p^* and adjustment of wages and other items which are inflation-prone quickly takes place. The acceleration of the growth rate of money has, if any, only temporary effects on the real economy but lasting effects on the price level.

As we are talking about economic dynamics the implications of this theory concerning the assumed knowledge of the average economic agent are of the utmost importance. The theory assumes that everybody knows the warranted growth rate of the economy in which he lives. Why should that be a feasible assumption in an open economy and society? For example, nobody had forecast that Europe as a whole would in the 1990s fall much behind the United States and its own historical performance in terms of the average growth rate. Who would assert that an increase in real growth in Europe in the next decade is not possible? If this information is not available the whole theory falls apart. Nothing is left but a file without contents.

The fact that we have to live up with is the increase of short rates in conjunction with long rates since the beginning of the 1980s. If there were real reasons for the rise in long rates like capital scarcity or increased demand for capital, short rates could have followed a different pattern. Short rates are determined by monetary policy and nothing else.[6] If monetary policy increases short rates beyond the point which is determined by the time preference of asset-holders it creates incentives to substitute long against short assets. The supply of long-term assets falls, compared with what would have been offered without the central bank intervention, leading to rising interest rates on the long side of the market too[7] and vice versa.

Thus, monetary policy destroys or creates capital by setting the short rate beyond or below the rate which reflects the undistorted portfolio selection of the average supplier of capital. Monetary policy shifts the supply curve of capital. It is important to note that this happens without any compensating repercussion on the real side of the economy. If monetary policy reduces the money supply in an attempt to stop inflation and asset holders switch to the short side of the market, shifting the supply curve to the left, there is no expansionary effect on the real side as in a case in which private households reduce their saving rate and increase consumption. This is due to the unique role the central bank holds among policy-makers. Only the money supply or the short rate are exogenous, all the other instruments have to bear the burden of being endogenous, being an integral part of the economic system.

Money and investment

There can be no doubt that monetary policy dominates the development of the nominal and the real long-term interest rate on the world level. Thus, the riddle of high rates and low world savings since the beginning of the 1980s has to be discussed under a new heading. It was indeed a shift of the supply curve of capital to the left which has brought about the global rise in interest rates. But the shift was induced by monetary policy in its attempt to fight inflation after the two oil price explosions in an environment of rigid nominal wages. And monetary policy was successful. Inflation in the OECD as a whole has come down year by year from 15 per cent in 1980 to 4 per cent in 1994. Given the fact that prices do react only with a lagged adjustment even to such fundamental changes in the course of monetary policy, the bulk of the burden had to be borne by the most vulnerable element of overall demand and supply, namely investment. Thus, the whole story of saving, investment and interest rates in the world has to be rewritten in a manner which had been known long before but seems to be forgotten by modern writers.

The fall in the world savings rate and the rise in short and long rates is perfectly compatible. The switch of monetary policy from accommodation in the 1950s and 1960s to restriction since the middle of the 1970s, which has mainly fallen on Europe, explains the fall in investment in the industrialized world. The fall in investment is the mirror picture of the fall in world saving. But to talk about saving without investment easily leads to confusion. Neither an 'act of individual saving' (J.M. Keynes) nor the saving of the whole group of private households or of governments, which we usually tend to associate with the word 'saving', is a phenomenon leading, quasi automatically, to an increase of saving of the economy as a whole. The repercussions of an increase of saving of these groups on the saving of the entrepreneurial part of the economy must not be overlooked. If private households and/or governments plan to save more (dissave less) out of a given income this will be detrimental to the target of increasing the sum of saving and investment if the planned increase in the supply of capital (diminished demand of capital) is not going to induce a fall of the long-term interest rate (nominal and real as a rule). This is definitely not the case if monetary policy at the same time restricts the supply of capital by giving incentives to restructure portfolios and to switch into short-term assets.

Given the irrefutable fact that monetary policy, mainly in Europe, acted in this way since the middle of the 1970s over longer periods than ever before, the fall in the growth rate of real income (output) in the world as well as the fall of the rate saved (invested) out of that income has, to a very large extent, to be attributed to this dramatic change in the role of monetary policy. Whether this change was justified or not is a question that has to be answered separately. But as it is irrefutable too that the spread explains much of the fall in the growth rate and the growth rates of real income and employment are highly correlated with fluctuations in investment (see Flassbeck and Spiecker 1998) we cannot escape the logic of the evidence.

The causality runs from (exogenous) short to long rates and from long rates to investment of the company sector of the world economy. Investment, being the main source of income creation and prone to the most grave fluctuations during the trade cycle, determines real income as a whole and thus consumption and saving of the other sectors. Take the case of a monetary shock induced by monetary restriction on the world level. Falling investment will be the initial result inducing a fall of expected real income due to falling employment and falling tax revenues of the government. The reaction of these sectors – increasing or decreasing their saving rate – is crucial for the ultimate outcome. If they smooth their consumption or expenditure by reducing the saving rate or increasing their demand for capital (increasing their de-saving) this will help to stabilize profits which otherwise fall as investment falls.

It would be absurd, for the world as a whole, to expect an absorption of a monetary shock by other sectors of the economy. If a market remedy for monetary shocks could be expected it would be more and more difficult for monetary policy to stabilize prices as markets would over extended periods learn how to deal with a monetary restriction and to avoid it by nominal adjustment. But there is no evidence for this. As we 'simply do not know' much about the future, monetary restriction or expansion still works on the real economy. If the trade cycle, as can be supposed by simply looking at the cyclical movements of the interest rate spread, consists of a series of alternating monetary shocks the average duration of restriction or expansion from the monetary side will not only determine the short-run performance of the world or a certain country but the long-run performance too. A country or a region which is not able to recover for a sufficiently long time after a negative monetary shock has occurred, will not be able to exploit its economic potentials as much as a region which has the time. The story of Europe and the United States in the last two decades consists mostly of this kind of situation.

Conclusions

The simple lessons to be learned from this investigation concern monetary and fiscal policy. Any national monetary policy is in danger of misinterpreting the data if their view is restricted to a national or regional point of view. With a world capital market the monetary policy of nations or even big global players has only limited influence on the long rate. But error creeps in any analysis concluding from this fact that the 'markets' play a role of their own in the determination of the long rate. The extremely close relationship between the long rate and the short rate on the world level proves that it is the influence of the other central banks and not the markets who limit the influence of a single central bank. A coherent view of the determination of long rates in a globalized world will not be found if central banks, like the German Bundesbank, are time and again led to perceive deviations of the long rate from the movement of short rates by 'inflationary' expectations or 'confidence' in their ability to stabilize prices.

Something quite similar is true for fiscal policy. To impute changes of the long (real) rate in a single country to changes in the public debt of that country is *a priori* misleading and usually wrong. Even the world public indebtedness is not decisive for the world level of long interest rates as other sectors may, as a result, be less indebted and the interference of monetary policy into the process of capital creation or destruction is much more important.

The more complicated lesson to be learned from these considerations concerns the role of saving and investment in industrial and developing countries. Remember the IMF's prescription for an economically healthy future. The IMF concludes its paper with observations about the 1960s of this century:

> Firm and committed actions are necessary to reverse the current pressures on saving. The 1960s started out with a high ratio of world government debt to GDP. But as the decade progressed and as governments enjoyed strong growth, they used the opportunity to run fiscal surpluses, cut the ratio of government debt to GDP sharply, and saw the world saving rate increase steadily. That is because government budget deficits *do* [italics in the original] matter for overall national and world saving . . . it probably was no coincidence that the strong fiscal positions in the 1960s were associated with relative affordable investment funds, a high ratio of investment to GDP and good macroeconomic performance.
>
> (IMF 1995: 89)

All in all it is just the other way round. The IMF is right by saying that governments in the 1960s 'used the opportunity' to cut deficits. But about the circumstances that created the opportunity the IMF is silent. Without monetary policy neither the opportunities of the 1960s nor the problems of the 1980s and the 1990s can be explained. The world investment rate increased throughout the 1950s and the 1960s because monetary policy, with short rates always below long rates, was expansionary without any exemption and thus gave way to the creation of 'forced savings' or the prefinancing of economic progress which had been recognized by former writers to be the necessary condition for a sound overall economic development. With monetary policy being, definitely in Europe but to a much lesser extent in the United States, nearly permanently on a restrictive course, fiscal policy in the 1980s and the 1990s had no alternative but to compensate for the lack of profits and investment opportunities which, in the least analysis, was the result of the long lasting conflict between monetary policy and money-wage policy.[8]

Thus, the policy lesson is a simple one. To restrict the dynamic development of a market economy from the demand side, namely by monetary policy, will, as a rule, force governments to expand on the demand side, that is to increase public budget deficits. This may for a single country, by increasing the company sectors profits, temporarily help to overcome the fall in investment which is the necessary concomitant of the monetary restriction if the country is large enough (the Reagan-boom is the best example) and not faced (as France in the first years of the 1980s) with a severe external constraint. For the world as a whole there is no solution but to change the course of monetary policy. This is, given the reasonable target of price stability, only possible if the danger of a quick acceleration of prices after the revival of investment and demand can be avoided from the supply side. This is where wages, wage policy or some form of incomes policy enter the stage. With wages being by far the most important cost component for the overall (vertically integrated) economy money-wage restraint is the only way out of the monetary policy trap in which Europe was caught in the last 20 years.

These considerations are of the utmost importance for the developing countries and the transforming countries of the East too. The usually given recommendations to these countries are based on the orthodox theory of saving and investment as represented by the analysis of the IMF. The recipes range from fiscal soundness to the explicit recommendation to keep the real interest rate sufficiently high to induce the increase of the saving rate of domestic private households or the inflow of savings from foreign countries. But austerity is not the way to prosperity. Has China, to cite the most striking example of a successful transformation (without the assistance of the IMF!), achieved a saving and investment rate of 35 per cent because the Chinese people one day decided to tighten their belts? China had, according to figures of the BIS, in the last ten years with the exception of 1990 always negative real short interest rates, since the beginning of 1993 in the range of 10 per cent.

Even if fiscal and monetary austerity may induce a bit higher saving rates of private households it will undermine the most important source of saving and investment, namely the increase of company profits. But monetary and fiscal laxity, so the argument at this stage, will quickly lead to renewed inflationary acceleration, once the phase of hyperinflation has been overcome. Nevertheless, there is no alternative. Sooner or later the phase of restriction, as in the industrial countries, must come to an end and give way to a policy which allows an increase of investment and real income for everybody. Then the test on monetary stability *without* monetary restriction is unavoidable. Either a developing country has successfully created the institutional arrangements which are necessary to allow the potentially inflationary process without leading to inflation or it has not. To keep it, by means of macroeconomic restriction, in a stage of stagnation is no solution at all.

But Schumpeter's phrase of the potential inflationary dangers of any kind of successful development highlights why it has been in the past so difficult to achieve the status of a NIC, a country catching up with the western world. And it may highlight why the Asian countries, as a rule, have been more successful to achieve this status than countries in Africa or South America or – in the years after the war – Germany more than the United Kingdom. Strong governments and the traditional search for consensus may have been the most important ingredients of their success. Only governments which are able to contain *a priori* the aspirations and claims of all the different groups of society to a level compatible with the potential production of the society and groups sticking to such an implicit contract, are able to combine the unavoidable macroeconomic laxity with stability of the price level.

Notes

1 The typical error as regards the informational contents of the identity can recently be found in Ball and Mankiw (1995: 97). They argue that 'This simple equation ($S = I$, H.F.) sheds considerable light on the effects of budget deficits'. But the equation has no light at all. Thus, Ball and Mankiw are misled from the beginning in their interpretation of what budget deficits do.

2 This is obviously a similar discussion as the one Keynes had fought against the 'classical theory of interest' (Keynes 1936: 14ff.). Keynes concludes that the classical theory is 'faulty because it has failed to isolate correctly the independent variables of the system. Saving and investment are the determinates . . . not the determinants of the system' (Keynes 1936: 183).

3 Ball and Mankiw seem to believe too that an increase of the government deficit 'leading' to a fall of national saving may induce a deficit on the current account too (1995: 100). There is no theory for such an assertion. If government deficits rise all over the world, as it happened in the 1980s, this will obviously not induce current account deficits everywhere. Only if governments are successful in inducing high growth rates and a positive growth gap between their countries and the rest of the world, as it was the case during the German unification, a current account deficit may occur. But then the government deficit will not have 'reduced' but increased national saving, i.e. increased investment.

4 Keynes flatly rejected the idea as he could not see how to make sense of it despite in the case of full employment where additional money – via inflation – may be necessary to shift resources from consumptive purposes to investment: 'But an attempt to extend this perfectly clear notion to conditions of less than full employment involves difficulties'. To Keynes the idea of forced saving cannot explain why 'the savings which result from this decision (the decision of a bank to grant a credit to an entrepreneur, H.F.) are just as genuine as any other savings' (Keynes 1936: 81, 83). This is undeniable but the term 'forced' is not the crucial point. Keynes misses this point by stating that '. . . these tendencies . . . which characterize the state of increasing output, H.F. will occur just as much if the increase in output has been initiated otherwise than by an increase in bank-credit' (ibid.). There may be no 'otherwise'. Then the notion of forced saving or better, about the role of money in the process of the creation of saving, gets an overwhelming importance.

5 Effective means including the relevant development of money demand, which is to say that effective money equals nominal output.

6 There is a lot of irritation around the way in which money is supplied by the central bank. But it should be clear that the state owned monopoly central bank has no supply schedule but determines a certain point on the money demand schedule so that all the arguments about a market process in the money market is useless. Additionally, the empirical evidence is overwhelming.

7 There is one argument usually brought forward at this stage. Holders of long assets could perceive the move of the central bank as bringing inflation down quickly. Then they would stay with the long market and not shift into short assets. The validity of this argument affords the same information implications as the general argument in the rational expectations debate with which we have dealt above. This

is not to deny that such a speculation may happen time and again for very short periods. To use it as a general assertion about the behaviour of the capital market involves, as we will see, a fundamental error.

8 In the first round the result of monetary restriction was a lack of profits, in the second round in most countries in Europe there was a remarkable fall of the wage ratio, i.e. a redistribution of income from wage-earners to entrepreneurs. But this redistribution could obviously not compensate the negative effects of an overly restrictive monetary policy.

12 Kalecki's investment theory reconsidered[1]

Anthony J. Laramie, Douglas Mair and Anne G. Miller

> the determination of investment decisions . . . remains, to my mind, the central *pièce de resistance* of economics.
>
> (Kalecki 1971b/1968: 165 [CW II: 435])

Introduction

Since Keynes' *General Theory* (1936), much attention has been given to the determinants of business fixed investment. Economists have recognized that investment is an important factor in determining aggregate economic performance. Investment contributes both to the aggregate level of spending and to the aggregate level of production. Investment not only adds to capital inputs but also brings new technologies to the market. Given the observed volatility of investment and its importance to long-run economic performance, many have argued that governments should pursue policies to stabilize investment and to ensure an adequate level of capital formation. Yet, despite the importance of its role, understanding what drives investment and what causes it to undergo periodic phases of expansion and contraction remains one of the major unanswered problems in present day economics.

From a Kaleckian perspective, modern investment models, be they of the neoclassical or *q* variety, are deficient for a number of reasons. First, while modern models typically emphasize microeconomic foundations, they ignore macroeconomic foundations. Kalecki, on the other hand, identified the macroeconomic foundations of investment in his profit function. The overall profitability of investment in a Kaleckian model is determined by aggregate expenditure and income flows, not by the marginal productivity of capital. Kalecki showed that aggregate profits, and, therefore, cash flow, are determined by business investment expenditures, the government budget deficit, the export surplus and the difference between consumption financed out of profits and savings financed out of wages.

Second, modern models have what post-Keynesians consider to be inappropriate microeconomic foundations. In a post-Keynesian/Kaleckian world, the distribution of aggregate profits is not simply determined by a set of relative prices established in perfectly competitive markets, but rather by the degree of monopoly as reflected in firms' or industries' price/cost margins. The degree of monopoly and therefore the intra- and inter-class distributions of income are influenced, Kalecki thought, by such factors as the level of industrial concentration, the ratio of advertising to sales and the power of trade unions.

Third, modern models typically ignore such things as true uncertainty, the separation of corporate control and ownership, financial constraints, and underemployment. As we show in this chapter, these factors do matter in a post-Keynesian/Kaleckian model by affecting how profits are re-invested. Finally, modern models treat the rate of economic depreciation as a parameter, even though somehow tied to the composition of the capital structure, without explaining explicitly the factors that make capital obsolete, and how these factors relate to the structure of the economy. In contrast, the post-Keynesian/Kaleckian approach explicitly considers the factors that influence the rate of economic depreciation. The post-Keynesian/Kaleckian model we present below addresses some of the more important shortcomings that are present in modern approaches.

Little attention has been given by policy-makers to the post-Keynesian/Kaleckian approach. We find this surprising because Kalecki's model has lain at the heart of many post-war investment models (Courvisanos 1996: 55–63). As our opening quotation indicates, Kalecki attached the greatest importance to understanding what drives investment. He regarded *Trend and Cycle* (Kalecki 1971b/1968), from which the quotation is taken, as another step in 'a continuous search for new solutions in the theory of investment decisions', a search on which he had embarked as early as 1935. An early pioneer of macroeconomics, Kalecki viewed business decisions on investment spending as one of the major determinants of output and employment in an economy that was subject to cyclical fluctuations. Thus, from a Kaleckian perspective, if we are to understand business cycles and growth, we have to understand what causes investment to fluctuate.

Issues arising in Kalecki's investment theory

There are four issues that we think should be addressed when attempting to specify and estimate a Kaleckian investment model. Two of these are identified by Sawyer (1985: 47). The first is to recognize that a major difference between Kalecki's approach and that of modern models is the sharp distinction Kalecki makes between investment decisions and actual investment expenditures. By making this distinction, Kalecki introduces a time lag that takes two factors into account: (i) many investment goods are not immediately available and that it takes time before they become operational; and/or (ii) businesses may reschedule investment orders or cancel them altogether in response to changes in economic or political conditions since the investment decision was taken. As we shall see in this chapter, the introduction of this time lag has extremely important implications for how a Kaleckian investment model can be estimated.

Thus, in Kalecki's investment theory, there are two investment functions to be considered, the *ex ante* decision function and the *ex post* expenditure function. If the object of the exercise is to understand the factors driving the business cycle and predict its turning points, then the appropriate function to consider is the *ex ante* measure of investment activity, i.e. with investment orders as the dependent variable. If the object of the exercise is to estimate the determinants of investment as one of the components of aggregate demand, then the appropriate function to consider is the *ex post*, i.e. with investment expenditures as the dependent variable. In this chapter, we consider both.

The second issue identified by Sawyer is that Kalecki's analysis is conducted at the aggregate level and incorporates conditions, such as the equality of investment expenditure and savings, which only apply at the macroeconomic level and not at the level of the individual firm. A further issue stems from Kalecki's rejection of the marginal efficiency of capital (MEC), an issue that applies equally to the neoclassical and *q* theories of investment. Kalecki had two criticisms of the MEC. The one that principally concerns us here is that the MEC depends on the aggregate level of demand and this in turn depends at least partly on investment expenditure. Thus, if firms plan to invest more in a future time period than they are currently doing, then demand and profits will be higher in that time period because of the higher investment. The MEC will have risen which will then induce firms to increase their investment. This feedback effect is missing in neoclassical and *q* approaches to investment.

The final issue is the one identified by Courvisanos and applies to the large number of other Kaleckian studies that he cites (Courvisanos 1996: 55–63). Courvisanos' argument is that while these Kalecki-inspired models provide strong theoretical and empirical support for a Kaleckian-based investment-cycle pattern, they all lack an underlying behavioural explanation of investment volatility. Thus, if the concern is to understand the role of investment in influencing the cyclical behaviour of a capitalist economy, a genuine Kaleckian model should specify an *ex ante* aggregate investment *decision* function using aggregate data and incorporate the behavioural and institutional factors that influence investment stability.

In this behavioural/susceptibility model, the fragility of investment orders is explicitly considered. Investment orders create tensions in the firm, tensions concerning the profitability and viability of the firm. These tensions are a function of exposure to risk and uncertainty (Courvisanos 1996: 116). The easing and building of these tensions over time create a business cycle that Courvisanos calls the 'susceptibility cycle'. By incorporating these tensions, or behavioural elements, into his model, Courvisanos provides a link between Kalecki's (1971a/1968) rather mechanical theory of the business cycle and Keynes' views on the role of conventions or rules of thumb in the investment decisions process. Essentially, as we show below, these behavioural elements can be reflected in profits, the gearing (debt to equity) ratio and in the level of capacity utilization.

We proceed in two stages. First, we specify a model based on Courvisanos' behavioural specification of Kalecki's investment theory. We use this specification to estimate investment *decisions* for the UK using quarterly data from 1980Q1 to 1996Q3. We find that this version generates what we consider to be satisfactory econometric estimates. We then specify as closely as we are able Kalecki's (1971a/1968) investment equation. This time, with investment *expenditures* as the dependent variable, we use UK data for the same time period to estimate Kalecki's investment expenditures equation. Again, we obtain what we consider to be satisfactory econometric estimates.

The *ex ante* version of Kalecki's theory of investment

We begin by considering Courvisanos' interpretation of Kalecki. Having reviewed the various versions of Kalecki's business cycle theories, Courvisanos (1996: 20) argues that an investment cycle emerges with three endogenous elements:

i profits and the mark-up;
ii financial constraints; and
iii excess capacity and accumulation.

Courvisanos (1996: 13–63) concludes that there exists a large number of investment models which provide strong theoretical and empirical support for the existence of a Kaleckian-based investment-cycle pattern. What they all lack, however, is any underlying behavioural explanation of investment instability. Courvisanos (1996: 69–113) argues that if one takes into account the technological, psychological and institutional factors, as well as the linkages between firm sectors, which have been developed in the literature on behavioural and evolutionary economics, then the rate of diffusion of a new technological paradigm is variable. The point at which new technological systems enter into the firm or the industry and the subsequent endogenous innovations have a strong impact on the investment cycle. These ideas can be incorporated into a Kaleckian investment cycle model. This leads to the development of a 'behavioural Kalecki' in which the evolutionary contribution provides the dynamics and the behavioural contribution provides the uncertainty.

The elements which have to be taken into account when considering the institutional behaviour of firms are identified by Courvisanos (1996: 94–113) as:

i competition between firms;
ii the role of agents in the firm;

iii the financial behaviour of firms;
iv the role of innovation; and
v the role of the state.

Susceptibility

Courvisanos introduces the concept of 'susceptibility' to explain the cyclical behaviour of investment in the following way. Susceptibility refers to the psychological tension felt by entrepreneurs in relation to their fragile confidence about a particular investment decision, given the level of investment orders already committed. The fragility of this confidence in convention-based investment decisions explains unstable investment behaviour. Increasing fragility arises when tension related to current investment decisions escalates as investment is eroded. This cumulative process renders entrepreneurs' confidence increasingly fragile (or sensitive) as investment order levels rise. When investment order levels are falling, cumulative pressures are being eased on the fragile confidence of entrepreneurs. In this formulation, the level of investment orders is susceptible to change. This susceptibility is a function of the tensions generated by the degree of fragile confidence felt by entrepreneurs from exposure to risk and uncertainty (Courvisanos 1996: 116).

In all cycles, the explanation of turning points is crucial. Courvisanos (1996: 118) identifies turning points in susceptibility cycles as occurring when entrepreneurs' susceptibility is such that current conventions used for investment decision-making are rejected leading to structural breaks in the pattern of investment behaviour. If the three observable Kaleckian elements of profits, increasing risk and capacity utilization can create the objective preconditions for confident investment ordering, this leads to a building up of tension as investment orders are increased. This expansion of investment generates cumulative tension that manifests itself as an inclination to decrease investment commitments and/or postpone investment plans. As tension increases, ultimately some factor (seasonal, secular or random) or combination of such factors will lead to a postponement or reduction of investment commitments. This will release tension, reduce susceptibility and the susceptibility cycle will start its contractionary phase which will be reflected in decreasing investment orders. The process is not symmetrical at the upper and lower turning points of the susceptibility cycle. At the lower turning point, Courvisanos (1996: 120) argues that it is a situation of increased resilience on the part of more adventurous entrepreneurs that will induce greater risk-taking and lead to higher levels of current and future investment commitments.

Profits

Courvisanos then proceeds to explain the behaviour of the three objective Kaleckian elements over the susceptibility cycle. First of all, the behaviour of profits. In the 1971a/1968 version of his business cycle, which is the one that concerns us here, Kalecki introduces a complex interaction between the increment in total profits and the increment in profits from new investment (see equation (13)). This latter term can be seen as a better expectations guide to future investment than the former. Thus, Kalecki's 1971a/1968 model is the appropriate version from the point of view of explaining susceptibility as it emphasizes the sensitive nature of incremental profits from new investment. During the upswing of the susceptibility cycle, as a firm invests more in new capital equipment, it exposes itself to greater tension as an increasing proportion of its profits will be generated by its new investment, thus leading to greater fragility. This becomes progressively more significant during the upswing of the susceptibility cycle. During the downswing of the susceptibility cycle, the fragility of confidence is reduced as the increments in profits become progressively more attributable to existing capital equipment whose rates of return are more predictable (Courvisanos, 1996: 127–8).

Thus, according to Courvisanos, the profits-related mechanism incorporates both systematic contradictory pulls between the increments in profits from new investment and the total level of profits. This gives rise to conflicting pressures on incremental profits from new investment which are related to the relative proportions of new equipment to existing equipment. The introduction of the concept of susceptibility into Kalecki's 1971a/1968 business cycle theory brings the advantage of providing an understanding of the contribution of profits to the dynamic nature of investment decision-making.

Increasing risk

The second of the objective Kaleckian factors that Courvisanos introduces into the susceptibility cycle is increasing risk. Kalecki (1937a) introduced the principle of increasing risk to argue that the marginal risk of investment increases with the amount invested for two reasons:

- i the greater the amount invested by an entrepreneur the greater the risk to his position of personal wealth in the event of the business being unsuccessful; and
- ii the marginal risk of investment rises with the size of investment because of 'illiquidity'.

The sale of a fixed asset such as a factory in the event of business failure will almost always give rise to a loss. Thus, a businessman who has invested his reserves in fixed assets and taken 'too much credit' will only be able to borrow at a rate of interest above the market rate. Assuming, as Kalecki did, a horizontal schedule of marginal efficiency of investment, then the operation of the principle of increasing risk will serve to curtail investment to a level lower than would prevail in its absence.

Courvisanos explains the process in the following terms. During an upswing of the business cycle, the growth in internally generated funds allows a firm to increase its borrowing and share issue. As outside funds become more easily available during the upswing, the increasing risk involved in committing funds to new investment seems to rise only minimally. Under these circumstances, the firm is well below its gearing ratio limit. Tension builds up only slightly as it relates to small borrowers' risk, when financial (liquid) assets that earn income are converted into illiquid [fixed capital] with a long gestation period before any income is received. As the boom continues, greater borrowings and share issue bring the principle of increasing risk into operation (Courvisanos 1996: 130).

This increasing illiquidity leads to increased susceptibility as tension builds up. As gearing ratios rise, lenders' risk becomes an increasingly serious short-term issue. Shifting investment funding increasingly to equity finance leads to rising share issue risk, allied with concerns about possible falls in share prices as the increment in profits from new equipment starts to fall relatively. These increasing risk factors force entrepreneurs to reduce the rate of new investment commitments. Thus susceptibility continues to rise (even if at a slower rate) threatening the firm's liquidity position. Again, contradictory pulls emerge. In relation to this element, continuing long-term competitive pressure to earn income through investment in illiquid [fixed capital] eventually creates the need to protect the decreasing short-term liquidity position by doing the exact opposite – reducing investment orders and cancelling (or modifying) current investment orders. This lowers the very high tension related to increasing borrower's and lender's risks (and share issue risk) which reduces susceptibility and, with a lag, reduces investment activity (Courvisanos 1996: 131).

In the downswing of a business cycle, increasing risk generates a reverse susceptibility behaviour cycle to the one described by Courvisanos in the upswing. Firms' gearing ratios are an important guide to the presence of increasing risk. Their behaviour over time can be examined to see how changes alter tension in relation to firms' investment commitments. The element of increasing risk can trace out an unstable cyclical path of investment orders.

Kalecki recognized, but did not stress, the role of financial factors in influencing the behaviour of the economy over the cycle. For example, Dymski writes:

> monetary concepts seldom appear in Kalecki's mature writings; when they do the author treats them sparingly. For example, in the various permutations of Kalecki's dynamic model, financial elements are incorporated only partially and the banking system plays a passive role. . . .

> Kalecki purposely set financial factors into the background of the business cycle.
>
> (Dymski 1996: 116, 133)

Dymski (1996) and Sawyer (1999a) have both recently explored Kalecki's monetary analysis in some detail. They argue that while Kalecki did have a clear understanding of the operation of the monetary system, he was concerned principally to develop a *real* rather than a *monetary* model of the business cycle. Thus, for Kalecki, the rate of interest was a monetary phenomenon rather than the equilibrating mechanism between savings and investment. But Dymski argues that it is essential to incorporate a monetary element into Kalecki's analysis. According to him, Kalecki's framework cannot be encompassed in a real analysis: his theoretical building blocks can be *consistently* combined only in a monetary analysis; this implies a monetary analysis irrespective of any conditions imposed on preferences and technology. Further, a disequilibrium analysis like Kalecki's is inherently 'monetary' because agents seeking to carry value forward must rely on nominal assets whose real value is not predetermined within the system (Dymski 1996: 122).

Sawyer (1995a: 4–7) concludes that any analysis of the market capitalist economy which draws on the work of Kalecki should retain the 'principle of increasing risk' as a component. This conclusion is reinforced by Dymski (1996: 123–6). He poses the question 'how important is it to incorporate finance constraints (and credit relations) explicitly in Kalecki models?' The answer depends critically on the phasing of the investment cycle. In Kalecki's short-period analysis, Dymski defines three critical phases: (i) the placing of investment orders; (ii) the delivery of investment goods; and (iii) the initial production phase of the investment goods. During the first phase, the short-term finance is required for construction finance for the supplier of the investment good. The risk factor for the lender is determined by his/her degree of liquidity in the money market and there is no risk factor for the borrower. During the delivery phase, the supplier of the investment good repays the loans provided during the construction phase; the lender's risk is now of default on the project of the borrower and the borrower's risk is now an operational one. In the third phase, the short-term finance is the provision of working capital to the user of the investment good; the risk factors for the lender are liquidity and the interest-rate risk on the lender's liabilities; the borrower's risks are again operational and associated with market conditions.

Against the background of this schema, Kalecki's effective analytical period is the short period. It is too short to allow for returns to start to materialize from projects with long payback periods. His investment multiplier has not had long enough to work itself out before new investment decisions must again be made. Dymski (1996: 124) identifies the critical steps in the chain of events as the conversion of investment plans into investment orders into *in situ* production facilities. What breaks the connection between changes in (corporate) savings and investment at this stage of the investment cycle is the flexible lending capacity of the banks. Thus, what makes Kalecki's analysis of the business cycle *monetary* and not *real* is the possibility of disequilibrium in financial markets because of credit rationing because of a reluctance of banks to become less liquid.

Thus, Dymski (1996: 133) concludes that Kalecki's dynamic disequilibrium approach is informed by a subtle and mature monetary conception. While Kalecki did not treat monetary factors in a methodologically consistent way and quite intentionally kept them in the background, nevertheless he did recognize the importance of such phenomena as increasing risk and credit rationing. Consequently, his aggregate dynamics necessarily involves both monetary and real factors.

Capacity utilization

The final objective Kaleckian element that Courvisanos identifies as contributing to the susceptibility cycle is capacity utilization. The existence of unplanned excess capacity is an element that is common to all versions of Kalecki's business cycle theory. Kalecki saw unplanned excess capacity appearing mid-way through a boom as the means of production rise at an increasing rate, due to investment orders being completed but demand not rising sufficiently quickly to keep pace with the expansion in the means of production. The influence of this excess capacity becomes greater as the increase in demand starts to slow down towards the peak of the business cycle at a time when the increment in firms' profits from new investment is starting to fall. The combination of contradictory pulls between delays in the production of investment goods and changes in effective demand create unplanned excess capacity. Thus, according to Courvisanos (1996: 134), tension builds up within a self-generating susceptibility cycle. As activity slows down, so inventory investment will rise leading to even higher undesired excess capacity with concomitant increasing tension and fragility of confidence. Thus, investment orders will start to decrease and although firms' productive capacity will continue to expand due to completion of previously committed investment outlays, the decreasing rate at which new capacity comes on stream will start to ease susceptibility.

Courvisanos (1996: 161) formalizes his susceptibility cycle model in an investment order function that provides the objective reflection of susceptibility:

$$D_t = f(P_{t-1}, \Delta P, g_{t-1}, c_{t-1}) \tag{1}$$

where D_t is the level of aggregate investment orders in the current period; P_{t-1} = the previous period level of profits; $\Delta P = P_{t-1} - P_{t-2}$, the actual increment in profit levels; g_{t-1} = the previous period gearing ratio; and c_{t-1} = the previous period capacity utilization.

The peak of susceptibility is reached when D_t is at its maximum value. At this point the contradictory pulls on profits, risk and capacity utilization create enough susceptibility tension for investment orders to turn down. The peak of susceptibility occurs when:

i when P is high and ΔP begins to decrease;
ii when g is greater than the minimum desired proportion of retained earnings; and
iii when c rises above a desired degree of utilization.

The trough of susceptibility is reached when D_t is at a minimum value. The trough occurs under the following conditions:

i when P is low and ΔP begins to increase;
ii when the lowest desired limit of g has been reached; and
iii when c falls below a desired degree of utilization.

Estimating the Kalecki–Courvisanos investment orders function

We now estimate equation (1) using quarterly data for the UK 1980Q1 to 1996Q3 as in Table 12.1. Investment decisions, D, are defined as real new orders received by the manufacturing and construction sectors of the UK economy, P is real net profits after payment of corporation taxes on income and capital and ΔP is the quarterly change therein. The gearing ratio, g, is [real net borrowing from banks by industrial and commercial companies and financial institutions] divided by [real retained earnings of industrial and commercial companies and financial institutions minus real net capital issues of industrial and commercial companies and financial institutions]. To avoid as far as possible the problems of interpretation when estimating a model with a mix of variables in levels and ratios, we define capacity utilization, c, as: $c \equiv (Y - Y^*)$ where $Y^* = \gamma K$, and where Y^* is the output associated with target capacity utilization which in turn is assumed to be a fixed proportion of capital stock, K. Thus, $c \equiv (Y - \gamma K)$. Adopting this procedure instead of the more conventional measure of capacity utilization as the ratio of actual output: potential output, has the advantage of providing an estimate for γ, the desired capital:output ratio. $1/\gamma$ provides an estimate of the optimum life for capital stock.

We specify the Kalecki–Courvisanos investment orders equation as:

$$D_t = \beta_0 P_{t-1} + \beta_1 \Delta P_{t-1} + \beta_2 g_{t-1} + \beta_3 Y_{t-1} + \beta_4 K_{t-1} + \varepsilon_t \qquad (2)$$

where the variables are as defined above and ε_t is the error term. From our interpretation of Courvisanos, we expect the coefficients to have the follow-

Table 12.1 Ordinary least squares estimation

Dependent variable is Real New Orders$_t$
66 observations used for estimation from 1980Q2 to 1996Q3

Regressor	Coefficient	Standard Error	T-Ratio[Prob]
Time	−9.1047	4.1888	−2.1736[0.034]
Real Net Profits$_{t-1}$	0.32968	0.059849	5.5085[0.000]
ΔProfits$_{t-1}$	−0.20226	0.058130	−3.4795[0.001]
Gearing Ratio$_{t-2}$	284.0496	81.8194	3.4717[0.001]
Real GDP$_{t-1}$.	0.15492	0.0074158	20.8912[0.000]
Real Capital Stock$_{t-1}$	−0.022328	0.0014605	−15.2876[0.000]
R-Squared	0.78883	R-Bar-Squared	0.77498
S.E. of Regression	559.3140	F-stat. F(4, 61)	56.9671[0.000]
Mean of Dependent Variable	6143.6	S.D. of Dependent Variable	1179.1
Residual Sum of Squares	1.91E+07	Equation Log-likelihood	−508.6131
Akaike Info. Criterion	−513.6131	Schwarz Bayesian Criterion	−519.0872
DW-statistic	2.0300		

ing signs: β0, β2, and β3 positive, β1 and β4 negative; β4 = −β3γ where γ is the proportion of capital stock associated with desired capacity utilization.

Thus, the Kalecki–Courvisanos susceptibility cycle model is formulated explicitly with investment *decisions*, *D*, as the dependent variable. We report in Table 12.1 our OLS estimate of the Kalecki–Courvisanos specification (equation (2)). In estimating the model, we found that the coefficient of g_{t-1} failed marginally to be significant at the 10 per cent level. For this reason we report the regression with g_{t-2} which is strongly significant. All of the coefficients are statistically significant and of the expected sign. Rbar^2 is 0.77 and the Durbin–Watson statistic confirms that it is not possible to reject the null hypothesis that the error term is non-systematic. The D–W statistic of 2.03 allows us to conclude that nothing further about the lag structure will be learned from an autoregressive distributed lag investigation. We consider that the results provide support for the Kalecki–Courvisanos susceptibility model. Real new orders are influenced by real net profits with a one quarter lag, by the gearing ratio with a two quarter lag and by capacity utilization. Examination of the β_3 and β_4 coefficients in Table 12.1 yields a value for γ of 0.144, implying an optimum life for capital stock of approximately 7 years.

Kalecki's theory of investment expenditures

Having estimated successfully Kalecki's investment *decisions* equation, we now proceed to examine his investment *expenditures* equation. We use the final version of Kalecki's investment theory, widely known as Version III, which is to be found in *Trend and Business Cycle* (Kalecki, 1971a/1968). This marked an important stage in the development of Kalecki's thinking on the determination of investment decisions. He recognized that in his earlier work, in which he had concentrated on developing a theory of the 'pure business cycle' in a stationary economy, he had missed certain repercussions of technical progress which affect the dynamic process as a whole (Kalecki, 1971a/1968: 166).

Investment decisions in a given year depend on two sets of considerations:

i those concerning gross entrepreneurial savings; and
ii those concerning the prerequisites for their investment.

The former, Kalecki argues (Kalecki 1971a/1968: 172), are linked with the problem of entrepreneurial capital being the basis of investment because of limited capital markets and the 'increasing risk' involved in making use of it. The latter are closely related to $I(\pi)$. If, in a given year, $I(\pi) = I$, then entrepreneurial savings are just being re-invested. Thus, Kalecki defines:

$$D = E + r((I(\pi) - I) \tag{3}$$

where D = investment decisions as before; E = entrepreneurial savings; I = actual investment; $I(\pi)$ = investment that yields the standard rate of profit; and r is a coefficient measuring the intensity of the reaction of entrepreneurs to the difference $I(\pi) - I$.

Kalecki rewrites equation (3) by finding an expression for $I(\pi)$. To find an expression for $I(\pi)$, Kalecki first explains the appropriation of profits:

$$P = I + C_k \tag{4}$$

where P = profits; and C_k = capitalists' consumption.

Neglecting the time lag between capitalists' consumption and profits, he argues that it is plausible to postulate:

$$C_k = \lambda P + A \tag{5}$$

where λ. is a rather small fraction and A is a semi-autonomous variable dependent on past economic and social developments and can be considered as a slowly changing function of time, $A(t)$.

From equations (4) and (5), Kalecki derives equation (6):

$$P_t = (I_t + A(t))/(1 - \lambda) \tag{6}$$

or, denoting $1/(1 - \lambda)$ by m:

$$P_t = m(I_t + A(t)) \tag{7}$$

Kalecki then defines q as the ratio of profits, P, to national income, Y, ($q = P/Y$) which although it may change in the long run, he treats as a constant.[2] This, he argues, can be justified on the grounds that, by assumption, all prime costs are labour costs. He reasserts his degree of monopoly theory of income distribution. This theory argues that the share of direct labour in national income, ω, depends on the mark-up of price over prime costs and on the relationship between wage and material costs; i.e. $\omega. = 1/[1 + (k - 1)(1 + j)]$, where k is the ratio of gross proceeds to prime costs and j is the ratio of material to labour costs. By assuming $q = P/Y$ is constant, Kalecki confines his discussion to cases where the pricing process does not cause a change in income distribution. However, he argues that assuming that q is a parameter which *may* be constant is quite incompatible with the approach which assumes q to be the instrument, through price flexibility, to achieve full utilization of resources (Kalecki 1971a/1968: 169). Thus, he postulates:

$$Y = P/q \tag{8}$$

Kalecki then proceeds to address the problem of the determination of investment decisions in what he considers to be a novel way by introducing the concept of that level of investment at which the new equipment would yield a certain definite gross rate of profit. This he defines as the 'standard rate of profit' (π); it is the reciprocal of the 'pay off period' during which capital invested is recovered (Kalecki 1971a/1968: 169). The level of investment which would fetch the standard rate of profit he defines as $I(\pi)$. If the rate of profit yielded by new equipment is higher than π. then $I(\pi)$ is higher than actual investment I, and vice versa.

What are the determinants of $I(\pi)$? Assuming, initially, no increase in productivity due to technical progress, Kalecki assumes that $I(\pi)$ is proportionate to the increase in 'real' profits (ΔP) over the year under consideration. Given his assumption of ample unused productive capacity, new investment captures only a (rather small) fraction of profits, nΔP. Thus, he writes (Kalecki 1971a/1968: 170):

$$I(\pi) = n\Delta P/\pi \tag{9}$$

Now, introducing technical progress, Kalecki defines 'real' labour costs as $(Y - P)$. These, he argues, will also approximate the labour costs associated with old equipment, because new capacity added in any year is small in relation to the existing capital equipment. 'Real' labour costs associated with old equipment will rise as a consequence of the improvement in productivity caused by technical progress. Consequently, the profits yielded by older equipment will fall by an amount equal to $\alpha(Y - P)$, where $\alpha.$ is higher the greater the rate of increase in productivity resulting from technical progress. Given no change in total profits, P, the loss in profits suffered by the old equipment equals the gain in profits from the new investment. It follows, therefore, that the profit generated by new equipment, if that new equipment earns the standard rate of profits should be multiplied by $I(\pi) = n\Delta P + \alpha (Y - P)$ so that:

$$I(\pi) = (n\Delta P + \alpha(Y - P))/\pi \tag{10}$$

As a first approximation, Kalecki treats n and α as constants. Equation (10) shows that the level of investment 'capturing' the rate of profit, π depends on two basic determinants:

i the increment in total profits; and
ii the transfer of profits from new to old equipment.

From equation (10), Kalecki writes:

$$\alpha(Y - P) = \alpha((P/q) - P) = P\alpha(1/q - 1) = \delta P \tag{11}$$

where $\delta = \alpha[(1/q) - 1]$.

Thus, equation (10) can be rewritten in the form:

$$I(\pi) = (n\Delta P + \delta P)/\pi \tag{12}$$

Substituting equation (12) into equation (3), Kalecki obtains:

$$D = E + r[(n\Delta P + \delta P)/\pi - I] \tag{3'}$$

Assuming gross entrepreneurial savings bear a constant relation to *rentier* savings, Kalecki defines:

$$E = eS \tag{13}$$

where $e < 1$.

Defining entrepreneurial savings as the difference between profits and capitalist consumption, i.e. $S = P - C_k$, we rewrite equation (12) as:

$$D = e(1 - \lambda)P + r[(n\Delta P + \delta P)/\pi) - I] - eA(t) \tag{14}$$

The important feature of equation (14) for investment decisions, which distinguishes it both from Kalecki's own earlier work and other work on the topic, is the term δP. The term δ captures the rate at which profits are lost to existing capital as a result of technical progress and, is, therefore, the rate of depreciation (Kalecki 1971a/1968: 171 fn). The term δP accounts explicitly for the stimulus to investment due to higher productivity of labour in the new plant enabling it to capture profits from old equipment (Kalecki 1971a/1968: 172–3).

Kalecki's argument so far depends critically on the relationship between the rate of profit on new actual investment and $I(\pi)$ and on the transfer of profits from existing to new equipment. It is, however, necessary to take account of an additional stimulus to investment that accelerates the increase in productivity from new investment. He therefore modifies his equation for investment decisions by including a term $F(t)$ – 'a slowly changing magnitude depending . . . on past economic, social and technological developments' – which he expresses as a slowly changing function of time (Kalecki 1971a/1968: 173). Thus:

$$D_t = e(1-\alpha)P_t + r[(n\Delta P_t + \partial P_t)/\pi - I_t] + B(t) \tag{15}$$

where $B(t) = F(t) - eA(t)$.

Finally, Kalecki argues that investment decisions taken in time period t are translated into investment expenditures in $t+\tau$, so that $I_{t+\tau} = D_t$. Thus, equation (15) can be rewritten as:

$$I_{t+\tau} = e(1-\alpha)P_t + r[n\Delta P_t + \partial P_t)/\pi - I_t] + B(t) \tag{16}$$

Estimating Kalecki's investment expenditures equation

We now proceed to specify and estimate Kalecki's model using investment *expenditures* I_t (equation (16)) as the dependent variable. Since we are testing a carefully specified model, we eschew the by now virtually mandatory techniques of time series analysis such as co-integration.

We follow Kalecki (1971a/1968: 174–5) in treating π as a parameter. Thus π becomes incorporated in coefficients α_2 and α_3 in equation (17):

$$I_t = \alpha_0 T + \alpha_1 P_{t-1} + \alpha_2[(P_{t-1} - P_{t-2})] - \alpha_3[(Y_{t-1} - \Pi^*_{t-1})] - \alpha_4 I_{t-1} + \varepsilon_t \tag{17}$$

where: I = real net investment by industrial, commercial and financial companies and institutions; T = time; P = real net profits after payment of corporation taxes on income and capital; Y = real gross domestic product; Π^* = desired level of real gross profits before tax of industrial and commercial companies and financial companies and institutions $[Y - \Pi^*]$ = 'real' wages.[3]

The interpretation of the coefficients is as follows:

- α_0 = [coefficient of time trend of technological change (equation 15) – coefficient of the time trend of capitalist consumption (equation 5)]; expected sign of α_0 is positive/negative;
- α_1 = $(1-\lambda)$ [λ = average propensity to consume out of capitalist income (equation 6)]; expected sign of α_1 is positive;
- α_2 = r/π [r = intensity of reaction of entrepreneurs to the difference between the level of investment which yields the 'standard' rate of profit $I(\pi)$ and the actual level of investment (I) (equation 15)];

Table 12.2 Ordinary least squares estimation

Dependent variable is Real Net Investment$_t$
66 observations used for estimation from 2 to 67

Regressor	Coefficient	Standard Error	T-Ratio[Prob]
Time	−9.1047	4.1888	−2.1736[0.034]
Real Net Profits$_{t-1}$	0.17774	0.046388	3.8316[0.000]
ΔProfits$_{t-1}$	−0.11019	0.044051	−2.5015[0.015]
Real Wages$_{t-1}$	−0.010937	0.0039910	−2.7405[0.008]
Real Net Investment$_{t-1}$	.97545	0.033337	29.2604[0.000]
R-Squared	0.95294	R-Bar-Squared	0.94986
S.E. of Regression	410.8833	F-stat. F(4, 61)	308.8365[0.000]
Mean of Dependent Variable	4259.9	S.D. of Dependent Variable	1834.9
Residual Sum of Squares	1.03E+07	Equation Log-likelihood	−488.2586
Akaike Info. Criterion	−493.2586	Schwarz Bayesian Criterion	−498.7327
DW-statistic	1.8946	'h' statistic	0.4448

n = proportion of profits captured by investment in new equipment (equation 10); π is the standard rate of profit; expected sign of α_2 is positive;
α_3 = $r\,\tilde{\underset{\cdot}{\alpha}}/\pi$ [$\underset{\cdot}{\alpha}$ = change in profits yielded by old equipment (equation 10); r and π are defined as above]; expected sign of α_3 is positive or negative·;
α_4 = r [defined above]; expected sign of α_4 is positive.

Table 12.2 shows the OLS regression of equation (17).

The 'h' statistic in the above regression indicates that the null hypothesis of no serial correlation in the residuals cannot be rejected. However, the regression results are not entirely satisfactory. The negative sign of α_2 is the opposite of what we expect and the results are dominated by the inclusion of the lagged dependent variable in the model. This might suggest parallels with conventional autoregressive investment models in which the coefficient of the lagged dependent variable represents a 'catch all' of all the otherwise unspecified factors that have influenced past investment. However, in Kalecki's Version III, the coefficient of the lagged dependent variable, α_4, specifically captures r, the intensity of reaction of entrepreneurs to the difference between the level of investment that yields the 'standard' rate of profit, $I(\pi)$, and the actual level of investment.

The Krawiec–Szydlowski business cycle theory

Thus, there are two investment functions to be estimated in the Kaleckian schema, an investment decisions function (Table 12.1) and an investment expenditures function (Table 12.2). The only difference that Kalecki specifies between them is the time lag, τ. An explanation for the emergence of these two distinct investment functions is provided by Krawiec and Szydlowski (1999) in their formulation of a new business cycle model deriving from Kaldor and Kalecki. Their model acknowledges the distinction between investment decisions and their implementation by means of second-order differential delay equations. Their results show that the dynamics of investment depend crucially on the time-delay parameter, the gestation time period of investment. The mathematics of the Krawiec–Szydlowski model involves the application of the Poincaré–Andronov–Hopf bifurcation theorem, generalized for functional differential equations. Their model demonstrates that even with a linear investment function, the introduction of Kalecki's time delay parameter can create a limit cycle for small values of the parameter. Depending on the length of the time delay parameter, Kalecki's investment model bifurcates to limit cycle behaviour, then to multiple periodic and aperiodic cycles and eventually tends towards chaotic behaviour. The overall conclusion of Krawiec and Szydlowski is that there can be no doubt that time lags in investment and their capacity for generating cycles should be taken into account in the analysis of business cycles.

It appears to us that the reason why it is necessary to specify two Kaleckian investment functions is to do with the dynamic properties of the time lag identified by Krawiec and Szydlowski. There is no way of telling, either from their model or from the data, the length of time lag in the UK between the placing of an investment order, its commissioning and ultimate generation of output. The lag will vary with the nature of the capital good and may range from a few to several years. What is important is that the Krawiec–Szydlowski model indicates that dynamic effects begin to kick in after even a short time lag.

Conclusion

In this chapter we have examined two versions of Kalecki's investment theory. The fact that we have been able to estimate Kalecki's investment *decisions* function provides a link between Keynes and Kalecki. Numerous attempts at estimating the objective formulation of Keynes' investment theory through the medium of q models have not been successful. For example, q models have not been noticeably successful in accounting for the time series variation in aggregate investment. Their explanatory power is low and serial correlation or dynamic structures using the lagged dependent variable are common. In addition, other variables reflecting liquidity constraints or the state of demand are often significant in the equations although the standard formulation of q does not provide a satisfactory rationale for their inclusion (Blundell *et al.* 1992: 233).

However, both Keynes and Kalecki recognized the importance of risk and uncertainty in determining investment decisions, although Keynes gave them much greater emphasis. Uncertainty is introduced into Keynesian models indirectly on an *ad hoc* basis via some measure of the spread of output and prices or of expert forecasts, on the assumption that spread or variance is an appropriate proxy for uncertainty (Baddeley 2001: 11–12). It is only recently that uncertainty has been formally introduced into Kaleckian theory via Courvisanos' concept of susceptibility. Our econometric results provide support for an objective Kaleckian formulation of the concept of susceptibility.

It is important to remember what Kalecki was attempting to do. As our opening quotation suggests, he was trying to find an explanation for the determination of investment *decisions* and this is what we think we have done via the Courvisanos behavioural reformulation. Where we think Kalecki was at fault was in failing to appreciate adequately the dynamic implications of the introduction of the time lag between investment decisions and investment expenditures. As the Krawiec–Szydlowski model suggests, the time lag can have the effect of fundamentally transforming Kalecki's investment decision function.

This conclusion has important policy implications. If the object of policy is to reduce the volatility of investment and raise its trend growth rate, the focus should be on those factors that influence business susceptibility. Courvisanos has argued that these can be objectified as profits, financial considerations and capacity utilization. Our results show that they have had a significant influence in explaining business susceptibility in the UK over recent years. Central to Kalecki's model is the recognition that both microeconomic and macroeconomic foundations are important. At the microeconomic level, it is those factors that determine the degree of monopoly that determine the *share* of profits. As Laramie, Mair and Reynolds have recently shown, the degree of monopoly is influenced by such factors as product differentiation, entry barriers and exposure to foreign competition.

Appendix

The definitions of the variables and the sources of the data are as follows:

Real net investment = {[gross domestic fixed capital formation of industrial and commercial companies (*Economic Trends*, Table 1.15) *plus* gross domestic fixed capital formation of financial companies and institutions (*Economic Trends*, Table 1.11)] *minus* [capital consumption at current replacement cost of industrial and commercial companies and financial companies and institutions (*National Income and Product Accounts*, Table 1.1)]} *divided* by implied GDFCF deflator (1990 = 100) (*National Income and Product Accounts*, Table 1.1).

Real net profits = [gross trading profits of industrial and commercial companies and financial companies and institutions – UK taxes on income of industrial and commercial companies and financial companies and institutions (*Economic Trends*, Table 1.12)] *divided* by implied GDP deflator (1990 = 100) (*National Income and Product Accounts*, Table 1.1).

Real wages = [wages and salaries before tax, not seasonally adjusted (*Economic Trends*, Table 1.6)] *divided* by implied GDP deflator (1990 = 100) (*National Income and Product Accounts*, Table 1.1).

Real new investment orders = new investment orders from manufacturing and construction sectors (*Economic Trends*, Table 4.4) divided by implied GDFCF deflator (1990 = 100) (*National Income and Product Accounts*, Table 1.1).

Gearing ratio (g) = {[net borrowing from banks by industrial and commercial companies and financial companies and institutions (*Economic Trends*, Table 1.16)] *divided* by [implied GDP deflator (1990 = 100) (*National Income and Product Accounts*)]} *divided* by {[retained earnings of industrial and commercial companies and financial companies and institutions (*Economic Trends*, Table 1.13)] *divided* by [implied GDP deflator (1990 = 100) (*National Income and Product Accounts*, Table 1.1)]} *minus* {[net capital issues and redemptions of industrial and commercial companies and financial companies and institutions (*Financial Statistics*, Table 6.2A)] *divided* by [implied GDP deflator (1990 = 100) (*National Income and Product Accounts*, Table 1.1)]}.

GDP = gross domestic product at market prices (*Economic Trends*, Table 1.3) *divided* by implied GDP deflator (1990 = 100) (*National Income and Product Accounts*, Table 1.1).

Capital stock = net capital stock at current replacement cost, all fixed assets of industrial and commercial companies and financial companies and institutions (*National Income and Product Accounts*, Table 14.8) *divided* by implied GDFCF deflator (1990 = 100) (*National Income and Product Accounts*, Table 1.1).

Notes

1 This is a revised version of a paper presented initially at the international Kalecki commemorative conference in Warsaw, 27–8 September 1999 and subsequently at the conference of the Eastern Economic Association, New York, 22–5 February, 2001.

2 In order to maintain consistency with Kalecki's notation we retain the use of 'q' in this section of the chapter. Kalecki's 'q' should not be confused with the q model of investment discussed above.

3 See the Appendix for a full definition of the variables.

Part IV

The developing economies

13 Kalecki's political economy of development of mixed economies

Employment-led growth[1]

Ignacy Sachs

Michal Kalecki devoted his whole life to comparative studies of functioning and dynamics of different economic systems. At the beginning of his career, first as an economic journalist, and later as a researcher with an economic institute in Warsaw, he concentrated his attention on problems of a peripheral and backward capitalist economy, with an obsolete agrarian structure and heavy dependence on foreign capital, striving to overcome the Great Depression of the 1930s. Though the notion of an underdeveloped country was not yet adopted at that time, his knowledge of realities of the Polish economy would help him later to address the problems of economic underdevelopment. It may be useful to remember that the theory of underdevelopment as we have it in mind today was formulated in a great part in England in the early 1940s, on the grounds of studies aimed at elaboration of a programme of reconstruction of Central and South-European economies from damages they suffered during World War II. Refugees from Eastern countries were to play a leading role in that intellectual venture.[2]

Since his early writings Kalecki approached the great theoretical problems of functioning of capitalism in a Keynesian way, well ahead of Keynes himself. In the years spent in England, on the eve and during World War II, his observation of the functioning of a mature capitalist economy and active participation – together with other left-wing Keynesians – in the organization of its war effort and the simultaneous building up of a welfare state, have refined and sharpened his reflection.

During his work, from 1946 to 1954, with the Central Office of the United Nations in New York, he was again called on to focus on the case of peripheral countries and their relations with economies of the centre. This time, it was no more the case of Poland but that of the Third World countries.

Kalecki continued to be lively interested in their development even after he left his UN office. Indeed, his main contributions to the theory of development came out after his return in 1955 to Poland where he spent the rest of his life. It is owing to his inspiration that Warsaw became the seat of a research centre on less developed economies and an international school of planners for those countries under protectorate of the UN. Their central subject has been comparative studies of socioeconomic systems.

However, having been invited, after his return to Poland, to take the post of a scientific adviser to the chairman of the Planning Commission, he gave priority to the study of the functioning and growth conditions of a socialist (or, in any case, non-capitalist) economy. In his lectures for planners of the Third World countries he identified the fundamental differences between demand-constrained developed capitalist economies, supply-constrained socialist economies and the underdeveloped economies which, owing to the under-development of their productive apparatus, had to suffer both evils, being supply-constrained like socialist economies, and sharing with the capitalist economies the constraint of insufficient effective demand.

In this way the circle has been closed. Among economists of his generation Kalecki was undoubtedly the most complete in having explored and compared all the principal systems in existence in the twentieth century. He was a subtle observer of the real world, gifted with an unusual capacity of both giving theoretical treatment to identified facts and situations and of drawing from it prescriptions for public policy.

Mixed economies

On the crossing of his studies of developed capitalist economies and the underdeveloped ones, Kalecki found an important category of mixed economies. They are composed of:

- i a big private sector where capitalist enterprises, both domestic and foreign, coexist with small market producers, both urban and rural;
- ii a public sector which, in spite of its possibly reduced weight in the GDP, does play an important, or even determinant, role in development;
- iii a planning apparatus which, for Kalecki, was indispensable for rational management of public affairs in a mixed economy.

In this regard he shared the view which, during World War II and after, was widely spread among economists and politicians except of the few extreme liberals like Hayek, who rejected even the mere idea of planning. His definition of the mixed economy has been therefore more restrictive than the one commonly used at present (Tsuru 1993; Kuttner 1997).

Kalecki's perception of the role of the state, its responsibilities and initiatives in the process of development, may be compared to the concept of *developmental state*, based on the recent experience of Japan and South-East-Asian *tigers* (Johnson 1982; Sautter 1987, 1996; Wade 1990). However, it differs from the latter in the priority Kalecki attached to social objectives of planning as well as his preference for models of state intervention limiting rather than tending to stimulate and strengthen private capitalism (Sachs 1962). It shows, instead, even more convergence with the ideas proclaimed by the radical current of CEPAL-based economists and Latin-American structuralists, from R. Prebisch, C. Furtado and A. Pinto up to J. Ocampo, at present the executive secretary of CEPAL (Ocampo 1999), M. Wolf, A. Ferrer, F. Fajnzylber and O. Sunkel (Sunkel 1993).

For Kalecki the state should be a programmer, a promoter or, if necessary, even a producer. His attitude was pragmatic. Not only should the state indicate the development priorities, but it had also to assure inflow of the necessary investment.[3] Hence, the state had to create incentives to attract private capital, but without pushing fiscal policy of subsidies or exemptions beyond certain limits which could make the projects counterproductive. Instead, he justified foreign borrowing for financing imports of investment goods in order to create export capacities, which had to assure an additional flow of exports for debt repayments.[4]

However, in the case of absence of private investment, it came to the state's duties to provide public investment so as to avoid a situation in which planned objectives would not be fulfilled. This is why the dynamics of a mixed economy was believed to depend on the existence of an active public sector.

Mobilization of domestic resources took the central place in the strategy of development as proclaimed by Kalecki, but without any concept of autarky. As far as the recourse to foreign aid was envisaged, he considered evaluation of its true impact not possible until account could be taken of its consequences for the whole economy. In fact, it might happen that an offer of foreign credit to finance a project of recognized priority would permit to shift resources previously designed to finance that project towards financing luxurious consumption, thus cancelling the usefulness of such foreign aid (Kalecki and Sachs CW V: 61–91).

The mixed economies of the Third World present a number of significant institutional variants. Kalecki attached much importance to comparative analyses of these variants in order to work out their typology. It was exactly in this connection that the concept of 'intermediary regimes' was born to characterize a relatively stable hegemony of petty bourgeoisie of town and country, grouped around the army, as was the case in Egypt, a model country in this regard. This phenomenon was made possible due to the rivalry, at the world scale, of two antagonist systems. It found a number of applications and raised long discussions in the countries concerned (Egypt, India, Bangladesh).[5]

The role of planning

Kalecki devoted a number of his writings to the institutionalization and methodology of planning, starting with the important manifesto published anonymously in a left-wing socialist review in England (CW III: 269–75).

A great part of his efforts in Poland was directed towards improving the methods and instruments of planning which were used there. He presented, in particular, methodologies for: constructing a long-term (perspective) plan;

evaluation of effectiveness of investment; optimization of foreign trade. Also, within the programme of cooperation between socialist countries, he made an endeavour to build up a rational system of international prices. Towards the end of his life his critical reflection inspired by the weaknesses of the Polish planning system turned to institutional conditions which he considered indispensable for efficient functioning of the decision-making mechanisms: separation of the functions of elaboration and evaluation of projects; necessity of a public discussion of plans which was to be made possible by means of free circulation of information; and respect for the right to err *bona fide*.

Although insisting on the importance of planning, Kalecki gave it a rather restrictive definition. Planning meant for him thinking in terms of variants: through comparing two or three alternative scenarios it would be possible to choose the one representing greater advantage in loosening bottlenecks which hampered full employment of labour force and productive capacity, or to construct a new one by finding a combination. He reserved the notion of optimization to the conditions where the objective function was homogeneous, as is the case with foreign trade.[6]

Having extended his concept of mixed economy to embrace both underdeveloped and developed economies, Kalecki was contemplating the minimum institutional conditions which had to be met if planning were to take place in a developed non-socialist economy (CW V: 183). These conditions – recognized by himself as difficult to be met – were as follows: control of investment; control of prices but not wages; and control of foreign trade. According to him these conditions could either imply a programme for implementation by a government of the popular front,[7] or to serve as a tool for comparative evaluation of existing situations.

The latter idea was of fundamental importance for Kalecki's thinking. As already mentioned, he was a convinced socialist, and in his prescriptions of economic policies he always gave preference to safeguarding the interests of working people: full employment; protection of purchasing power of wages and, as far as possible, wage increases; involvement of the government in the satisfaction of social needs; and, with regard to peasantry, urgent agrarian reforms. However, he was realistic enough to be aware that the necessary conditions for progressive policies rarely could be met simultaneously.[8] But planning as he conceived it could at any rate serve as a standard enabling to assess the divergences between desirable and real situations.

For countries of the Third World the need for planning resulted from rather important reasons. Because of underdevelopment of their productive apparatus and the immense social debt to be filled in, these countries had no moral right to waste their resources by spending them for non-priority purposes or enjoying the luxury of letting productive capacities lie idle. Instead, they had to increase considerably their investment in order to accelerate the expansion of their productive capacity. For this purpose they had to plan not only the volume but also the structure of investments and their allocation between production of essential and non-essential consumer goods and capital goods (Kalecki CW V: 13–19).

What they really needed was to mobilize all their ingenuity in order to loosen the bottlenecks and to find the best possible solutions in an unfavourable international setting and with scarcity of foreign exchanges, the very joker in the planning game. The foreign trade barrier is ultimately the principal bottleneck of 'import-sensitive' economies (Sachs 1963). Kalecki didn't take any *a priori* position relative to the respective merits of export promotion or import substitution. He contented himself to say that, under conditions of equal net cost, expressed in domestic currency, of the foreign exchange either earned or saved, it was the import substitution that offered more advantage by providing for the country a shelter against turmoils in world markets.

Evidently, import-sensitive countries were interested in having recourse to imports of foreign capital, provided, however, that they would not lose control of the process of development nor pay an excessive price in the form of debt service increasing in a snowball way. Kalecki expressed his preference for public credits to serve development plans at reduced discount rates. As already mentioned, he was in favour of repaying debts in the form of exporting a part of the output produced due to foreign loans. He recommended, however, that the impact of foreign aid should always be examined in relation to changes brought about in the economy as a whole, and not by single projects.

Employment[9] and growth

In his writings Kalecki used a deliberately trimmed and concise style which served to present highly rigorous thinking in terms of essentials, and nothing more than essentials. The growth rate of economic systems, he said, depends first of all on investment and technical progress and, additionally, on the rate of real depreciation and the degree of utilization of the existing productive apparatus. This is expressed in the following formula:

$$r = i/k - a + u \quad (1)$$

where r is the rate of growth of GDP; i is the share of gross investment expenditure in GDP; k is the capital/output ratio; a is the coefficient of real depreciation; and u is the coefficient of optimum utilization of the existing productive apparatus.

This formula constituted the starting point of the Kaleckian theory of growth of a socialist economy. However, in one of his last writings (Kalecki 1970, CW IV: 111–17) he came to the conclusion that it applied to all economic systems, provided that coefficients k, a and u would be given a different interpretation. In a capitalist economy they acquire a cyclical pattern of behaviour to reflect changes of effective demand. In depressions, u may take a highly negative value; on the other hand, a is increased by 'creative destruction'. In the socialist economy a can be modified by a planner's decision, while u is as a rule positive due to the effects of organizational progress and the resulting economies in the use of resources.

According to another formula used by Kalecki the rate of growth of the economy is roughly equal to the sum of the rate of growth of employment e and the rate of growth of labour productivity p resulting from technical progress:

$$r = e + p \tag{2}$$

Employment appears here both as an essential factor of growth and as the main objective of the latter.

In this way, the objectives of full employment and protection of labour incomes constitute for Kalecki a moral imperative and a condition *sine qua non* of his engagement on the side of social justice. His numerous and important contributions to studies of policies to promote full employment in developed capitalist economies, and his famous text, so often quoted, on the political aspects of full employment (CW I: 357–76 and 347–56) constitute the distinctive part of his thought. On the other hand, in the context of the socialist economy, it is the pursuit of full employment that underlies the planner's choice of the shadow price of capital which plays an essential role in Kalecki's formula for evaluation of the effectiveness of investment.[10] Consequently, creation of jobs constitutes, all the more, the foundation of his theory of development and its financing.

Let us precede analysis of the main aspects of this theory by providing a simple typology of growth trajectories, derived from formula (2):

i intensive growth is accompanied by non-creation of employment; it is then entirely driven by rising labour productivity ($r = p > 0$; $e = 0$). An extreme case of modernization with perverse social effects would be represented by growth accompanied by a reduction of employment ($p > r > 0$; $e < 0$);

ii by contrast, extensive growth is driven entirely by increasing employment ($r = e > 0$; $p = 0$); in the case when e increases more than r at the expense of p, implying a decline in social productivity, we have to do with an extreme case of creating unproductive or fictitious jobs.

The rate of growth of labour productivity p is the foundation for both economic and social progress and improvement in living standards, provided the gains in productivity are equitably distributed within the society; a part of these gains can be assigned to shorten the working time without affecting wages, or to extend training. Industrialization is the principal leverage of structural transformation for an underdeveloped economy. It has a multiplier effect on the supply of jobs in the services sector. It also permits these countries to overcome their status of exporters of raw materials and to aspire at a more equitable access to the world economy. Moreover, one of the important objectives of development is elimination of painful and noxious jobs, which can be done by means of mechanization or even, in some cases, automation of production, whatever the country's level of development.

This is why there is no reason to propose, for the long-run, a strategy of development based solely on extensive growth, irrespectively of the existing burden of unemployment and under-employment. Both types of growth are to find their place in the development strategy. Countries with abundant supply of under-employed labour, experiencing excessive rates of demographic growth, should explore all the possible ways of jobs creation, and concentrate on those showing moderate capital/labour coefficients in sectors of activities demanding low import inputs. One should not confuse the capital/labour coefficient t with k, the capital/output coefficient: they are linked with one another by the identity: $t = k\ p$, where p means labour productivity. Many handicraft activities are characterized by low t, but their labour productivity p may be extremely low which can make their capital coefficient k rather high.

Insistence on employment-led growth is all the more necessary as private enterprises, pushed by market logic and competition, tend to pursue intensive growth, particularly in the form of perverse modernization, which leads to premature obsolescence of productive equipment (with the Schumpeterian creative destruction losing its creative quality).

The combination of the two types of growth should be thus biased in favour of extensive growth. Since the latter does not collide with the barrier of insufficient import capacity, as is the case of economic sectors where only intensive growth matters, insistence on the potency of extensive growth is tantamount to the acceleration, *ceteris paribus*, of the rate of growth of the national economy.

How far can this manoeuvre be pushed? I think that the most original part of Kalecki's development theory turns exactly around this question.

In view of the deprivation of workers, it may be assumed that any increase in the purchasing power of labour income through the creation of new jobs would be spent entirely on essential consumer goods and, first of all, on food products. Then, in such circumstances, the productive capacity in that sector would constitute the principal limit to the creating of new jobs in such a way as to secure growth without inflation.[11] Consequently, the increase in the supply of necessities would be reduced to the real need of financing employment-led growth, while at the strictly financial level this kind of development could be based on interception of a part of incomes of the well-to-do classes (CW V: 23–44, 45–60.

Hence, in his article on development of India (CW V: 122–8) Kalecki lays stress on the point that the problem of avoiding inflationary pressures in economic development is not a 'monetary' one. It is solved by securing, by means of various methods, an appropriate structure of national expenditure.

Three pre-conditions have to be met: an adequate supply of necessities, limitation of expenditure on non-essential goods in order to create adequate savings for financing public and private investment, and limitation of private investment so as to use a part of private savings to finance public investment (this element, let us recall, was of great importance in the development strategy adopted by India). Fiscal reform in India could thus consist, on the one hand, in complete tax exemption of a strictly limited number of essential goods which compose more or less total consumption of underprivileged social strata and, on the other hand, in highly progressive taxation of non-essential goods.

From the above one can understand the great importance Kalecki attached to agrarian reforms. In the absence of the latter, the supply of food products would not increase at a sufficient rate with a consequent rise in inflationary pressure which would lead to an unacceptable erosion of the purchasing power of labour incomes.

In general, it was considered important to take the best advantage of the latent potentialities of the peasant economy with its reserves of family labour force as evidenced in the writings of Tchaianov (1990) whose work was widely discussed in Poland after 1956.[12] An effort of the peasant agriculture was thus of double importance: it helped to relax a major constraint on the creation of non-agricultural employment, and it served to improve the living standards of the majority of inhabitants of the Third World. Thus industrialization of the Third World had to proceed without 'depeasantization' or, at least, without precipitate depeasantization (Abdalla 1979).

Yet, Kalecki did not envisage any expansion of large-scale public works which would mobilize dozens of thousands of workers equipped with shovels and spades, as was the case in China at the time of the 'big leap'. He was well aware of the related problems of management and organization as well as of the authoritarian implications of 'human investment' and forced labour.

The choice of techniques

Kalecki took an active part in the debate on the choice of techniques (CW V: 188–90) that had been provoked by well-known books of M. Dobb (1960) and A.K. Sen (1960). He did not share the views of these two authors who recommended maximization of the investible surplus rather than of output, which implied recourse to capital-intensive techniques. His opinion was that countries with abundant manpower should, whenever possible, use labour-intensive techniques.

This was all the more so, as the margins of freedom were limited in a double way: by techniques already embodied in the productive apparatus, whose transformation would spread over long years; and by the branch structure of new investment if account is taken of the fact that certain branches were not suitable for employment-creating solutions. An extreme example of the latter is oil extraction. By contrast, there are activities which, of their very nature, require much manpower, like services, construction or agriculture, and therefore should be granted a possibly important part in the goal function.

In the long run, the range of available techniques with desired parameters would depend on the orientation given to research and on the financial means assigned to it.[13]

Modernization of agriculture is a case which needs some more consideration. In fact, capital invested in agriculture plays the role of a substitute either for manpower (mechanization brings about an increase in labour productivity) or for land (irrigation, fertilizers, pesticides contribute to a rise in output per unit of land) (Sachs 1970).

In the first case the direction of development is towards agriculture without manpower, implying destruction of employment due to perverse modernization (David 1997). In the second case, technical progress is often accompanied by a rise in employment, especially if it is combined with types of activity which by their very nature require much manpower (horticulture, floriculture, certain kinds of animal breeding). This is the reason of Kalecki's insistence on treating the increase in output per hectare as a major objective of development.[14] But things become more complicated when mechanization is needed to accelerate certain field works so as to permit the passage from one to two harvests per year.

In any case, the choice of techniques in agriculture depends, to a large extent, on the composition of cultures and other activities performed by increasingly multifunctional peasant families.

Finally, let us mention the 'pure' technical progress, which consists in application of inventions that do not require significant investment, as sometimes happens in agriculture (e.g. in the field of genetics) or, more generally, disembodied progress (methods of management). Kalecki was very sensitive to this aspect. He felt that countries possessing highly qualified scientific cadres whose salaries were considerably inferior as compared to those of scientists in industrialized countries, had a *forte carte* to play in matters of specialization in foreign trade by offering for exports the products of highly skilled labour. Since 1955 he kept suggesting (alas to no effect) that Poland starts production of electronic components, taking advantage of its excellent mathematicians and abundant offer of cheap female labour needed in the electronic industry. The present successful software exports from India prove that he was right.

Thirty years later

Kalecki did not live long enough to witness the revenge of monetarists on Keynesians, the thunderous ascension (in a double sense) of the neoliberal counter-revolution and the application *urbi et orbi* of policies known under the name of the Washingtonian Consensus, rather remote from what he had recommended.[15]

It is no doubt too early to speak of the end of the neoliberal interlude. Nevertheless, the recent crises in South-Eastern Asia, Russia and Brazil have seriously impaired the hegemony of monetarist and neoliberal theories and their prestige with the World Bank. Its chief economist, Joseph Stiglitz, talks about a Post-Washingtonian Consensus (Stiglitz 1998a). John Gray, on his part, argues that the *laissez-faire* economy has been in England but a short-lived historical aberration which, after all, was made possible owing to interventions of the British government. In his view the setting-up of a global *laissez-faire* system as aimed at by the United States cannot lead but to a tragedy. The Asian crisis appears to his eyes as the first historical manifestation of the disastrous effects of free flow of capital for economic stability (Gray 1999).

In a penetrating book D. Rodrik draws the conclusion from his econometric studies (Rodrik 1999) that policies of openness do not necessarily lead to growth, the latter being dependent essentially on the rate of investment and appropriate macro policies. Policy-makers are reminded not to trust the changing fashions in economic thought and the orthodoxy preaching reduced government and *laissez-faire*. International policies should create space for national development efforts, necessarily plural in their philosophy and contents. It is absurd to impose on all countries a unique model of development, taking at that into account that its pretended superiority is doubtful. The structure of social institutions, the acceptable degree of inequality, the types of public goods which the governments have to supply – these are the issues which have to be dealt with at the national level.

Possibly, the best way of shaping the policies of the Post-Washingtonian Consensus may be to go back to the policies of the 1950s and 1960s. It is in this context that Kalecki's theory of development appears to regain its relevance.

Some Indian authors were aware of this when they proposed that employment and *ex ante* distribution of income between compensation of labour and profits be used as the starting point to an iterative process leading to elaboration of a development strategy or plan. Nothing else is needed than to reverse the sequence in which employment and income distribution are treated as outcome of the process of growth driven by the market (Chakravarthy 1994; Gosh 1996; Kurien 1996). Employment policies – not to be confused with measures to make the labour market more flexible – should once again take the central place in the strategies of development.

In fact, more than at any time, employment and self-employment constitute nowadays an absolute priority. Even in rich countries the remedy to negative situations is no longer to be found solely in income distribution. Structural unemployment, precariousness of jobs and the resulting social exclusion are today the common fate of rich and poor countries alike. Both of them are affected by a split of their societies into duality. In the circumstances it may be justified to speak about '*thirdworldization*' of our planet. This is why the social democratic paradigm entered into a crisis.

From the viewpoint of the pursuit of employment-led growth the actual situation of a number of countries of the South permits a certain optimism. At first glance this may seem surprising. But they possess important reserves of jobs whose activation should be possible by making an appeal for mobilization of internal resources, both real and financial[16] without taking recourse to foreign capital and without creating pressure on the balance of payments thanks to their very limited imports content. Five paths seem to be particularly interesting:

i *Intensification of peasant agriculture* which can be stimulated, where necessary, by agrarian reforms, as well as by programmes of modernization of small holdings and, more generally, by integrated programmes of rural development based on increasing multifunctionality of family farms. In a report, which passed almost unnoticeably, the International Commission for Peace and Food notes the existence of one milliard direct and indirect rural jobs in the world as a whole, extrapolating an Indian study which proposed to create, over ten years, 100 million jobs composed of 45 million strictly agricultural jobs, 10 million jobs in food processing, 45 million rural and urban jobs as a result of the multiplier effect of increased consumption of the rural population; at the same time the rural sector would constitute a source of biomasses (food, fodder, bioenergy, green fertilizers and industrial raw materials) and a market for industrial products and services (ICPF 1994; Abramovay and Sachs 1972).

ii Jobs connected with *eco-efficiency, resource management and maintenance of equipment, infrastructure and buildings*, able to bring about an extension of productive life of equipment and thereby a reduction of demand for reinvestment. In Kalecki's terms, this would mean reducing the coefficient *a* (the rate of real depreciation) and augmenting *u* (the coefficient of optimum use of productive capacity) through re-utilization of materials, recycling, economies in the use of energy, water and other natural resources, in other words, through activating sources of growth that do not require investment. In macro terms, many of these jobs connected with eco-efficiency may finance themselves through induced economies of natural resources.

iii Employment and self-employment related to *construction and subsidized self-construction of popular housing* in urban and peripheral slum areas of the Third World. There are now at least 600 million people deprived of decent housing. Urbanization of the refugees from the countryside requires that they get access to decent housing, stable jobs and conditions for effective exercise of citizenship.

iv *Public works* which are of essential importance for the modernization and expansion of underdeveloped economies, especially at a time when they are about to undertake the task of reconstructing their internal capacity to invest and to open the Keynesian virtuous circle of investment – saving (Ocampo 1993). Their particular importance results from the fact that the systemic competitiveness of these countries depends, to a considerable extent, on their progress on the way to rehabilitation and expansion of infrastructure. In so far as *non-tradeables* are concerned there exist margins of freedom for the choice of job-creating techniques, but such advantages are seldom used. Of course, one would not advocate going to the extreme of works based on the use of shovels and spades, not more than importing the most efficient and highly automated equipment, the usefulness of which may be questionable even in the richest countries.

v Finally, mention should be made of *services*, and in particular *social services* in the widest sense. Demand for the latter is far from satisfied even in the richest countries if looked at in terms of needs rather than effective demand. Countries where wage levels are low produce these services at much lower cost than those with high wages. This may be their chance for advance in the direction of a welfare state without waiting until their incomes per capita reach levels comparable to those in industrialized countries (Sachs 1971).

Abandoning his habitual modesty, in the Preface to the re-edition of his juvenile writings dated 1964, Kalecki expressed his conviction that he had raised and resolved a certain number of problems which later absorbed the attention of economists for two decades (Kalecki 1962). *Mutatis mutandis*, 30 years after his departure from this world, the same applies to his theory of development. But, over the last two decades, the mainstream of economic thought preferred to ignore his teachings.

Notes

1 Translated from the French by Adam Szeworski and Zdzislaw Sadowski.

2 In London, a committee was created at the Royal Institute of International Affairs to deal with problems of the post-war reconstruction of the economy. Its secretary, P. Rosenstein Rodan, assisted by H.W. Arndt, was working in close co-operation with a group of economists and sociologists refugees from Eastern Europe, who had found asylum in Britain. A parallel group was formed at the Oxford University Institute of Statistics where Michal Kalecki and E.F. Schumacher had become the main animators. Among the economists who later on were highly influential in discussions on economic development there was a number of Hungarians (Balogh, Kaldor, Mannheim, Polanyi, Scitovsky) and Poles (Lange, who was then working in the United States, Malinowski and Rudzinski, and later also H.W. Singer and Mandelbaum alias Martin). An article by Rosenstein-Rodan on problems of industrialization of countries of Eastern and South-Eastern Europe, published in 1943, has been often referred to as the starting point of development economics as an autonomous branch of economics (Arndt 1972, 1984).

3 This might, in addition, make necessary putting a brake on non-priority investment, be it private and profitable at the micro-level, in order to prevent detracting country's scarce resources, and especially, foreign exchanges.

4 This proposition of Kalecki appeared highly attractive to S. Chakravarty (1994: 239–40). In general, Kaleckian thought exerted a strong influence on Indian

planners and economists (e.g. P. Mahalanobis, P. Pant, K. Raj, S. Chakravarty and A. Mitra).

5 The article written by Kalecki on this subject in 1964 (CW V: 6–12, 200–4), which gave rise to a number of articles by various authors, was a generalization of the conclusions arrived at in an empirical study I undertook on his suggestion, entitled 'On the nature of the economic and social system in Egypt' (both texts were published together in Polish).

6 Optimization is possible in that case using foreign exchange as a common denominator: it consists thus in choosing the best opportunities for earning foreign exchange by means of exports or saving it by means of import substitution, at the lowest cost in domestic currency per unit of foreign exchange (earned or saved).

7 Or in a situation like the historical compromise of Christian Democrats and Communists, as was the case in Italy.

8 When an interviewer asked him, why he did not suggest to the Indian government to make agrarian revolution, his answer, which then became famous, was: *a country which likes to make revolutions does not appeal to foreign consultants.*

9 This term is to be understood as embracing both employment and self-employment, in the countryside as well as in urban areas, so to cover all the forms of production of subsistence means ('livelihood' as used by Polanyi).

10 For the sake of equilibrium in the balance of payments investment should be kept at the lowest level compatible with full employment of the available labour force (Kalecki 1970, CW IV: 204).

11 Kalecki was the pioneer of the structuralist theory of inflation which has been particularly relevant to the conditions prevailing in Latin America (Dell 1977; Arndt 1985).

12 In this connection it is advisable to remind the reader of the peculiarity of the Polish model of development: the idea of collectivization of agriculture was quickly abandoned, and Poland's transition to socialism was accommodated to the existence of a large sector of peasant economy.

13 For any economy considered as a whole there exists, at any time, a concave curve CC' of efficient technical solutions, which combines various quantities of capital and labour. Technical progress shifts this curve to the left and downwards. In contrast to the widely adopted prejudice, technical progress is not necessarily biased in favour of higher capital intensity. It can be neutral or even biased towards higher labour intensity. However, there are only a few points on that continuous curve that represent solutions feasible of being applied in practice. Future research should be, therefore, aimed also at increasing the number of such points on the relevant segment of that curve.

14 This thesis requires some modification in view of the present state of our knowledge of ecological consequences of the abuse of chemicals.

15 The only common point would be the preoccupation with avoiding of inflation and the ensuing erosion of the purchasing power of wages.

16 Either, as already mentioned, in the way of absorption of a part of incomes of the well-to-do strata of population or raising savings above the initially assumed level, in form of non-monetary investment of both peasants and urban inhabitants participating in supported residential self-construction.

14 The opportunities and dangers of international capital inflows for developing countries from an effective demand perspective

Amit Bhaduri

Overview

It is widely recognized that the phenomenal magnitudes of international capital flows from private sources present the most dramatic face of contemporary globalization. Global turnover in foreign exchange trading rose from an average daily figure of US$18.3 billion in 1977 to US$1.23 trillion in 1995, a figure which rises even higher to about US$1.30 trillion dollars daily, if foreign exchange options and related derivative are included. Over the same period 1977–95, the ratio of daily global foreign exchange turnover to the value of global exports rose from 3.5 to 64, while official reserves declined from 15 to less than that of a day of the daily foreign exchange turnover (Felix 1998).

At the same time, in so far as the developing countries are concerned, only a narrow band of about a dozen of them, mostly belonging to the 'newly industrializing countries', became recipients of capital flows on any significant scale (IMF 1998).

The process of massive deregulation, that began in the international capital markets around the mid-1970s, and was by and large completed in OECD countries by the mid-1980s, undoubtedly drove this phenomenal growth in private capital flows. Not accidentally, this also coincided with the period when market-oriented ideology reached its peak. Both developed and developing countries were advised to turn to the private capital market, and rely on 'the magic of the market place', both as a disciplining device and as a promoter of economic growth. Those fortunate, but relatively narrow band of about a dozen developing countries, which could attract significant international capital inflows from private sources, saw in this an unprecedented opportunity for faster economic development. However, the danger that is intertwined with this opportunity also unfolded itself through the varied experiences in several developing countries, especially in Latin America, and more recently in South East Asia. The danger of a financial crisis driven by external debt, usually with an accompanying banking crisis at home, seems to present an awkward choice. Attaining higher economic growth with capital inflows seems to make that growth process also more fragile and exposed to large fluctuations. The choice, it appears from experience, is between a slower but steadier trend rate of growth and a faster but unsteady one.

It is probably justified to say that in the present stage of our understanding, we do not have a unified theory as to how and why heavy reliance on the international private capital market leads a developing country so frequently towards financial collapse. It is a problem which seems to involve 'complexity' in the sense that there exists no short-cut common analytical description, reducible to a single unified explanation. Somewhat like the variety of models of oligopoly and industrial organization in economics, several formulations trying to capture different aspects of the problem coexist. However, they are not necessarily contesting theories, but simply a variety of analytical descriptions, intended at highlighting different aspects of the same problem. It is very much like several blind men (or economists) trying to describe an elephant to touching different parts of its body! A plethora of explanations, running in terms of corrupt government and 'crony capitalism', moral hazards inducing over-borrowing or over-lending by domestic or foreign banks, lack of adequate supervision of capital markets and misalignment of the exchange rate are offered as explanation. They may all be touching different parts of the same complex problem of how such a financial crisis gets precipitated, while none of them may be sufficient to capture adequately the entire problem.

It is not the purpose of this chapter to offer yet another such partial, explanatory model; instead, it takes a different route. We decompose the problem for analytical convenience into several separate parts. Assuming a developing country to be the recipient of significant capital inflows, we first analyse how its levels of output and economic activity are affected by autonomous capital inflows in the short-run. In the intellectual tradition of Kalecki and Keynes, we postulate that output and economic activity are determined by aggregate demand (see following section). Therefore, this analysis of 'quantity adjustment' focuses on the impact of capital inflows on the real economy through aggregate demand. It is assumed that the impact operates entirely through the channel of trade balance, while the other relevant macroeconomic variables like investment and consumption remain unaffected. In the third section we analyse how capital inflow might impact on some of these other relevant macroeconomic variables to affect aggregate demand. Since, the channel of operation is mostly through the markets for money and other financial assets, the total effect on aggregate demand and output is considered in this light.

Throughout the analysis, we oversimplify the problem deliberately for convenience of exposition, by assuming that the exchange rate remains fixed to focus exclusively on quantity adjustments. This artificial assumption rules out by definition any financial crisis precipitated by a collapse in the exchange rate. Nevertheless, the analysis might be still useful in a more limited sense. It hopes to capture the mechanisms of transmission through which international capital inflows impact on the real economy through aggregate demand that might even create a 'financial bubble' in the process.

Output or quantity adjustment through capital inflows: the trade channel

Keynes' as well as Kalecki's analysis of the problem of aggregate demand was set, almost self consciously, in the context of a closed economy. The generalization of this analysis to an economy open to foreign trade through various ramifications of the 'foreign trade multiplier', had one common thread running through them. Import, like saving, was assumed to be induced by income. Thus, with both saving and import as increasing functions of income, the effect of the foreign trade multiplier on aggregate demand could be derived in terms of saving and import propensity.

With capital inflow in the liberalized trade regime of a developing country the problem needs to be viewed somewhat differently. Capital inflow is an autonomous variable decided by private traders in the international foreign exchange market. In many situations we may plausibly postulate that higher import, and trade deficit, is not only sustained, but driven by the volume of autonomous capital inflows into a country. Thus, in contrast to the more traditional Keynesian model, import is assumed to be induced, not by income, but by capital inflow. Its consequence is evident. A higher capital inflow in a liberalized trade regime permits sustaining a higher trade deficit, which in turn, has a contractionary impact on income through the standard multiplier mechanism (Bhaduri and Skarstein 1996). More formally, in familiar notations of national income accounting:

$$X = \text{GDP} = C + I + E - M$$

where C = Consumption, I = Investment, E = Exports and M = Imports.

Deducting consumption expenditure (C) from both sides, we have:

$$\text{saving } S = Y - C = I + E - M \tag{1}$$

Moreover, for simplicity, we assume average and marginal saving propensity to be a fixed proportion of GDP (X), i.e.:

$$S = sX, \; 1 > s > 0 \tag{2}$$

The solution of demand-determined GDP is given from (1) as:

$$X = (1/s)[I - (M - E)] \tag{3}$$

If a higher level of capital inflow (F) simply sustains higher trade deficit, but does not affect investment (I), it is evident from (3) that such capital inflow will be contractionary through the multiplier mechanism in its impact on demand-determined output. This is shown explicitly by rewriting (3) as:

$$X = (1/s)[I - F] \tag{4}$$

where $F = (M - E)$, i.e. the level of trade deficit sustained by capital inflow F.

Despite the elementary nature of the above algebraic calculation, it has an important economic message which deserves emphasis, because it goes against the conventional wisdom about trade liberalization sustained through capital inflow. As equation (4) shows, a higher inflow of foreign finance F, could reduce income through the multiplier mechanism for a given level of investment. However, the multiplier mechanism driving the contraction of aggregate demand and income in equation (4) does not depend merely on the substitution of less competitive, 'inferior' domestically produced goods by 'superior' imported goods to enhance consumers' welfare, as conventional theory would often have us believe. This is because the substitution of domestic by imported goods provides only the initial impulse to the Kahn–Keynes multiplier process. However, as the output of domestic goods decreases through substitution, so do profits, wages and employment in these domestic industries. This sets in motion further decline in demand and output of domestic industries in a chain reaction captured by the usual convergent geometric series of the multiplier process, as implied by (4). Note that these successive rounds of contraction in demand and output need not involve any further substitution of domestic by foreign goods. Therefore, they also do not imply that the decline in domestic output in these successive rounds is due to its lack of international competitiveness, because they could be driven entirely by the contraction in domestic demand.

The unambiguously contractionary impact of capital inflow on the level of aggregate demand and output, represented by equation (4), is an extreme case. Yet, it may not be altogether irrelevant in some situations. Tanzania was advised by the IMF in the 1980s to liberalize imports by bringing most imported items under the 'Open General Licence' (OGL) scheme, while major aid donors agreed to sustain the higher trade deficit of the liberalized trade regime through augmented capital inflows, mostly in the form of official development assistance (ODA). Without a marked increase, either in public or in private investment, the higher ODA, supporting a larger trade deficit under the OGL scheme without much variation in the exchange rate as assumed in the analysis above, resulted in a strong contractionary impact on domestic demand and output. In an altogether different context, it is arguable that the massive transfer of income from the West to the East of united Germany, right after the political as well as exchange rate reunification, had a similar effect. A large part of the transferred income as well as accumulated private saving in the eastern region were spent on imports from West German industries to set in motion a similar contractionary process of demand for goods produced by the eastern region.

Equation (4) is, however, misleadingly simple even in macroeconomic accounting terms. It assumes that the entire capital inflow to the developing country is available for sustaining only trade deficit. Some recent calculations on the other hand suggest that, on average capital outflows in various forms including service payments account for some 30 per cent and the change in reserve for another 20 per cent of capital inflows to developing countries. Only the remaining 50 per cent is available for covering trade deficits $(M-E)$ of developing countries as a whole (UNCTAD, unpublished tentative estimates, 1999). Thus:

$$F = Z + \Delta R + (M - E) \tag{5}$$

where F = capital inflow (including factor income earning by the country);
ΔR = change in foreign exchange reserve;
Z = 'outflow' which is assumed to be equal to net factor payment for simplicity; and
$(M-E)$ = trade deficit.

Since, by definition, GNP (Y) is GDP (X) minus net factor payment (Z) i.e.:

$$Y = X - Z \tag{6}$$

We may substitute this in (1), and use (5) to obtain:

$$Y - C = S = I + \Delta R - F \tag{7}$$

Therefore, if saving is assumed to be a fraction (s) of GNP (rather than GDP), we obtain in place of (4):

$$Y = (1/s)[I - (F - \Delta R) \tag{8}$$

In other words, the contractionary effect of foreign capital inflow at a given level of investment discussed earlier in equation (4) remains similar qualitatively to equation (8). The support such inflow provides to trade deficit, net of the change in reserve (ΔR) operates through the multiplier leading to demand contraction. And, the two formulae (4) and (8) coincide on the right-hand side in case of no change in reserve ($\Delta R = 0$).

Quantity adjustment: the channel of financial assets

Our theoretical analysis so far suggests that, 'other things being equal', capital inflow used to cover trade deficit has a contractionary effect on the level of economic activity, operating through the multiplier mechanism. However, this contradicts the recent experiences of many developing countries which have enjoyed rapid expansion in the levels of output and economic activity in regimes of significant capital inflows. This is easy to incorporate formally in the analysis, once it is recognized that 'other things' do not remain 'equal' under capital inflows. In particular, investment might be stimulated either directly through foreign direct investment or indirectly through the influence of capital inflows on the domestic interest rate and the stock market.

The indirectly stimulating effects of capital inflows on investment can be seen most clearly by considering for analytical convenience, logically extreme situations. Suppose first that all capital inflows are in the form of reserves held by the domestic financial system, in the central or in the commercial banks so that no output contraction operates through the channel of trade deficit (equation 8). Since, by standard accounting, liabilities of the financial system to the public is some definition of the supply of 'money' (M^s), this must be matched by its corresponding asset position which is credit advanced (A) plus foreign reserve (R), i.e:

$$M^s = A + R \tag{9}$$

It follows from (9) that an increase in reserves would be associated with an increase in money supply. However, it is more correct to see this money supply as potential, rather than realized. The potential is realized to the extent the public demands the increased potential supply of money. More formally from equation (9):

$$M^d(i, Y) = M^s = A\ (i) + R \tag{10}$$

so that, on total differentiation:

$$\mathrm{d}i = \frac{(\Delta R - M_y^d\,.\mathrm{d}Y)}{(M_i^d - A_i)} \quad \Delta R = \mathrm{d}R \tag{11}$$

where (as in all succeeding algebra) the subscript represents the partial derivative with respect to the relevant variable.

The usual transaction and speculative demand for money enters as arguments in the money demand function M^d on the left-hand side of (10); amount of credit that the banks wish to advance increases with the interest rate on the right-hand side of (10). Thus, we may plausibly assume:

$$M_I^d < 0,\ A_I > 0 \text{ and } M_y > 0 \tag{12}$$

Consequently the denominator of (11) is unambiguously negative, and I increases or decreases due to capital inflow according to:

$$\Delta R \,{}^{<}_{>}\, M_{y.}\mathrm{d}Y \tag{13}$$

From (5):

$$\Delta R = F - (M + Z - E) = F - B \tag{14}$$

where $B = (M + Z - E)$, i.e. the magnitude of current account deficit on the balance of payments. Thus, a sufficiently large capital inflow which not only covers current account deficit (equation 14), but also contributes to reserve after covering the additional transaction demand for money in a growing economy would tend to lower the domestic rate of interest from (13). It might also stimulate investment, thus establishing a link between equations (8) and (11).

In so far as large foreign capital inflow has this tendency to depress the domestic interest rate through larger money supply, it might not only stimulate investment, but also private consumption through greater hire-purchase, housing loans etc. However, these effects are likely to be felt more strongly in industrially advanced countries with wider networks of financial intermediation and consumers' credit than in most developing countries.

A lower interest rate, by raising the prices of bonds might also create a positive 'wealth effect' for various bond-holders. In so far as the commercial banks in many developing countries are major holders of government bonds, their asset position and capital base for lending would improve correspondingly, just as private bond holders many spend more and save less due to the positive wealth effect.

However, the main channel through which foreign capital inflow might influence private investment is the market for private corporate equities, rather than bank-financed debt.

Thus, foreign institutional and other investors would exchange foreign currency with domestic banks to purchase financial assets denominated in domestic currency. If they purchase equities in the *primary market* to finance the issue of new equities, this would directly lead to higher investment. Capital inflow would then have a stimulating effect on real investment without equity prices necessarily rising, as more new equities are issued. However, if foreign capital inflow goes mostly into the *secondary market* in the acquisition or merger of existing ownership rights, equity prices would rise and interest rate driven down. Its effect on real investment would be positive, if this more favourable climate for financing long-term real investment through higher prices of equities is seized by the investing firms. However, it is also possible that rising prices of equities in a bullish stock market would divert investment more towards the acquisition and merger to create a 'financial bubble', rather than provide support to long-term real investment. The same story, with only slight modification, can be repeated for investment being diverted into land and real estates. Note in this context that prime land properties being more or less in fixed supply, tend to resemble more closely the secondary market for financial assets, where the acquisition of existing ownership rights rather than financing *new* ownership rights, is the name of the game.

The preceding analysis of the impact of capital inflow on the real economy can be summarized more formally. On the basis of our analysis we assume that investment, saving as well as current account deficit are influenced by the inflow of foreign capital through the various routes only some of which are mentioned above. In addition, we assume as before that trade deficit increases generally with both income and capital inflow due to higher import in most developing countries. Thus using (14) in (7), we have:

$$S(Y,F) = I(Y,F) - B(Y,F) \tag{15}$$

Which yields on total differentiation:

$$\frac{\mathrm{d}Y}{\mathrm{d}F} = \frac{I_F - (S_F - B_F)}{(S_Y + B_Y) - I_Y} \tag{16}$$

Note, by assumption, $by > 0$, $S_Y > 0$, $I_Y > 0$ and $B_F > 0$.

By chain rule, and assuming the interest rate, i.e. bank credit to be the main channel of transmission:

$$I_F \equiv \frac{\partial I}{\partial F} \equiv \left\langle \frac{\partial \overset{-}{I}}{\partial i} \right\rangle \left\langle \frac{\partial \overset{-}{i}}{\partial F} \right\rangle > 0 \tag{17}$$

$$S_F \equiv \frac{\partial S}{\partial F} \equiv \left(\frac{\partial \overset{+}{S}}{\partial i} \right) \left(\frac{\partial \overset{-}{i}}{\partial F} \right) < 0 \tag{18}$$

(The signs assigned to the partial derivatives are shown above the relevant brackets.)

If we assume the single variable income adjustment process of the Keynesian system to be stable, the denominator in (16) is unambiguously positive, i.e.:

$$(S_y + B_y) > I_y \tag{19}$$

Thus, the impact of capital inflow on the level of income would be positive. Unless the deficit on current account is stimulated too strongly by capital inflows, the inequality condition (20) may be satisfied for capital inflow to stimulate growth, i.e.

$$(\partial Y/\partial F) > 0, \text{ if } I_F > S_F + B_F \tag{20}$$

However, in the special case of a 'financial bubble', condition (20) tends to be violated. This condition is more transparent, as discussed earlier, if we concentrate on the case of foreign capital inflow entirely into the secondary market for equities. As large inflow pushes up equity prices, i.e. $\frac{\partial p}{\partial I} < 0$ p is equity price, this leads to diversion of funds in the expectation of quick capital gains in the secondary market, instead of new equity investment. This results in lower real investment due to higher equity price.

It is also possible that higher equity prices lead to even higher demand for bank credit met through capital inflow to finance the speculative bubble in the secondary stock market as well as fixed supply real estate market. Instead of condition (17), we would, then have, with asset or real estate price as the main channel of transmission:

$$IF = \frac{\partial I}{\partial F} = \left(\frac{\overset{-}{\partial I}}{\partial p}\right) \cdot \left(\frac{\overset{+}{\partial p}}{\partial F}\right) < 0 \tag{17a}$$

This is the extreme case of a financial bubble with foreign capital inflow, where domestic real investment stagnates or even falls i.e. $(\mathrm{d}I/\mathrm{d}p) < 0$ while the (secondary) stock market as well as the real estate market boom. Nevertheless, interestingly enough, as condition (20) shows, the effect of foreign capital inflow on income may still be positive, if S_F is negative and large enough in absolute magnitude. This would be the case when a financial or real estate bubble creates a strong enough wealth effect to raise aggregate demand and output through higher consumption. One might add that such a situation characterized by a consumption-led expansion in aggregate demand and output is more likely to arise in an advanced, industrial country like the United States with very extensive participation of the public in the stock market. It is less likely in most developing countries where the stock market is less extensive, and perhaps even in most countries in Western Europe. Nevertheless, the fixed-supply real estate market with economic characteristics similar to the secondary stock market may play a similar role, of fuelling a consumption-led bubble of expanding demand and output.

15 On Kalecki's contribution to development economics[1]

Rune Skarstein

Introduction

Michal Kalecki was sceptical to the possibility of underdeveloped economies to attain development under a regime of free trade or economic liberalization in general. His contributions to the theory of economic development were therefore conceived for centrally planned or mixed economies. However, in his papers on economic development, as well as in his theoretical work in general, he made assumptions and opened up perspectives which are highly relevant to any theory of economic development, also under the conditions of a liberalized underdeveloped economy attempting to follow the path of *laissez-faire* capitalism.

His contribution to development economics covered mainly five areas. First, he revised the Domar type of growth theory to make it applicable to centrally planned and mixed economies under the condition of unlimited supplies of labour (Kalecki 1972: 10–16, 27–36). Second, he made significant contributions to the theory of taxation in developing countries as well as industrialized economies. Third, in his brilliant articles on 'intermediate regimes' he provided important insights into the political and institutional constraints to economic development (Kalecki 1976: 30–7, 198–203). Fourth, in his articles on the financing of economic development he showed convincingly that the growth in the supply of food grains and agricultural growth in general represent the major constraint to overall economic development (Kalecki 1976: 41–63, 98–115). Fifth, in extension of these articles, he made influential studies on the impacts of foreign aid and foreign direct investment. The focus of this chapter will be the fourth part of his contribution, which will be compared particularly with Nicholas Kaldor's work on the same theme.[2]

An important point of departure: Kalecki's theory of prices

In the early 1940s, Kalecki elaborated his price theory, classifying price changes into two broad groups, i.e. '. . . those determined mainly by changes in the cost of production and those determined mainly by changes in demand' (Kalecki 1971a: 43). While the price of agricultural products is determined more or less in line with the standard neoclassical textbooks, by changes in demand and supply, the price of industrial products is 'cost-determined'. Industrial prices react slowly or insignificantly to changes in demand but change in response to changes in variable costs, particularly wage costs. Kalecki assumed that the industrial firms add a mark-up on the variable cost per unit of output, essentially the unit wage cost. This mark-up is in turn determined by the market power of industrial capitalists, which Kalecki called the 'degree of monopoly' (Kalecki 1971a: 45ff).

We use the following notation: the average industrial mark-up is m, the industrial money wage rate is w_i, industrial value added in terms of industrial goods is Y, and industrial employment is L. When the average productivity of labour in industry is $\lambda = Y/L$, which is assumed to be constant in the short period, up to full capacity utilization, the money price of industrial output (value added) p_i can be expressed as:

$$p_i = (1+m)\frac{w_i}{\lambda}, \qquad \text{for } Y \leq Y^c,\ L \leq L^c \tag{1}$$

where Y^c and L^c are full capacity production and employment, respectively.[3]

Kalecki's price theory has inspired later discussions of price formation, for example Hicks' distinction between 'fixed price' and 'flexible price'. More importantly, as we will discuss subsequently, Nicholas Kaldor used Kalecki's price theory in his contributions on the economic interaction between agriculture and industry in economic development.

The problem of 'financing' economic development (I)

Kalecki wrote two important papers on this theme (Kalecki 1976: 41–63, 98–115, respectively). In the first article, originally published in Spanish in 1954, the same year as W.A. Lewis published his seminal paper on economic growth with unlimited supplies of labour, Kalecki used Marx's scheme of reproduction, dividing the economy into two major sectors, Department I producing industrial investment goods, and Department II comprising both industrial and agricultural production of consumer goods. Throughout his analysis he assumed that workers and small proprietors, including peasants, 'consume all their income and no more', so that 'the total saving is equal to the saving out of profits of the capitalists' (Kalecki 1976: 42).

Using Marx's scheme he first amplified the Keynesian proposition that

> in a sense, investment finances itself . . . investment as it is carried out creates its counterpart in saving. A part of saving arises directly in Department I. The second part of saving is equivalent to the selling of the surplus of consumption goods of Department II to workers and capitalists in Department I.

From this he concluded that

> There are no financial limits, in a formal sense, to the volume of investment . . . the crucial point in the problem of whether a certain level of investment creates or does not create inflationary pressure is the possibility of expansion of supply of consumer goods in response to demand.
>
> (Kalecki 1976: 43–4)

He further argued that in the industrial sector of Department II the supply of consumer goods would be elastic owing to idle capacities in that sector. On the other hand, in the agricultural sector of Department II, supply would in general be 'fairly rigid'. For two reasons, the existence of surplus labour in agriculture would not contribute much to relieving this constraint. First, the reduction of surplus labour owing to rising industrial investment and employment would not affect agricultural production noticeably. Second, the 'extra surplus' of food arising in this process 'will frequently be used to increase the food consumption of the peasants'. From this Kalecki concluded that the rise in industrial investment 'may create a strong pressure on the available supplies of food' (Kalecki 1976: 47).

This pressure will lead to rising food prices which would imply a reduction of the industrial real wage at the given money wage. The higher price of food could potentially lead to increased demand for industrial mass consumer goods on part of the countryside, and in that way stimulate industrial production and investment. However, Kalecki argued that the benefits of higher food prices would to a large extent 'accrue to landlords, merchants or money lenders. . . . In this case, the high demand generated by a rapid development involving large scale investment will not create a market for industrial mass consumption goods' (Kalecki 1976: 47).

Without making the point quite clear Kalecki assumed that the rise in food prices would partly lead to an increase in the money wage, which would in turn result in higher industrial price through mark-up pricing as shown in equation (1), and partly it would lead to a lower real wage, because the price of agricultural products, particularly food, would rise more than the money wage. Let us denote the agricultural price as p_a and the real wage in terms of food as w^*.[4] Then $w^* = w_i/p_a$, and $w_i = p_a \cdot w^*$. Denoting the terms of trade between agriculture and industry as $p_i/p_a = p$, we can reformulate equation (1) as:

$$p = \frac{p_i}{p_a} = (1 + m).\frac{w^*}{\lambda} \tag{2}$$

Equation (2) shows that an increase of p_a at a given industrial price must lead to a proportionate reduction of the real wage w^* if the mark-up m and labour productivity λ are kept constant. On the other hand, if the price increase of agricultural output is partly transmitted into an increase of the industrial money wage, the price of industrial goods will rise in accordance with equation (1), and the result will be a combination of reduced real wage and an overall price increase. Kalecki summarized his argument as follows:

> We can conclude that the increase in investment under conditions of inelastic food supply will cause a fall in real wages and will generate an inflationary price–wage spiral. Moreover, this type of inflation may not be associated with any considerable rise in demand for industrial consumption goods. Thus, it is clear from the above that the expansion of food production, paralleling the industrial development, is of paramount importance for avoiding inflationary pressures.
>
> (Kalecki 1976: 48)

Kalecki's main point was to show how excess demand for agricultural goods gets propagated into general inflation in the economy as a whole even when there is excess capacity in the industrial sector. This contradicts the conventional view that excess demand for industrial goods is required for producing inflation in that sector.[5] He added that 'While an adequate supply of food is of basic importance for preventing inflation, in the course of economic development, the increases in industrial productivity work in the same direction' (Kalecki 1976: 48). As is evident from equation (2), an increase in industrial labour productivity will imply less reduction of the real wage when the agricultural price rises at given industrial price and given mark-up. This will in turn lead to less upward pressure on the industrial money wage and have a dampening effect on inflation.

On the other hand, at a given volume of industrial output, the increase of industrial labour productivity will mean lower industrial employment which will worsen the situation of 'surplus labour'. Thus, 'The rise in productivity mitigates inflationary pressures, but at the same time it slows down the rate at which surplus rural labour is absorbed into industry' (Kalecki 1976: 51).

So far, Kalecki has assumed that the mark-up is constant. However, 'Since, in the course of economic development, there will be a tendency towards increased concentration in industry, a rise in the degree of monopoly may easily take place' (Kalecki 1976: 50). At a given money wage this will lead to an increase of the industrial price in accordance with equation (1). Moreover, since the profit share rises with the mark-up (see note 3), and industrial wages purchase mainly agricultural products, 'the final result will be a shift in the distribution of income from wages and agricultural incomes to industrial profits' (Kalecki 1976: 50). The reaction of the workers to the reduction of real wages associated with this 'forced saving' will be 'a demand for higher money wages, and thus a price–wage spiral will be initiated' (Kalecki 1976: 44).

Kalecki's theory of inflation in a developing economy has inspired the whole school of structural theory of inflation (cf. Arndt 1985: 154–5). Indeed, the different varieties of the structural theory of inflation may be considered as mere elaborations or refinements of Kalecki's theory, which makes their very cornerstone although he is not often referred to.[6] These theories also appear to me to leave the same questions open as Kalecki's original version. In my assessment, these questions are, first: how is the industrial money wage determined, and second: is there any lower limit to the industrial real wage? (cf. e.g. Cardoso 1981; Taylor 1982).

Nicholas Kaldor suggested a solution to this problem, following W.A. Lewis' assumption that, with 'unlimited supplies of labour', the industrial real wage in terms of food, i.e. w^*, is constant at a 'subsistence level'. With reference to Smith, Ricardo, Mill and Marx, Kaldor argued that the 'subsistence wage' in terms of agricultural goods may be determined by 'custom and convention or by sheer biological needs' (Kaldor 1978: 207). This implies that at $w_i/p_a = w^*$, any increase in the food price p_a must lead to a corresponding increase in the industrial money wage w_i, which through mark-up pricing in accordance with equation (1) will result in a proportional rise in the industrial price p_i. Thus, an increase in the price of agricultural goods will leave the real wage as well as the intersectoral terms of trade more or less unaffected (cf. equation (2) above), while leading to overall price–wage inflation. A problem with this solution is why the industrial money wage should rise *pari passu* with the price of agricultural goods. One could, of course, conceive of some kind of wage indexation, but such a mechanism is hardly more convincing than Kalecki's assumption that the rise of the agricultural price will lead to a combined reduction of the industrial real wage and increase of the industrial price.

It may also be noted that Kaldor's assumption of a fixed real wage w^* in terms of food, makes the intersectoral terms of trade p independent of production conditions in agriculture and dependent only on factors which are internal to the industrial sector, i.e. the mark-up m and the productivity of labour λ. Therefore, p cannot play any role as an 'adjusting variable' in the interaction between the two sectors.

The problem of 'financing' economic development (II)

Kalecki's second article on 'financing' economic development was first published in the *Festschrift* to Roy Harrod in 1970.[7] In that article he made the following two 'basic assumptions' or 'postulates' on the financial aspects of planned economic development:

(a) There must be no inflationary price increases of necessities, in particular, staple foods.
(b) No taxes should be levied on lower income groups or necessities.

He noted that 'these two assumptions are of considerable significance for the course of economic development because they make it dependent to a great extent on the rate of increase of the supply of necessities' (Kalecki 1976: 98). He then derived the well-known equation:

$$c_n = q + e(r - q) \tag{3}$$

where c_n is the rate of increase of demand for necessities, q is the rate of increase of population, r is the rate of growth of national income, and e is the average income elasticity of demand for necessities.

Kalecki emphasized that e is a weighted average of the income elasticities of demand for necessities for various classes of the population, depending on the income distribution between these classes. It is not quite clear to me how he defined 'necessities', apart from assuming that e is less than one. Also in this version of his theory, a reduction of the real wage to restore equilibrium plays an important role. For that reason, he could not mean a given basket of goods in a *subsistence wage or income*. On the other hand, he pointed out that, 'the chief item in necessities are staple foods' (Kalecki 1976: 98). In any event, the composition of the 'basket' of necessities must be considered as constant during the period under consideration, because a change in its composition or the inclusion of new goods, would, of course, imply a change in the value of e.

When there are no imports, the actual rate of growth of demand for necessities will, of course, be equal to the rate of growth of domestic supply. Kalecki commented that

> in underdeveloped mixed economies, it is the rate of increase of supply of necessities (c_n) that can be considered as given. The increase in production of necessities, especially of staple food, is limited by institutional factors, such as feudal landownership and domination of peasants by merchants and money lenders.
>
> (Kalecki 1976: 104)

From this point of view, c_n is the 'autonomous', and independent variable in equation (3) which may more appropriately be written as:

$$r = \frac{c_n + q(e - 1)}{e} \tag{4}$$

where, as Kalecki emphasized

> the rate of increase of supply of necessities . . . as fixed by institutional barriers to the development of agriculture, determines the rate of growth of national income (r) which is warranted without infringing our basic postulates. . . . According to this conception the main 'financial' problem of development is that of adequate agricultural production. The key to 'financing' a more rapid growth is the removal of obstacles to the expansion of agriculture, such as feudal landownership and domination of peasants by money lenders and merchants.
>
> (Kalecki 1976: 104–5)

An important issue in Kalecki's discussion is what happens if actually the rate of growth of national income exceeds the growth rate warranted by the rate of increase in the supply of necessities as expressed in equation (4). He argued that, as the supply of necessities becomes inadequate to meet their demand, their prices must rise. At a given money wage, this price increase leads to a fall in the real income of workers. The fall in workers' real income implies a redistribution of income from workers to capitalists which, in turn, will bring about a fall in the value of e. Thus, the demand for necessities is brought back in line with supply through a reduction of e. Or in Kalecki's words:

> As the supplies of necessities forthcoming are inadequate to meet demand their prices rise. Equilibrium is restored through a fall in the real income of the broad masses of the population while the extra profits of the capitalists do not increase the demand for necessities, since they are spent on non-essentials or accumulated. . . . Thus this type of growth involving inflationary price increases of necessities – against the first of our basic postulates – is definitely to the advantage of the upper classes.
>
> (Kalecki 1976: 106)

Kalecki showed that the constraint on growth 'resulting from agrarian conditions' can, to some extent, be relieved through foreign trade, i.e. imports of necessities. However, he argued that this option

> comes into consideration only for countries that are favourably endowed by nature with easily accessible mineral deposits, such as oil, which can provide a substantial volume of exports per head of population. Such conditions, however, are exceptional and in particular are unlikely to prevail in a large country. India in order to be in the position of Iraq, for example, would have to possess oil deposits sixty times greater than those of that country.
>
> (Kalecki 1976: 19)

But he pointed out that also more generally there is a clear limit to the potential of foreign trade to lift the 'warranted' rate of growth of national income. The main reason for this is that the higher the growth rate r is, the more rapidly will the demand for imports other than necessities rise, in particular the demand for investment goods. In addition there may be limitations to the economy's capacity to export or limited demand for the exported commodities in foreign markets. Thus, it will become increasingly difficult to raise imports of necessities at a rate which permits a persistently rising gap between their demand and their domestic production. Kalecki concludes that

> In general, the basic prerequisite for rapid industrialization of an underdeveloped economy and in particular for the solution of the problem of

> unemployment and underemployment is a revolutionary upsurge in agricultural production.
>
> (Kalecki 1976: 19)

The role of effective demand

We have noted that the second version of Kalecki's model is highly aggregated. The income elasticity of demand for necessities is an average for the entire economy, and he did not analyse the interaction between agriculture and industry apart from agriculture's role in providing workers in industry with necessities. Because he considered only the aggregate supply of necessities, he did not make any distinction between the part of total agricultural production which is used for self-consumption and the *agricultural surplus* which is 'exported' to the non-agricultural sectors of the economy.

It is noteworthy that Kalecki, this pioneering and outstanding theorist of effective demand, did not analyse the role of the agricultural surplus in generating effective demand for industrial output in the developing economy. Instead he argued that while in developed capitalist economies

> unemployment arises on account of inadequacy of effective demand . . . unemployment and underemployment in underdeveloped countries are of an entirely different nature. They result from a shortage of capital equipment rather than deficiency of effective demand.
>
> (Kalecki 1976: 17)

This statement is all the more significant, because, with Kalecki's assumption of mark-up pricing as expressed in equation (1), the volume of production in industry cannot be determined by price. How much the industrial capitalists can produce and sell will be determined solely by *effective demand*. A considerable part of effective demand will originate from the investment and consumption of industrial capitalists and the consumption of industrial workers. However, since the industrial sector depends on imports from agriculture, particularly food for the workers, and must finance these imports, some part of total effective demand must be 'external', originating from agriculture.

In other words, to the extent that industry depends on supplies of necessities 'imported' from agriculture, it will also depend on agriculture's demand for its 'exports' to finance those imports, at least as long as industries are at an 'infant' stage and cannot compete in foreign markets. Like most theorists of the development of the dual economy, from W.A. Lewis to Fei and Ranis, Dixit, Jorgenson and many others, Kalecki ignored this problem and analysed the agriculture–industry interaction only from the supply side of industry, as well as agriculture.

The problem of 'external' effective demand in the early stage of industrialization has first and foremost been addressed by Nicholas Kaldor (1967, 1978, 1989, 1996). Kaldor emphasized that:

> the growth of the agricultural surplus is an essential condition for providing the growth of *purchasing power* necessary for sustaining industrial expansion. . . . This means that, whereas the growth of industrial production is primarily governed by the growth of effective demand, in the growth of agricultural production (in the early stages of development, at any rate), the element of *response* to outside stimuli plays a much smaller role. Agricultural production has an autonomous momentum which is mainly dependent on the progress of land-saving, as distinct from labor-saving, innovation.
>
> (Kaldor 1967: 56)

Using Kalecki's assumption of agricultural prices being determined by demand and supply and industrial prices being cost-determined, through mark-up pricing, while assuming a constant industrial real wage in terms of food, Kaldor apparently suggested two different approaches in his analysis of the interaction between agriculture and industry. In the approach he suggested first, he argued that since industrial prices are determined through mark-up pricing and the real wage in terms of food is constant, any rise in agricultural prices 'results in general inflation rather than in a fall in industrial prices in terms of primary products'. Therefore, industrial production is

> determined by demand, or rather the exogenous components of demand which in turn determine through the usual multiplier and accelerator effects, the endogenous components of demand. . . . Hence, it is the income of the agricultural sector . . . which really determines the level and the rate of growth of industrial production.
>
> (Kaldor 1978: 209)

To demonstrate this point formally, Kaldor used a simple foreign trade multiplier, where industrial output is equal to agriculture's demand for industrial products divided by the share of expenditure on agricultural products in total industrial income. In a later paper, he emphasized along the same line that it is 'the "foreign trade multiplier" which, over longer periods, is (an) . . . important and basic factor in explaining the growth and rhythm of industrial development' (Kaldor 1989: 423).

He also noted that it is not at all sure that the sales proceeds from agricultural surplus are transformed into effective demand for industrial goods. However, in the very same paper, he apparently left this approach. Instead, he presented the long-term industrial growth rate as an increasing function of the intersectoral terms of trade p and the growth rate of agricultural production as a decreasing function of p. In this context, the terms of trade p is industry's '*supply price*' for its own output and agriculture's '*demand price*' for industrial output. Therefore, the point of intersection between the two curves appears as a supply-demand equilibrium, with p as the equilibrating variable. As a consequence, the role of effective demand in determining the growth of industrial output disappears in this approach. In other words, this means central reliance on the price mechanism rather than effective demand.

A major problem with this approach is why and how the mark-up factor in the industrial sector should work as an ultimately adjusting variable (given the constant real wage in terms of food) to make *p* gravitate to the 'equilibrium point' where the 'supply curve' of industry and the 'demand curve' of agriculture intersect (cf. Kaldor 1989: 430–1; 1996: 43–5). In other words, this solution contradicts the assumption of mark-up pricing in the industrial sector (cf. also Dutt 1992: 158–60).

In addition to this contradiction and the strong semblance with traditional general equilibrium theory, this approach which was followed up and elaborated by Targetti (1985) and Thirlwall (1986)[8] appears to have another basic weakness: it is implicitly assumed that the demand parameters are equal for agricultural and industrial goods. In equilibrium, industrial and agricultural production will therefore grow at the same rate, and there will be no *structural change*, which 'as is well known' is a most fundamental aspect of modern economic growth.[9]

Moreover, Kaldor's argument that effective demand for industrial 'exports' is created solely by an 'autonomous' growth of agricultural surplus, requires serious qualification, because the agricultural surplus in physical terms has to be realized into purchasing power. That, in turn, depends on the export market for agricultural surplus which is provided by industry. In this sense, the generation of agricultural surplus and the *potential* demand for industrial goods which it creates, depend on the agricultural sector alone. But its *realization* into purchasing power and *actual* effective demand depend on industry. From this point of view, the two sectors mutually reinforce each other's growth, in a circular process of positive feedbacks (cf. Bhaduri and Skarstein, 2003).

The question of the price responsiveness of the agricultural surplus

Obviously, Kalecki did not believe that agriculture's supply of necessities could be raised substantially by improving the terms of trade of such goods. By contrast, he argued that agricultural production in underdeveloped economies is 'limited by institutional factors', that, 'the key to "financing" a more rapid growth is the removal of obstacles to the expansion of agriculture, such as feudal landownership and domination of peasants by money lenders and merchants' (Kalecki 1976: 104–5). This perspective of Kalecki has stimulated important studies of the influence exerted by agrarian production relations and class structures on agricultural growth (cf. e.g. Bhaduri 1973, 1991). On the other hand, he has been criticized, even by scholars who are sympathetic to him, for ignoring the alleged price responsiveness of agricultural production and the agricultural surplus. Thus, E.V.K. FitzGerald writes:

> Kalecki . . . has a fixed food supply (or at least a fixed growth thereof) which, while rather implausible, was a common view in the 1950s. . . . All the evidence points towards a considerable response (at least of *marketed* food supply) to variations in the internal terms of trade.
>
> (FitzGerald 1990: 189)

FitzGerald does not cite any published evidence on this issue. Referring to the evidence I have come across, I will therefore assess whether he is justified in his criticism of Kalecki on this point. Here it should first be noted that an increase of agricultural producer prices does not necessarily mean an improvement of agriculture's terms of trade. As we have already seen, under the assumption of mark-up pricing in the industrial sector and a constant industrial real wage rate in terms of food, a rise of the money price of agricultural output will drive up the industrial money wage, which – through the mark-up mechanism – will lead to a correspondingly higher money price of industrial products. This process will leave the intersectoral ('internal') terms of trade constant or near constant and result in general inflation rather than a fall of industrial prices in terms of agricultural products.

On the one hand, if we assume that an increase of the agricultural producer price is not totally transmitted to the price of industrial goods, then it can be shown that the supply elasticity of the surplus with respect to the intersectoral terms of trade, may be *negative* although the elasticity of total agricultural production is positive.[10] On the other hand, it is evident that the question whether the supply elasticity of the surplus is positive, negative or insignificant cannot be settled by formal analysis, but has to be answered by empirical studies, which may well yield different results in different situations.

Here it should be noted that the few empirical (econometric) studies which have been undertaken, do not deal with the elasticity of the agricultural surplus, but with *total production*. In general, these studies show that even the price elasticity of total production is not significantly positive, and in many instances it is negative. The most comprehensive of these studies is that by Binswanger *et al.* (1985), which includes data from 58 developing countries in the period from 1969 to 1978 and takes as explanatory variables not only the agricultural producer price level, but also data reflecting the extent and character of government activity towards agriculture, such as agricultural research expenditure, the degree of literacy, life expectancy, length of roads and extent of irrigation in agricultural areas. The study estimated very low positive price elasticities for the time series analysis, varying between zero and 0.18 for the short term and between 0.01 and 0.23 for the long term. On the other hand, the cross-country comparison yielded only negative elasticities. In both cases, the greater part of changes in aggregate agricultural output was correlated not with the price variable, but with the indicators of government activity (cf. Binswanger *et al.* 1985).

These findings are supported by a more recent study of Indian agriculture based on district-level time series data and using sophisticated econometric techniques (Binswanger *et al.* 1993). This study arrived at a very low short-term price elasticity of aggregate agricultural output of 0.045 with respect to domestic prices and 0.13 with respect to international prices. On the other hand, it was found that rural infrastructure facilities, such as roads, electricity, rural banks and education, play an overwhelming role in determining agricultural investment, inputs use and aggregate output. For example, increased number of commercial bank branches appears to raise private agricultural investment in draft animals (estimated elasticity is 0.54) and pump sets for irrigation (0.38). Similarly, a 10 per cent increase in the number of villages with electricity supply increases investment in irrigation pumps by 4 per cent (elasticity 0.4). The impact on aggregate output of individual infrastructural variables, in particular length of rural roads and number of primary schools, turned out to be significant and much stronger than that of prices, with elasticities of 0.20 and 0.33, respectively (Binswanger *et al.* 1993: 355–60).

The results arrived at by Binswanger *et al.* (1993) were broadly confirmed in another study of 20 districts in seven Indian states, applying several econometric models (Schäfer 1997). It may also be noted that an econometric study of Indian agriculture covering the period from 1950 to 1983, arrived at a result which apparently contradicts the predictions of neoclassical economists:

> sharp declines in agricultural output were associated with significant increases in the relative price of agricultural products *vis-à-vis* manufactures, while significant increases in agricultural output were associated with only moderate declines in the relative price.
>
> (Ghose 1989: 324)[11]

When we keep in mind that the supply elasticity of the agricultural *surplus* may well be *negative* although the elasticity of total output is positive, then these results become even less encouraging for the advocates of economic liberalization and price reform as the major means of increasing the surplus. My conclusion is that FitzGerald was wrong in his criticism of Kalecki on this issue and in his claim that, 'all the evidence points towards a considerable response (at least of *marketed* food supply) to variations in the internal terms of trade'.

Concluding remark

Kalecki's contribution to development economics stands in sharp contrast to the contemporary mainstream approach whose characteristic features are methodological individualism (actually implying that social classes are non-existent) and attempts to explain economic underdevelopment in terms of 'market failure', non-excludability of public goods, rent-seeking in the state, 'moral hazard', etc. In view of this, a comment by Joan Robinson in her Introduction to Kalecki's *Essays on Developing Economies* still appears to be worth quoting: 'Most of the "development" literature is aimed at disguising the truth of Kalecki's argument...' (Kalecki 1976: 10). Maybe Kalecki's most important contribution to development economics was that he taught us to ask the relevant questions.

Notes

1 Revised in August 2002. I wish to thank Amit Bhaduri and Julio López for most helpful comments on earlier drafts of this chapter.

2 For a useful survey of Kalecki's overall contribution to development economics, see Chakravarty (1997).

3 As is well known, there is a definite relationship between the mark-up and the share of profits in industrial value added. When α is the profit share, it can easily be shown that, $\alpha = m/(1+m)$. Thus, a particular profit share corresponds to a particular mark-up factor.

4 Kalecki assumes that the industrial workers consume both agricultural and industrial goods. To arrive at the real wage we should then divide the industrial money wage with a weighted price index, $P = p_a^s . p_i^{1-s}$, $0 < s \leq 1$, where s is the share of food (i.e. agricultural goods) in the industrial workers' total consumption. However, Kalecki argued that the overwhelming part of workers' consumption is agricultural goods, which means that the value of s is close to 1. On this assumption, the essentials of his argument are retained by deflating the money wage by the price of agricultural goods. It may also be noted that the rise of the industrial price in this particular context will not contribute to the fall in the real wage, because it is proportional to the rise in the money wage, through mark-up pricing.

5 This is also my understanding of Sukhamoy Chakravarty's statement that Kalecki in his analysis of the developing economy, 'helps in showing that a "demand problem" may coexist with the problem of inflation' (Chakravarty 1997: 115).

6 For example, the widely cited article by Cardoso (1981) makes no reference to Kalecki, while Taylor (1982) has one reference to Kalecki's theory of mark-up pricing (i.e. Kalecki 1971a: 43–61).

7 Kalecki may have felt good reason to publish the article in the *Festschrift* to Harrod, since his concept of 'warranted growth' of the underdeveloped economy was apparently inspired by Harrod.

8 Both Thirlwall and Targetti write that they assume mark-up pricing in industry, but none of them makes use of this assumption in their formal models which show clearly that the terms of trade is the equilibrating variable. Thirlwall makes no comment on this, while Targetti (1985: 85) claims that his result is 'compatible with the pricing of the sector'. On the other hand, Molana and Vines (1989) omit the assumption of mark-up pricing and therefore avoid the contradiction we have discussed here.

9 In his Mattioli Lectures of 1984, Kaldor (1996: 47) argued that, 'these complications could be introduced into a more complex model without destroying its important characteristics...'. However, he did not indicate how this could be done.

10 On the assumption that the price elasticity of total agricultural production is positive, it can be shown that the sufficient requirement for the elasticity of the agricultural surplus being positive is that the absolute value of the elasticity of substitution effect of agriculture's self-consumption exceeds the elasticity of income effect multiplied by one plus the price elasticity of total production. In plain words this means that the increase of agricultural production must not lead

to a corresponding increase of agriculture's self-consumption (cf. Nowshirvani 1977; Skarstein 1999: 119–22).

11 Historically, this is no news. For example during the agricultural revolution in England, from about 1680 to 1750, there was a pronounced fall in grain prices at the same time as production and productivity increased strongly (cf. e.g. Jones 1965: 9–14).

16 Economic crises in Latin America

Some considerations in the light of Kalecki's theory

Julio López

Introduction

Since the demise of their high-growth period, which lasted from the 1950s through the beginning of the 1980s, Latin American economies have seen their long-run average growth rate decline. Simultaneously, they have been subject to several and in some cases dramatic foreign exchange crises. The crises and subsequent recoveries are very idiosyncratic. Still, there seems to be a certain typical pattern amongst Latin American semi-industrialized economies,[1] which allows for some generalizations.

The objective of this chapter is to analyse Latin America's crises and recoveries (economic cycles, for short) within a broad perspective, and particularly to consider these episodes in the light of Michal Kalecki's theory of effective demand in capitalist economies. The chapter can thus be read from two different angles. It can be read as an analysis of Latin American economic cycles, with the help of M. Kalecki's theory. It can also be read as a present-day reflection on certain aspects of Kalecki's theory of the capitalist economy, illustrated with particular episodes of Latin American economies.

The chapter is organized as follows. In the first section I describe the course of a representative economic cycle in Latin America. In the second section, I discuss some analytical issues involved. I initially consider the role of investment and compare the typical Latin American cycle with Kalecki's and Keynes' theory of business cycles. Second, I look at the economic policy measures implemented to cope with the crisis. In this context I first analyse currency depreciation, then I reflect upon credit contraction, and lastly I deal with governmental expenditure and its deficit. In the final section I summarize the main findings of the chapter.

Perhaps a warning is in order before getting into the matter. In attempting to generalize on the basis of particular experiences of countries that differ in many respects, one runs many risks. I am conscious of these risks. I think my generalizations are quite accurate with respect to Mexico, a country I have been able to study in depth. But I would concede, if proof were bestowed, that some of my statements may be less valid for other countries, where I have only second-hand knowledge.[2]

The course of the crisis and recovery

I shall first give a concise account of what seems to be the stylized course of a typical economic cycle in Latin American semi-industrialized economies (Latin American economies for short). The following common features stand out:

i The crisis usually follows an extended period of current account deficit (which may be accompanied by capital flight), and is triggered by an external shock that brings about the collapse of the value of the domestic currency.

ii The onset of the crisis comes with the downfall of private expenditure, i.e. private fixed investment and private consumption. The drop of the latter is due to the decline of employment, but most of all results from a large decline of real wages.

iii The fall of investment takes place abruptly and without any previous signs that investment incentives are faltering. All components of private investment, i.e. fixed investment and stocks, residential construction and machinery and equipment, decline and their fall explains a large percentage of the drop in final demand and output.

iv Government expenditure, and especially government investment, also falls at the onset of the crisis, greatly contributing to the decline of aggregate demand.

v The balance of trade improves. One reason is the expansion of exports, which tends to be the higher, the larger the share of manufacturing exports in total exports. But the contraction of imports and especially imports of investment goods and industrial inputs explain most of the improvement in the trade balance. In fact, total imports fall at a higher rate than output, i.e. the coefficient of import declines. But this is not the consequence of import substitution ensuing from a change in relative prices between domestic and foreign goods. Rather, the decline is mostly explained by the higher-than-average import content of investment demand.

vi Real wages drop, and a shift from wages takes place. Notwithstanding the fall in wages, inflation tends to accelerate due to the higher domestic prices of imports. On the other hand, the rate of open unemployment jumps, though not necessarily much – but then mostly because open unemployment is usually very low since no unemployment insurance exists in Latin American countries.

vii The crisis may be drawn out, and a necessary – though not sufficient – condition for the recovery to take place is a positive external shock, which is usually a rise in the price of export commodities. In the more recent experiences, such as Mexico's, Argentina's and Brazil's, an important aid package has been indispensable in order to avoid a huge and prolonged crisis.

viii Just as the decline of demand and output in the course of the downswing is mitigated thanks to the growth of exports, the latter is normally the single most important factor contributing to the recovery, with both manufacturing and non-manufacturing exports growing. Imports recover, and at the upper point of the recovery they may actually exceed their pre-crisis level. In any event, the trade balance improves, dragging with it demand and output.

ix Government expenditure also grows at the onset of the recovery. The fiscal accounts are normally – and especially during the most recent period – kept in balance. This is the consequence of the conditions imposed upon these countries by international financial institutions; but it is also the result of the new wisdom prevailing amongst policy-makers in Latin America.

x Once the recovery is underway private expenditure starts growing and replaces exports and the government expenditure as leading demand factor in the upswing. However, private expenditure may not fully recover from its decline during the downswing. In fact, both consumption and fixed investment may be lower at the upper point of the recovery than they had been prior to the crisis.

xi The economic recovery, though it may be strong, is normally also lopsided, and the working classes hardly benefit. Although employment is after a time restored to its pre-crisis level, average real wages do not recover until after quite a long time.

xii When the recovery is completed and output is back to its pre-crisis size, investment may still be below its former level. However, domestic savings, and especially private savings, usually are higher, and the share of private savings in output is well above its pre-crisis level.

With this background description of the course of the typical Latin American economic cycle in mind, I turn next to some analytical issues involved.

Some analytical issues

Private investment and the cycle

I will analyse Latin American crisis experiences in the context of business cycle theories. I will take Kalecki's theory of business cycle as a starting point because, besides its intrinsic importance, it inaugurated the theoretical development of, and thus also represents a whole class of business cycle models. In this class of models the cycle is entirely endogenous, and its course is governed by the course of private investment.[3]

Summarizing to the utmost Kalecki's model, private investment follows with a lag in investment decisions, which are dependent (among other factors) upon the rate of profit. Thus, the turning points of the cycle follow, after a lag, changes in the economic conditions, and in fact follow to a large extent the turning points of the rate of profit. Moreover, investment decisions are essentially irrevocable. That is, events occurring between the moment the decision was taken and its implementation do not normally lead to their cancellation or even revision.

Kalecki also introduced external shocks into his model (1954a: ch. 13). But these were not of the kind that could derail the 'normal' course of the cycle, in the sense that they do not determine its turning points. Thus, although he recognized that particular situations might lead to the cancellation of investment orders (1954: 201, 49), he did not consider this phenomenon in depth.

In order to understand the reason for these simplifications it may be useful, I think, to take into account Kalecki's theoretical objective. As I have argued elsewhere (López and Mott 1999), Kalecki's objective was very broad indeed. In fact, his theory of effective demand and of investment was just a stepping-stone into a much grander purpose – to develop a theory of the overall dynamics of a capitalist economy. A theory, that is, adequate to explain why long-run growth goes hand in hand with cyclical movements around the trend. Thus, his theory was not meant to analyse particular episodes; and he left out of the picture those atypical periods when 'disorder', rather than 'conditional stability' characterizes the economic record (to use the very apt distinction established by Crotty (1994: 117)). Indeed, at a very early stage of the elaboration of his theory, Kalecki (1933a) recognized that his model would not remain valid under shocks capable of provoking a 'crisis of confidence'.

Now, most of Latin American economic cycles take place exactly in those atypical periods of disorder rather than conditional stability mentioned above. Besides, they tend to closely conform to the pattern of 'financial crises' caused by an exogenous shock, which Keynes (1936, ch. 22) did analyse, and about which one of his most eminent followers extensively theorized (Minsky 1975, 1982, 1986).

We have already depicted the course of a Latin American representative crisis. As stated, the collapse of private investment, which is normally the most weighty factor triggering the crisis, is not usually caused by a prior downfall of the rate of profit, but rather follows instantaneously a shock that causes a sudden change of expectations. Expectations are further deteriorated after the announcement by the economic authorities that government expenditure will be curtailed and credit will be reduced. It appears that frequently many previous investment decisions and orders are cancelled, thus leading to the abrupt and violent fall of actual investment.

The recovery from the common Latin American crisis does not either follow the typical pattern of business cycle upswings, in the sense that it is not usually triggered by a revival of private investment, following the restoration of the rate of profit. But neither does it come about solely as a result of an improvement of (long-run) expectations[4] – although an improvement of expectations is a necessary condition for the recovery of private investment. Rather, it is almost invariably initiated by the improvement in the trade balance, and also by the increase in government expenditure. Both raise profits and stimulate private investment.

Once initiated, the recovery develops very much in line with Kalecki's theory. Higher profits stimulate private investment, employment, wages and private consumption. Thus, at a certain stage private expenditure replaces exports and government expenditure as the leading demand factor in the recovery. Higher domestic demand brings about a rise in imports, and may abate the rise of exports, especially if exports of basic goods weigh heavily in total exports, as in Argentina for example. The trade surplus diminishes which directly or indirectly tends to dampen the economic upswing. The upswing loses momentum much earlier than full utilization of the productive capacities has been reached.

We shall now analyse more in depth the points briefly sketched above, in the context of an inquiry into the typical economic strategy response with which the authorities tend to confront the crises.

Economic policy in the crisis and the recovery

When confronted with a crisis, Latin American economic authorities have usually responded with the following set of measures:

- i freeing of the exchange rate;
- ii reduction in bank credit; and
- iii contraction of public expenditure.

In the typical adjustment package, it seems to be implicitly assumed that the crisis is always the final outcome of a previous expansion beyond the productive potential of the economy, and that the contraction in external credit will further reduce the supply capacities. Then, the central bank's withdrawal from the foreign exchange market unleashes a currency depreciation. The currency depreciation would eventually reduce the external deficit to its equilibrium level. It would also stimulate aggregate demand, because exports would grow even as import substitution would be stimulated.

Since the domestic supply is assumed to be at its potential level and imports are assumed to be greater than those that could be financed, inflationary pressures would be kept high. In order to cope with them, and also to help redress the external sector, it is necessary to contract aggregate demand by reducing credit to the private sector and government expenditure[5] (and simultaneously putting a cap on the growth of money wages).

The main results achieved with this set of economic policy measures have been briefly sketched in the preceding section. Although the external imbalance is corrected and the country is soon able to regain access to the international capital markets, output, real wages and investment all fall, sometimes dramatically. Finally, inflation will accelerate unless the fall of real wages is indeed huge.

These results normally come as a surprise to the authorities and to the international financial agencies involved in the adjustment package. However, they should not surprise anybody. In fact, the collapse of the economy during the downswing closely follows Kalecki's theory of effective demand. The drop of private investment reduces effective demand, profits and the profit rate, thus further discouraging new investment (and also aggravating the financial crisis and setting off a wave of bankruptcies). Furthermore, the reduction of real wages does not improve profits or stimulate investment decisions. Rather, it intensifies the drop of consumption and aggregate demand.

The fall of private demand is magnified when, as is normally the case, government expenditure is also curtailed. Finally, the course of the crisis is normally mitigated thanks to the improvement in the trade balance, which sustains private profits and effective demand (Kalecki 1933b). The improvement in the trade balance, and the shift to profits, bring about an expansion of domestic, and especially private savings, and a rise in the share of private savings in output.

We shall now elaborate on the economic policy issues involved in the management of the crisis, and we shall contrast the conventional adjustment package with Kalecki's theory.

Currency depreciation and domestic demand

As mentioned, freeing of the exchange rate is an important component of the typical adjustment package. Government authorities, as well as international financial institutions, seem to be of the opinion that currency depreciation ensuing from the freeing of the exchange rate is indispensable in order to diminish the depth of the crisis and to stimulate the recovery. This is based on the expenditure-shifting effect of currency depreciation; that is, it invigorates exports even as it brings about a decline of the coefficient of imports. It is alleged that the trade balance will improve with the currency depreciation, dragging with it demand and output.

Kalecki, on the contrary, was very sceptic about the alleged beneficial effects of currency depreciation. Unlike Keynes, he did not accept the theory of diminishing marginal returns or (its corollary under perfect competition) that real wages passively adapt to the level of output and employment. Hence, he thought that money and real wages could actually fall with unemployment.

We can easily understand the importance of analysing the effect of currency depreciation for Kalecki's theory of capitalism (and, more in general, for the theory of effective demand). Kalecki (1939a: 38) noted that 'a reduction of wages in an open system is very much the same as that of a currency depreciation'.[6] Now, if the fall in money and real wages and the consequent depreciation of the currency (and improved competitiveness) do bring about an expansion of employment and output, capitalist economies would have a built-in full employment mechanism. Unemployment would bring about a reduction of wages, which would result in a currency depreciation, and the latter would stimulate effective demand and thus the re-absorption of unemployment. In fact, the previously described mechanism might be even stronger than e.g. the so-called 'Pigou-effect', which Kalecki so thoroughly demolished, and which the theory of effective demand has never accepted.

From his analysis Kalecki concluded:

> even in such a case [in an open system, J.L.] the reduction of wages does not necessarily lead to an increase in employment, and the prospects of raising the aggregate real income of the working class are even dimmer. In particular, under the system of high and rising tariffs it is very likely that a reduction of wages will have an adverse effect on employment also in an open economy.
>
> (Kalecki 1939a: 38)[7]

Kalecki's analysis is rather laconic, but we can elaborate on it, and rigorously examine the effects of currency depreciation with the help of his theory.

Consider the effects of a currency depreciation that leads to a rise in the real exchange rate. In the short run, when capitalists' expenditure is given, the effect of the depreciation on profits will depend on the elasticity of exports and imports with respect to the real exchange rate. That elasticity is probably higher today than in Kalecki's times, because nowadays trade is much less restricted – in other words, the so-called 'Marshall–Lerner condition' is probably fulfilled.[8] Still, it is well known that the response of exports (and import substitution) to the change in relative prices may be slow, and that in the short-term the currency depreciation may result in a worsening of the balance of trade and in profits. The latter may be further reduced if private investment does fall in the short term. This may in fact come about as a result of worsening expectations and of the increase in the indebtedness ratio of firms indebted in foreign currency, ensuing from currency depreciation (Kalecki did not consider the latter possibility, probably because it was unimportant in his times).

This is not the end of the story, for besides total profits, the relative share of wages in output is likely to fall too with a currency depreciation, magnifying the drop of demand and output. Indeed, the currency depreciation brings about, in the first place, a rise in the ratio of the materials bill to the wage bill, and in the second place an increase in the price of competitive imports, which probably will stimulate a rise in the degree of monopoly.[9]

Summing up, in Kalecki's theory several factors may produce a contraction of output as a result of currency depreciation, and this fall may take place even if the Marshall–Lerner condition is fulfilled. Moreover, the contraction of output and employment may be drawn-out, due to the detrimental effects of the fall of profits and of the decline in the degree of utilization of capacities on investment decisions and on investment.

All in all, it appears that the Latin American experience is closer to Kalecki's than to the conventional anticipation.

Financial conditions in the crisis

It is generally accepted that the financial aspects of capitalism are relatively undeveloped in Kalecki's theory and empirical analyses. However, he had very definite views concerning the effects of monetary policy and financial conditions.

Kalecki argued that, provided the economy was not pushed beyond full employment, even a large budget deficit need not raise the rate of interest. But to avoid the rate of interest from rising the central bank should provide the requisite bank reserves. In his view, then, monetary policy was required as a complement, but by itself its power was rather limited. Let us consider in more detail Kalecki's perspective on the subject.

On the basis of his 'principle of increasing risk', Kalecki (1937b) thought credit rationing was a permanent feature of capitalist economies. Only firms with capital and profits of a minimum size would be willing to demand and able to obtain external savings to complement their own internal accumulation of capital, and the rate of interest charged to them could vary with the size of borrowing in relation to their own capital. Now, in his business cycle model the ratio of 'internal' accumulation of capital to total investment is assumed to be constant.[10] The latter implies that the degree of credit rationing would not vary in the course of the cycle. That is, lack of external saving would not further depress private investment in the downswing, and a higher elasticity of credit supply would not either stimulate additional investment decisions in the course of the upswing.

The reduction of the long-term rate of interest would stimulate investment by increasing its net profitability. Here again a substantial fall in the rate of interest is necessary in order to make the effect significant[11] (Kalecki 1946a: 403).

Now, one of the most outstanding changes in capitalist economies since Kalecki's time is the deepening of financial relationships. Today, the relative share of financial assets and liabilities in the balance sheet of both firms and individuals (capitalists, rentiers and workers) is much larger than in the past – a phenomenon Hyman Minsky aptly labelled 'financial fragility'. This situation brings about an increased sensibility of demand towards developments in the financial markets – both domestic and international.

Latin American economies have also followed this tendency. As a result, typical Latin American crises depart considerably from Kalecki's model in that increases in the interest rates and drastic reductions in bank credit play a large role and exert a huge influence in the downswing. In fact, immediately after the onset of the crisis the central bank usually announces that domestic credit in real terms will be reduced, and that the monetary policy in general will be very stiff.

The announcement and implementation of an inflexible monetary policy, by itself, would lead to a curtailment of credit and to a rise in interest rates. But this basic tendency is magnified because banks' lending capacity and expectations worsen due to the deterioration of their balance sheets ensuing from the rise of non-performing loans caused by the crisis, and from the increase in the service of their debt contracted in foreign currency.

Thus interest rates skyrocket and credit rationing occurs on an enlarged scale, which not only depress demand, by contracting fixed investment and consumption, but also decrease aggregate supply, further intensifying the decline in demand.

A rise in interest rates and curtailment of credit affect both investment and consumption demand. Normally, large firms are not much impaired because they have on-going credit lines with banks and, in any case, they can have access to foreign credit – particularly when, as is increasingly the case in Latin America, they are branches of or have long-term agreements with multinational concerns. But the higher price and lower availability of credit hit medium- and especially small-sized firms drastically. They are thus forced to curtail fixed and inventory investment, and the latter in turn impairs supply capacities in the short term, as will be argued shortly.

The higher price and lower availability of credit also affect consumption. Consumption of the higher-income brackets is not particularly reduced but mass consumption is severely harmed because – unlike in Kalecki's times and model – wage earners in today's Latin America do have access to credit. Thus, the workers' saving rate is forced upwards and the workers' consumption rate is reduced during the downswing, which further depresses demand and profits.

Because demand falls so drastically in the crisis that there seems to be little room for supply to play a role, an analysis of supply conditions is sometimes overlooked. This lack of interest may be valid for a closed economy, where supply accommodates demand (below full employment). However, supply conditions do have an importance in an open economy, and particularly so when a crisis, rather than a simple business downswing, takes place, because in a crisis demand is also affected. For example, if supply conditions deteriorate during a crisis, exports, and substitution of imports, will be lower than they might have been.[12] The trade balance will thus improve less than otherwise, and the drop in final demand and in output will be consequently larger, owing not only to the smaller trade balance, but also to the smaller internal demand induced by the smaller trade balance.

The worsening of the supply conditions of firms in the typical Latin American crisis can be explained as follows. In the first place, the rise in real interest rates deteriorates firms' equity position due to the higher service on debt. A second factor is credit restriction, because many small- and medium-sized firms are credit-rationed. Last, but not least, production risks become higher. Thus, managers facing either productive or financial investments are likely to opt for the latter because these become relatively more profitable and less risky.

The deterioration of the supply conditions brings about a leftward shift of the supply function, which also provokes a leftward shift of the demand function. This is a consequence of the reduction in output, and the ensuing fall in employment, wages, and the demand for intermediate and wage goods.

Thus, due to credit restriction, during the crisis firms are not able to take advantage of the competitive gains brought about by the currency depreciation. Normally exports are not much affected, because large and financially solid firms are the main exporters. But firms producing for the domestic market, which are usually smaller and financially weaker than firms catering to the world market, are greatly affected by the contraction of and by the rise in the price of credit. Probably the latter goes a long way in explaining a phenomenon that seems to be quite common in the typical Latin American economic cycle. Namely, the fact that the coefficient of imports is reduced very little, if at all, in the upper point of the recovery as compared to its value before the crisis, in spite of the phenomenal rise of the real exchange rate and in competitiveness of domestic producers.

Government expenditure and the recovery

We mentioned above that in the typical Latin American cycle export growth is usually one of the triggers for recovery. We also emphasized that the improvement of the trade balance, by itself, would not be sufficient to spearhead the recovery. This is because during the downswing private investment and government expenditure fall, even while the multiplier of autonomous expenditure declines due to the drop of the share of wages in output and the rise in the rate of saving. We suggested, finally, that together with exports, government expenditure is usually one of the triggers for recovery. In fact, we can posit that the recovery would not take place without the joint expansion of both exports and government expenditure.

The improvement in the trade balance and the fall in the utilization of the productive capacities and in employment caused by the downswing, leave ample room for expansionary fiscal policies. On the other hand, the worsening of the economic situation heightens public criticism of the authorities and brings with it political pressures on the government in order to do something. Finally, government accounts improve and the government is able to expand expenditure without incurring in deficit. I turn now to an analysis of the economic factors involved.

A large relative share of export taxes in total government revenues is one important characteristic of Latin American economies. Thus, government expenditure and exports are peculiarly intertwined in Latin America, in a relationship that helps in transmitting the export cycle into the domestic economy in a very distinct way. In this context I think outlining the Kalecki theory of fiscal policy may be useful as a previous step in understanding the general processes entailed.

At a very early stage of the development of his theory, Kalecki (1932,

1933b) emphasized the influence of government expenditure on effective demand. More particularly, he showed that deficit financing would have a strong expansionary effect, and would add to private profits. Somewhat later he added that financing expenditure with taxes exacted on the private sector would also have an expansionary effect, provided those taxes were levied on business profits and firms did not pass on those higher taxes via higher prices (Kalecki 1937a; Mott and Slattery 1994).[13]

Referring now to Latin American economic cycles, the effect of government expenditure in spearheading the upswing is usually not given much credit, insofar as – at least during the last decade – governments have in general avoided incurring in deficits. However, we know from Kalecki's theory sketched above that even when the budget is balanced government expenditure can have an expansionary effect. We shall contend now that in most Latin American recoveries, and especially when the latter come as a result of a rise in exports, that expansionary effect may be quite large.

Consider first those economies where one important export industry is government owned, such as in Colombia, Mexico and Venezuela (the oil industry), and in Chile (the copper industry). In these cases, when the price of exports recovers government revenues swell and the government can expand expenditure without incurring in a budget deficit. However, the expansionary effect on aggregate demand of the government expenditure thus financed is as high as in the case of a deficit, because the government is spending more without levying higher taxes from the private sector.[14]

When the main export industry is not government-owned the process is somewhat altered, but not drastically. In fact, in this case the rise in exports brings about a rise in profits and wages. The additional government revenue does not either involve a reduction in private earnings, nor does it stimulate a rise in domestic prices, which could reduce the purchasing power of the population (as might be the case if the government raised taxes levied on producers catering to the domestic market). In this sense, its expansionary effects are again much like a budget deficit.

In conclusion, the role of government expenditure in spearheading the recovery after the typical Latin American crisis should be given due credit. All in all, the recovery is normally not the outgrowth of judicious economic policies that correct previous distortions, or the spontaneous consequence of the working of market forces set free from their previous constraints after the crisis completed its process of creative destruction. The recovery appears to be usually the final upshot of the interplay of economic and political factors. These factors can come into force thanks to a positive external shock that creates the material possibility of implementing expansionary policies, and thanks also to the political pressure on the government to go somewhat beyond the orthodox recipe.

Final remarks

I will now summarize the main arguments developed in this chapter.

i In Latin America's typical economic crisis the immediate and most significant trigger is usually the fall in private investment. This fall cannot be attributed to a previous decline in the rate of profit, but rather to the worsening of expectations ensuing from the collapse of the domestic currency, and also to the credit squeeze. The fall of government expenditure, the result of a restrictive fiscal policy, also contributes to the crisis. Manufacturing exports respond swiftly to the currency depreciation. Imports fall mostly due to the contraction of output, and import substitution practically does not take place, because the supply conditions of firms deteriorate due to the credit restriction. Firms catering to the domestic market are thus hampered from taking full advantage of their higher competitiveness, even as they suffer the contraction of their market. The improvement of the trade balance offsets the fall of domestic demand, but much less than it would if import substitution on a larger scale were to take place. The fall of the autonomous components of demand causes a decline of consumption. The latter decline is magnified due to the decline of real wages, and the shift to profits, ensuing from the currency depreciation. Thus the fall of real wages does not restrain the depth of the crisis, but rather tends to intensify it. Consumption is also hampered due to the rise in the saving rate of the population ensuing from the lower availability and higher price of credit.

ii Growth of exports is an important factor spearheading the recovery. Growth of government expenditure, and particularly the increase in the government expenditure financed with export taxes, appears to be usually another important trigger of the recovery. Since government expenditure financed with revenues accruing from exports does not encroach upon the purchasing power of the population, it has an important expansionary effect and can make a proportionally large contribution to increases in domestic demand, even as the fiscal and the external balance are kept in check. Imports rebound in the recovery, and the coefficient of imports falls little, if at all, compared to its pre-crisis level. Accordingly, the export surplus is below the level it would have reached if substitution of imports had taken place, thus restraining the recovery. The restoration of profits ensuing from the correction of the trade deficit, the enlargement of government expenditure financed with taxes on exports, and the (usually milder) recovery of private investment, lead to an improvement in business supply conditions.

iii Though private expenditure recovers, it does not necessarily reach its level prior to the crisis. In fact, both consumption and investment may be lower at the upper point of the recovery than they had been prior to the crisis. The recovery of private investment may be significant, but usually private consumption rises rather modestly during the upswing, because of the fall in real wages.

iv International financial institutions tend to present the upswing following the crisis as a successful story of a recovery from a crisis, and praise the economic authorities for their skills. However, their vision seems highly misleading, to put it mildly. On the one hand, the recovery, though it may be swift and strong, is usually very lopsided, and the working classes hardly benefit. On the other hand, the important change in the fiscal policy stance, which in most cases is essential for the recovery to take place, is forced on the government by the deterioration in the economic situation. The latter goes usually much beyond expectations, and gives rise to strong pressures from public opinion. Moreover, the expansionary fiscal policy stance, which spearheads the recovery and sustains private profits, is commonly made possible by the rise of the price of exports, or their volume or both. This gives the government the possibility of enlarging its expenditure without incurring in a deficit, even as it amplifies the expansionary effect of government expenditure.

v Kalecki's theory of effective demand appears to be very useful in understanding the course of the typical economic cycle in Latin America. Since Kalecki did not analyse crises but business cycles, the turning points of both the downswing and the upswing in a typical Latin American cycle do not follow along the lines conceived in his cycle model but rather are caused by exogenous shocks. More specifically, expectations, on the one hand, and government expenditure on the other, tend to trigger the crisis and the recovery. But the general pattern of the upward and downward movement of the economy follow in general terms Kalecki's theory of effective demand.

vi One exception to the previous statement must be made with regards to the financial conditions and monetary policy in present-day capitalism in general and the course of the cycle in particular. The study of the financial aspects of capitalism is an area where Kalecki's theory certainly needs to be completed and updated. Capitalism has greatly changed, and finance is probably the field where those changes are most significant. Most importantly, a high relative share of financial liabilities and assets in the balance sheets not only of firms but also individuals, is a prominent feature of present-day capitalism. Unlike in Kalecki's model, changes in financial variables exert today a strong influence in the course of the evolution of capitalist economies. A great deal of work needs to be done in order to enrich Michal Kalecki's theory.

Notes

1 I refer to Argentina, Brazil, Chile, Colombia, Mexico, Uruguay and Venezuela.

2 I provide statistical support for most of my statements for Mexico in López (1998).

3 One cannot lose sight of the fact that Kalecki (1943b) had also another political, and accordingly much less mechanistic, theory of economic cycles. In this chapter I do not refer to Kalecki's political cycle.

4 For example, not even the huge aid package given to Mexico after the December 1994 crisis could improve expectations enough to stimulate private investment, which did not lead but rather followed the recovery in 1995.

5 There is an ambiguity here. At a theoretical level, it is assumed that government expenditure does not affect aggregate demand, since it only crowds out private expenditure. However, at a practical level, policy-makers acknowledge that government expenditure does expand demand.

6 *Grosso modo* a nominal currency depreciation is equivalent to a fall in money wages with a constant nominal exchange rate; while a real currency depreciation (i.e. a depreciation capable of improving price competitiveness) necessitates a fall of real wages.

7 In their otherwise excellent paper, Krugman and Taylor (1978) do not mention Kalecki as one precursor of the theory of the contractionary devaluation.

8 However, if export firms do not reduce by much their international prices in foreign currency (because they price to the circumstances of the market in which they are selling rather than to their costs), then export demand is unaffected and everything depends on the price-elasticity of imports. I owe this observation to Malcolm Sawyer.

9 Firms catering to the domestic market may actually respond differently to a currency depreciation than firms catering to the export market. In both cases the 'degree of monopoly' may rise, but more so in firms catering to the export market because their price in foreign currency will fall by little, if at all, in spite of the fall in their costs in foreign currency.

10 An exception is in Kalecki (1942). But the reasons and the consequences of varying this ratio receive only a cursory treatment.

11 Since he did not deal with periods characterized by 'crisis of confidence' Kalecki left out those cases 'when during the depression, the rate of interest rises' (1933a: 74).

12 Recall that price and income elasticities of exports and imports depend on elasticity of demand and on elasticity of supply.

13 Kalecki also devised a very novel and detailed methodology for analysing the role of government demand on the cycle, which he applied in his studies on the US economy (Kalecki 1956, 1962). During the 1950s he directed a small team of economists at the Polish Academy of Sciences, devoted to the study of the economic situation in capitalist countries, which published a series of booklets on the subject (see e.g. Kalecki and Szeworski 1957; Dobrska and Szeworski, 1958, 1959; Dobrska, Kalecki *et al.* 1960. See also Szeworski 1965). It is unfortunate that Kalecki had almost no following regarding his empirical studies of capitalist economies.

14 When both the price and the volume of exports rise, the expansionary effect is magnified because higher wages entail higher workers' consumption.

17 Kalecki's arguments for socialism

Jan Toporowski

Beyond Marx and Keynes

In the century since the birth of Michal Kalecki political economy has been dominated by three schools of thought: the Austrians and neo-classical marginalists, who saw in the market the perfect form of economic coordination and were therefore inclined to idealize capitalism; the Marxists, who saw capitalism as prone to crisis because of inconsistencies arising out of the process of production, rather than market exchange, and who argued for political action to bring about a new form of economy, socialism, which would avoid these inconsistencies; and the Keynesians. Because of the variety of the latter, it is necessary to distinguish the neo-classical Keynesians who were most influential in the capitalist countries during the quarter-century after World War II and who merely believed in fiscal activism to overcome market imperfections (a view which would have been quite acceptable to Keynes' old opponent Pigou) from Keynes himself and his more fundamentalist, post-Keynesian, followers. Broadly, the Keynes of the *General Theory* (as opposed to the Keynes of the *Treatise on Money* and before) saw neo-classical and Marxist political economy as being based on stylized 'Ricardian' economies producing and exchanging commodities, whereas the signal feature of capitalism in the twentieth century is its monetary character. This gives rise to its most fundamental flaws in the system of finance, which are responsible for the instability of capitalism and its propensity towards under-investment. Keynes therefore recommended not only fiscal activism to stabilize capitalism, but also the reduction of the influence of finance (the 'euthanasia of the rentier'). Furthermore, Keynes was critical of socialism. He considered the concentration of power arising from state ownership of the means of production to be incompatible with political freedom and pluralist democracy, a view amply borne out by the Eastern European experience of socialism.

A fourth school of political economy, institutionalism, became very influential in the United States during the 1920s and the 1930s and the work of John Kenneth Galbraith in the second half of the twentieth century testifies to the fertility of its ideas. This chapter argues that the analysis of capitalism given by the founder of institutionalism, Thorstein Veblen, is complementary to Kalecki's analysis of capitalism, and that their views on the proper functioning of the socialist economy coincide.

Kalecki fits uneasily into this political economic trichotomy. While there has been some attempt made to see in his early 'Three Systems' paper a prototype of the plainly neo-classical Hicks/Hansen IS/LM system (Chapple 1996), Kalecki never idealized market relations and regarded their natural outcome as neither just nor efficient, nor stable. Similarly, Nuti's attempt to read into Kalecki's socialist investment efficiency analysis a neo-classical kind of teleological equilibrium strains the meaning and purpose of that analysis (Nuti 1986).

As Joan Robinson noted on more than one occasion Kalecki's analysis of capitalism nestles neatly in between those of Marx and Keynes and is, in some respects, superior to their systems (e.g. Robinson 1964). Kalecki quite evidently derived the fundamental concepts of his political economic analysis from Marx. His was a Marxist class analysis in which capitalists (entrepreneurs and rentiers) and workers are distinguished by their incomes in a society characterized by capitalists' 'power in society', as well as in the factory, based on their ownership of the means of production (Kalecki 1942). His business cycle theory is a revised exposition, using the interpretations of Rosa Luxemburg and Mikhail Tugan-Baranovsky, of Marx's theory of crisis. This led him independently to the central doctrine of Keynes' macroeconomics, the Principle of Effective Demand as the determinant of economic activity, and under-investment as the cause of economic depression so that for many neo-classical Keynesians he remains a part of the 'Keynesian' school of thought (Patinkin 1982: ch. 3). Even though he agreed with Keynes over the importance of finance, even the most enthusiastic Kaleckian has to admit that finance is underdeveloped in Kalecki's work. While he gives considerable thought to the analysis of money and finance, it is very much as an afterthought to his business cycle analysis, rather than lying at the centre of his theory of capitalism and being the key flaw in its operations, as the theory of liquidity preference is in Keynes' analysis (Sawyer 1985: ch. 5). Notwithstanding the interpretations of Chapple and Nuti above, Kalecki is also distinct from Keynes in rejecting equilibrium and marginal analysis. This, his pessimism concerning the possibilities of Keynesian stabilization of capitalism (Kalecki 1944a) and his consequent socialism put Kalecki firmly outside the Keynesian school and in the Marxist camp. On more than one occasion, Kalecki was happy to express his macroeconomic theories in a Marxian two-sector model of the commodity, rather than monetary or finance, kind (e.g. Kalecki 1958).

However, two features of his analysis separate Kalecki from Marx, and from many Marxist economists in this century. First, he did not adhere to the labour theory of value and did not consider any of the pricing issues deriving from it, such as the transformation problem, of any consequence. In this regard he was no more distinct from Marx than were, for example, Rosa

Luxemburg, Baran and Sweezy, or even Lenin. Wlodzimierz Brus was later to recall that Kalecki 'felt . . . a strong distaste for the Marxian theory of value, which he considered metaphysical . . .' (Brus 1977). In this regard he seems to have unconsciously shared Veblen's view that the labour theory of value was a pre-materialist 'natural right' metaphysic (Veblen 1906). Second, Kalecki did not believe in what Josef Steindl called the Marxian 'Katastrofenpolitik', according to which, instead of seeking measures to improve the conditions of working people and their families, socialists should look forward to the final catastrophe that would engulf capitalism, from whose ashes would arise socialism and general welfare and prosperity (Steindl 1964). In this regard he too seems to have shared, unconsciously, Veblen's criticism of Marx's Hegelianism, whereby the abolition of private ownership of the means of production would give rise to a wholly new and better situation simply because the product of labour would now belong to the labourer (Veblen 1906).

The consequence of 'Katastrofenpolitik' for the economics of socialism was to encourage 'voluntarism' and arbitrary direction of the economy by those who claimed to represent the 'objective' interests of the workers. Kalecki was not alone in criticizing this kind of 'scientific' millenarianism during the 1950s and 1960s. The unusual, if not unique, characteristic of his economics of socialism was that it was not based on *a priori* assumptions about how a socialist economy should operate, but on his analysis of what makes capitalism unjust and inefficient. This is further examined in Toporowski (1996). It turns out that Kalecki's analysis of capitalist inefficiency is very similar to Veblen's conclusions about capitalist efficiency, in which a central role is played by finance, in a way that is missing in Kalecki's work, but to which Kalecki adds a system of aggregate income and expenditure that is a fundamental lacuna in Veblen's analysis (see Sweezy 1958). Most important of all, for the subject of this chapter, Kalecki's system of economic control under socialism is virtually the same as the one which Veblen advocated in the latter years of his life.

In the next section, Kalecki's criticisms of capitalism are compared with those of Veblen. This is followed by a comparison of their respective views on socialist economic administration.

The economic inadequacies of modern capitalism

Kalecki's views on capitalist inefficiency are too well known to require more than just a summary here. They centre on its instability which Kalecki examined systematically in the form of business cycles, which he regarded as a distinguishing feature of the capitalist economy. The business cycle reveals three kinds of inefficiency. In the first place, full employment is not a constant, or even a normal outcome of the free operation of the capitalist economy. At best it occurs around the peak of the economic boom, so that involuntary unemployment is more usual:

> something like full employment is approached only in exceptional cases. In general unemployment (manifest or disguised) is sufficient to permit the boom to develop, and it is not the scarcity of labour which brings it to an end.
>
> (Kalecki 1939a: 115)

Second, while the capital stock may be more efficiently used than the labour force (since slavery or feudalism there have been no 'owners' of labour whose dependence on earning a return on their labour assets gives them an interest in its full utilization) the efficient utilization of plant and equipment depends on the state of aggregate demand. Periodically, and systematically as the peak of an economic boom is approached, demand fails to rise as rapidly as the capital stock. The emergence of excess capacity reduces the rate of profit and discourages further investment. The recession that follows lasts until that excess capacity is eliminated by factory closures. The higher rate of profit on the remaining, now more fully utilized capital stock encourages new investment and a new boom ensues (Kalecki 1939: ch. 6).

The third inefficiency arises because the level of investment is not determined by new opportunities for investment and available resources, as is indicated by neo-classical microeconomic analysis. Instead, it is determined by the degree of capacity utilization of existing capital, the rate of profit, which is also affected by the degree of capacity utilization, and the financial accumulation of entrepreneurs out of past profits (Kalecki 1939a: 128–41). In his last version of his business cycle theory, Kalecki added technological innovation as a factor in new investment (Kalecki 1968). However, taken together these factors do not automatically evoke investment whenever new investment opportunities or unused resources occur. Their failure to do so is most notable during recessions. As a result, investment tends to veer between over-investment and under-investment (Kalecki 1939a: 146–9). On more than one occasion Kalecki argued that among the advantages of socialism is the fact that it allows the central authorities to regulate investment in accordance with investment opportunities and the degree of under-utilized resources, rather than leaving it at the mercy of the vagaries of market demand and profits (e.g. Kalecki 1986: 30, 52).

(Although this argument is not based on the re-appropriation by workers of the surplus they produce, it is by no means 'unMarxist': Paul Sweezy makes a similar argument for socialism in the context of the long-term development of capitalism (Sweezy 1953).)

Veblen's argument about the inefficiency of capitalism is perhaps less formal, but adds finance and a socio-political dimension that are absent in Kalecki. In his first book, *The Theory of the Leisure Class*, Veblen argued that, with modern industrial technology, labour is sufficiently productive to secure current levels of output using less than the whole available labour force. The resultant 'leisure' is very unequally distributed between those forced into leisure with no income (the involuntarily unemployed) and those who enjoy leisure with income derived from their claims on the product of the employed (Veblen 1899: ch. 1). The book itself is a famously ironic exposé of how the leisured income-earners justify their unproductive consumption by occupying themselves with a variety of useless endeavours, including 'the higher learning' at universities.

Veblen returned to the analysis of capitalist inefficiency more systematically in his next book *The Theory of Business Enterprise* (Veblen 1904). Here he expanded upon a notion of 'capitalist sabotage' according to which 'vested' or business interests with a 'pecuniary' interest in economic activity hold back production and manipulate markets in such a way as to maximize profits. The result is that underproduction (in relation to technical and resource constraints, if not in relation to market demand) is the normal condition of the capitalist economy. Speculative booms may emerge with additional credit from the financial system. But this enhances the pecuniary influence over industry. It also gives those with access to 'credit extensions' or finance a competitive advantage that results in a proliferation of finance in excess of industrial productivity. The eventual over-extension of finance gives rise to financial crisis and depression. Veblen therefore may be regarded as the first theorist of financial crisis. Apart from finance, he postulated another stimulus to business activity in the form of what he called 'government waste' or unproductive expenditure. One particular fiscal stimulus he identified as being especially favoured by 'vested interests'. This is war, which in his view has the advantage over other kinds of government expenditure that the patriotic fervour associated with it is conducive to an unquestioning social and industrial discipline that is very agreeable to businessmen. It was precisely this kind of discipline which Kalecki argued was undermined by full employment (Kalecki 1943b).

Veblen ended his analysis by arguing that the capitalists' claim to a share in the proceeds of industry is a property right which has no objective foundation: the ownership of property being no material precondition for production. Echoing John Stuart Mill's view that the distribution of income is a social convention, Veblen pointed out that property rights are a metaphysical 'natural right' that is only legally enforceable because the law makes them so. When the 'technicians' or 'engineers' who actually organize and carry out productive economic activity realized how systematically disruptive and inefficient is the influence of business, they would get rid of 'absentee ownership'. The system that would replace it is remarkably like Kalecki's socialist economic planning.

The economic organization of socialism

Veblen was inspired by the Russian revolution to reconsider the prospects for socialism in the United States. He concluded that the likelihood of a Soviet America was minimal and that, if a revolution did succeed, it would be a revolution of technicians and engineers, since they are the only class capable of properly organizing and running industry. He envisaged the replacement of the vested interests by a 'directorate' of technicians who would organize industry centrally to avoid the most obvious failings of the capitalist system. They would therefore ensure

> the due allocation of resources and a consequent full and reasonably proportioned employment of the available equipment and man-power; (on) the avoidance of waste and duplication of work; and (on) an equitable and sufficient supply of goods and services to consumers.
>
> (Veblen 1919/1921: 446)

in other words the 'maximization of national income', given full employment, that Kalecki saw as being the purpose of socialist economic planning (Kalecki 1959: 295; Osiatyński 1988: ch. 4). This, in their view is thwarted under capitalism because there the purpose of production is to maximize profits rather than output.

A crucial feature of this 'directorate', or the central economic planning organization in Kalecki, is that its personnel consists of technicians or engineers. There were two reasons for this. First of all, both Kalecki and Veblen believed that it was important to reduce the influence of economists committed to planning in 'market' terms, by using instruments analogous to those obtaining in market or capitalist economies, such as prices or interest rates, or by econometric calculation. In Kalecki's case this was because he felt that econometrics does not provide objective data, which is subject to large margins of error (Osiatyński 1988: 61). But both also distrusted the economists' advocacy of instruments which, in mimicking capitalist markets, would reproduce in socialism capitalist instability and under-production and, as Veblen put it, shift the 'controlling purpose of industry' from a 'serviceable output of goods' to 'profits on absentee investment' (Veblen 1919/1921: 450; Kalecki 1986: ch. 5).

Their second reason for keeping central economic planning under the influence of engineers and technicians was because industrial coordination is principally a matter of matching the operations of machines and production (what was called the 'material balances' system of planning in the Eastern European countries). Kalecki used examples drawn from heavy industry, factory construction and coal-mining, when discussing the efficiency of central planning of investment (Kalecki 1986: 94–6). Both of them used railways as the example of an industry whose investment and current operations are disrupted by their subjection to business objectives (Veblen 1904: 39–41; Kalecki 1986: 20). Charles Bettelheim also stressed the superiority of the technical coordination of industry over its more unstable business direction (Bettelheim 1975).

However, his own observation of planning practice during the Stalinist industrialization drive, and his subsequent practical experience of economic planning, left Kalecki sceptical that engineers and technicians would be able to resist committing the economy under their control to excessive investment and a wasteful pursuit of technical novelty. In September 1964, he remarked to a conference of professors of political economy that

> Just as economists have a weakness for calculation, technicians want to have the latest technical toys and we should not hold this against them, but we do not need to offer them these toys immediately.
>
> (Kalecki 1964: 322)

The answer in his view was to establish a system of planning which would minimize the investment required for given levels of consumption. Major investment projects were to be centrally determined by desired levels of employment and industrial development priorities, with only alternative variants of a project being subject to decision by calculation. At the same time, minor, locally determined, investments would be financed with interest-bearing credits to exclude unnecessary investments (Kalecki 1986; Osiatyński 1988: ch. 6).

The other lesson of Stalinist industrialization was the danger of excessive concentration of industrial power. Kalecki's answer to this was to have central economic planning balanced by workers' councils in the factories. This would both secure the participation of the workers and their commitment to the system of economic administration. This combination of syndicalism and central administration was to ensure that the concentration of economic power was not abused (Kalecki 1986: ch. 3). But the failure of the Polish workers' council's movement in 1958 was not the only reason why Kalecki spent the last years of his life arguing against arbitrary and inefficient state planning in Poland (Osiatyński 1988: ch. 4). There was also a clear problem of undue concentration of political power.

Conclusion

Kalecki shared with Veblen a conviction that the capitalist industrial management was inefficient, and a distrust of business methods in the socialized sector of the economy. Kalecki's direct experience of socialism enabled him to develop a sophisticated view of how socialist economic planning should be conducted. However, in his maturity finance was not yet a dominant factor in capitalism, as it was when Veblen was writing. Had the Polish central planners understood more of Kalecki and finance, then many of the problems of the Polish economy since the 1970s might have been avoided. If the present post-communist governments understood more of Kalecki and finance, many of the present and future problems of post-communist economies might still be avoided.

Epilogue

18 Some concluding remarks

Zdzislaw L. Sadowski

As co-editor of this book and the organizer of the Warsaw 1999 Conference I feel obliged to add a few remarks, though without any intention of trying to summarize the contents. I am writing, of course, under a strong influence of what I read in all the preceding chapters and what I noted from the discussions at the Conference. But, of course, for what I write none of the contributors can feel in the least responsible.

Counting myself, as several other contributors, among the disciples of Michal Kalecki, I was happy to see that the Warsaw Conference based on papers now collected in this book served well its double purpose. On the one hand, it commemorated Kalecki owing to the effort of a group of eminent scholars who represent a thorough knowledge of his ideas. On the other hand, and perhaps more important, it gave at the same time much insight into some of the most pertinent problems of today's world economy, taking up the issue of relevance of Kalecki's ideas in the modern market economy.

Michal Kalecki left a rich legacy pertaining to the theory of capitalist market economies and to economic policy-making. He was much more than a neutral observer and analyst. He had his clear concepts of the objectives of development and of how they should be served.

His primary concern was unemployment. This was perfectly natural in the midst of deep stagnation of the 1930s. His analysis led him to the conclusion that it was possible to attain and maintain full employment in a capitalist market economy if economic policies of the right kind were applied. Maybe this explains the growing interest in Kalecki's thought in the world of today, in which unemployment is not only much higher than it used to be in any earlier period, but became a chronic economic disease which badly needs treatment. It has also been on the increase all over the 1990s with growing incidence of long-term unemployment, at least in OECD countries (United Nations 2001: 148, 151).

If one were to identify the basic tenet of Kalecki's theory, it would probably be the idea that, in a capitalist market economy, the volume of output and employment depend ultimately on demand, particularly investment demand. This idea, closely akin to that of Keynes, led to reasoning in which unemployment appears as caused by insufficient demand.

Ever since David Ricardo took up the issue of unemployment for the first time, economic theory had enormous difficulty in fitting this malady into the image of an economic system supposed to be orientated towards full employment equilibrium. Kalecki and Keynes were the first ones to show that the market economy in actual fact was not so orientated, its tendency being towards equilibrium with unused resources. This, however, implied that full employment was not attainable automatically by the interplay of market forces. It required deliberate macroeconomic policy of the government aimed at bringing aggregate demand to a sufficient level. This could be done by raising investment demand both by public expenditure with the possibility of deficit financing and by stimulation of private investment through appropriate tax policy.

The demand approach led both Keynes and Kalecki to a search for ways to stimulate demand when insufficient. Their prescriptions are parallel in attaching decisive importance to investment. Where they differ is the social aspect of income distribution which enters into the picture when stimulation of investment does not suffice. While Keynes stressed the importance of increasing private savings out of profits, Kalecki's line was to stress the need to stimulate consumption demand of the low-income groups by redistributing income from profits to wages through taxation.

Kalecki did not see any economic limitations to the application of full employment policies. What he perceived, however, was a decisive political constraint. He believed that businessmen are basically opposed to the idea of full employment, as it would strengthen the position of labour and impair their own. This makes them basically opposed to government expenditure aimed at the promotion of employment. Instead, they tend to favour policies of equilibrating the budget.

In the present book a subject recurrent in several contributions and widely discussed at the Warsaw Conference is the contrast between economic policies which prevailed in the capitalist countries in the third as compared to the last quarter of the twentieth century. The first of these two periods, often denoted as the 'Golden Age' of capitalism, was characterized, at least in Europe, by full employment, high growth rates, relative growth in the share of wages in national income, and income distribution free of increasing inequalities. This highly satisfactory performance was partly attributable to extended state control of the economy. Governments followed policies of the Keynesian type which helped to maintain high aggregate demand owing particularly to liberal monetary policy.

To avoid oversimplification it should be noted that the performance of the 'Golden Age' was probably not fully attributable to successful government policies. In most countries it was accompanied by budget surpluses which shows that full employment resulted from private rather than government spending. With sufficiently high levels of private expenditure active fiscal policy was not needed. But this situation was by no means contradictory to Kalecki's analysis, indeed it might have supported the view that a kind of consensus was reached between business and labour.

The second period, beginning in the late 1970s, brought a general shift to policies which were in full contradiction to the Keynes–Kalecki approach, but were much better suited to the interests of capitalists, with financial stability instead of growth and employment as the main concern. The cases of United Kingdom and Germany as scrutinized in this book represent a broader picture which shows that these policies, supported by legal constraints on trade unions, led to an increase in the share of profits in GDP, marked increase in unemployment and stagnation of real investment in manufacturing.

Writing in the first of these two periods, Kalecki could have been under the impression that what happened in the advanced capitalist countries was what he called 'the crucial reform of capitalism'. This was supposed to mean the reaching of a political consensus between labour and business which made it possible to overcome the political constraint and pursue the goal of full employment by active policy of the government. Kalecki could have believed that the 'crucial reform' became a real fact. But what happened in the next decades showed that, even if it was implemented, it became subject to a reversal. By the end of the 1970s inflationary tendencies triggered off by the oil crisis caused a shift to restrictive monetary policies. The fear of budget deficits ruled out active fiscal policy as well as every thought of demand policies.

Thus, the political constraint re-emerged. The orientation of macroeconomic policies returned to old ideas of market liberalism, limited role of government and financial stability. The basic role was assigned to central banks which were to control money supply and curb inflation. Growth and employment lost their role of primary objectives.

For about 25 years this neoliberal ideology dominated in the world of market economies. It brought about clearly negative effects. As a result, the present stage of the world economy does not provide much ground for optimism with regard to the future. Globalization which was expected to enhance overall welfare through liberalization of trade and capital movements, sadly failed. Free international flow of capital, instead of stimulating economic growth and sustained development, brought about financial instability, successive financial crises and overall slowdown. Unemployment is high and rising both in the developed and in the developing countries. Large areas of the globe cannot find their way out of utter poverty. The gap between rich and poor countries tends to widen, though the impressive economic performance of China makes the overall picture less clear. But even in the highly developed countries income inequalities are on the increase and tend to undermine social cohesion. Very obviously there arises the need to find new institutional and policy solutions which would reconcile the driving force of market competition with social concerns to which ecological concerns are now added. This can be considered the primary challenge for the human community.

At the time when the neo-liberal doctrine was born (or re-born) it could have been justified by the fact that the problem facing the world in the 1970s and 1980s was inflation rather than deficient demand. But eventually the situation evolved. The danger of the day is no longer inflation but deflation. This brings Keynesian and Kaleckian ideas again into the focus of attention.

Paradoxically, the neo-liberal doctrine still maintains its influence in financial circles. In spite of what happens in the world economy, the issue of unemployment acquires in these circles less attention than that of inflation. The main policy emphasis continues to be laid on curbing inflation and reducing budget deficits. The Maastricht Treaty with the absence of unemployment indicators among its policy requirements is mentioned in this book as an important example. This policy bias shows a serious discrepancy between facts of life and the policy approaches. This can perhaps be partly explained by fear of departing from the doctrine born in the late 1970s, and partly by the lack of confidence in the feasibility of combating unemployment when the prevailing tendency is towards its growth. What may also count is that, contrarily to inflation, unemployment does not directly affect decision-makers who are therefore less sensitive to its implications.

But a policy change is badly needed. The question arises how far it is possible now to reinstate the basic features of the 'Golden Age'. Is it possible to design policies based on the theories of Keynes and Kalecki in the substantially changed conditions including the institutional set-up of today's market system? It is tempting to think in terms of re-invoking Kalecki's dream of the 'crucial reform of capitalism' as a broad socio-political consensus with regard to the objectives and main policy instruments of development.

But it must be recognized that direct relevance of Kalecki's ideas is limited by the fact that, over the past several decades, the ways in which the market system works, the nature of competition, the organization of production processes and the institutional set-up were substantially changed. Present-day policies, to be applicable, have to be adjusted to these new circumstances.

In the era of the new civilization of information, economic development in the advanced countries is now driven by innovation rather than investment (Porter 1990). Though Kalecki recognized the role of innovations as one of the driving forces of economic progress, he treated them as exogenous to the market mechanism. They now became its fully endogenous, continuously active component. Also, the very notion of investment became something quite different from what it used to be. Investment today means largely expenditure on education and scientific research on which the processes of innovation are based. All this must have changed substantially the attitudes and policies of firms as well as those of the governments.

A very important new factor is the greatly expanded role of financial markets in the world economy resulting from the broad liberalization of capital flows. The impact of financial liberalization on world growth performance, initially expected to be highly favourable, proved the contrary. Instability in financial markets made both governments and private business more risk-conscious and prone to change their objective function from growth to monetary stability which eventually led to falling growth rates.

The free flow of capital makes it impossible to coordinate monetary and fiscal policies and therefore also to make use of such policies to stimulate effective demand. The leading role was assigned to monetary policy aimed at preventing inflation and stabilizing the exchange rate so as to create safeguards against outflow of capital. But the results are far from satisfactory. Repeated calls are being made for international action to create a new world monetary system. One of the recognized authorities in dealing with financial markets represents the explicit view that market discipline can no longer remain the goal, but needs to be supplemented by public policy aimed at maintaining stability in financial markets (Soros 1998: 176).

Against this background it is not surprising that a satisfactory answer to the question how applicable can Kalecki's recommendations be in the changed institutional set-up is difficult to reach. The problem remains open and invites further discussion. Only the basic approach seems clear. What is needed is policy orientation towards economic growth and high employment rather than towards damping economic activity by assigning top priority to financial stabilization and the fight against inflation. To reach these goals, in the new institutional set-up an active role of democratic governments in supporting the market mechanism is needed, whether at the national or supranational level. Solutions must ultimately be found of a contractual type to which the idea of the 'crucial reform' may serve as a guide.

Kalecki's search for the measures to deal with the diseases of the capitalist system eventually led him to look for an answer in the logic of long-term central economic planning. He was very much aware of the dangers of autocracy and therefore put forward a concept of democratic central planning based on cooperation of the planners 'from above' with labour organizations 'from below'. However, the actual institutional shape of such cooperation remained virtual and can hardly be considered today anything more than an attractive utopia.

At the same time account must be taken of the negative lessons of excessive state interference into the economy. Central planning based on state ownership failed as an economic system because it proved impotent in the sphere of technological progress, and failed as a political system because it served as a foundation for unacceptable autocracy. Market competition proved to be unbeaten as the most efficient known mechanism of resource allocation and the state cannot be expected nor allowed to replace the market mechanism in any of its basic functions. The active role of the government should consist solely in exerting indirect influence on the working of the market system through macroeconomic and related policies to provide safeguards against deficient resource utilization and unjust income distribution. This role of the government can be adequately performed only in a democratic set-up. The free market system of the present time is unduly named liberal, as the main objectives of liberalism cannot be successfully pursued in a society tormented by mass unemployment, poverty and marginalization of large parts of the society.

The part of Kalecki's legacy which seems most fully relevant to present-day issues is his contribution to development economics. His growth theory remains valid with regard to economies with unlimited supplies of labour. His insights into the political and institutional constraints to industrialization of less developed countries remain valid as well. His treatment of food supply as the major constraint to economic development is of continued relevance.

There is much similarity in the story of developing countries to what was said about the Golden Age in advanced countries. Before 1980 there was a general adherence to industrialization policies based on public investment expenditure and protection by tariffs and administrative controls. This was a period of relatively high growth rates in many areas, notably Latin America and even Africa. But after 1980 a general slowdown, even with downturns, occurred.

In the 1980s and 1990s the new line based on the so-called Washingtonian Consensus was almost generally adopted, with trade liberalization, privatization of state-owned companies, financial stability and control of inflation as the main objectives. The outcome was by and large negative. Neo-liberalism led to greater inequalities and increasing poverty. It became clear that, if poverty is to be brought down, the IMF line has to be abandoned in favour of deliberate policies promoting employment and growth.

One of the serious problems not dealt with in Kalecki's theory but faced nowadays by many developing countries (as well as economies in transition) appears to be that demand stimuli are hardly applicable in situations of growing imports penetration which are typical for many weak economies with low competitive power. It is not possible to improve the employment situation by means of such stimuli, as increase in aggregate demand, instead of enhancing domestic output and employment, would lead to an increase in imports and eventually to a growing current account deficit.

In broader terms one may say that, for a developing country, imports are needed to secure growth of GDP. This requires ability to pay. Thus the need arises to rely upon inflows of capital. But it seems that, with some exceptions, the general tendency is for the inflow of foreign capital to cause increases in imports and decreases in aggregate demand. As shown by experience, it can easily lead to the 'trap of indebtedness' when the foreign debt becomes too large to be serviced.

An example of an economy with high unemployment and a sizeable imports surplus with increasing current account deficit is provided by Poland of the years 1996–2001. With domestic demand orientated largely towards imports rather than to domestic output, the trade deficit and with it the deficit in the current account had a built-in tendency to increase. A few decades ago the problem of the balance of payments could have been dealt with by introducing quantity controls on imports. Today, in view of international commitments within the WTO it is not acceptable. Thus there is no visible escape from growing unemployment and Kalecki's recipe does not help in this situation. The message is that only really competitive economies can go for demand-side policies.

To conclude let me express the hope that, in the years to come, world economics will evolve towards a re-absorption of the ideas of Michal Kalecki and of their re-application – in their modernized shape – in the practice of policy-making.

Bibliography

References to Michal Kalecki's writings

Publications included in the English edition of *Collected Works of Michal Kalecki* are annotated by CW and a Roman numeral for the respective volume (I to VII).

1 Collected Works of Michal Kalecki (edited by Jerzy Osiatyński, Oxford, Clarendon Press)

(1990) Vol. I *Capitalism: Business Cycles and Full Employment*, pp. XV, 614.
(1991) Vol. II *Capitalism: Economic Dynamics*, pp. XIV, 631.
(1992) Vol. III *Socialism: Functioning and Long-Run Planning*, pp. XVIII, 449.
(1993) Vol. IV *Socialism: Economic Growth and Efficiency of Investment*, pp. XIII, 369.
(1993) Vol. V *Developing Economies*, pp. XV, 264.
(1996) Vol. VI *Studies in Applied Economics, 1927–1941*, pp. XXIII, 575.
(1997) Vol. VII *Studies in Applied Economics, 1940–1967, Miscellanea*, pp. XXIII, 680.

2 Selected books and articles

(1932) 'The Business Cycle and Inflation', CW I: 147–55, 483–5.
(1933a) *Essay on the Business Cycle Theory*, CW I: 65–108, 436–46.
(1933b) 'Stimulating the World Business Upswing', CW I: 56–64, 485–6.
(1933c) 'On Foreign Trade and "Domestic Exports"', CW I: 165–71, 486.
(1934) 'Three Systems', CW I: 201–19, 491–6.
(1935a) 'The Essence of the Business Upswing', CW I: 188–94, 487–9.
(1935b) 'A Macro-dynamic Theory of Business Cycles', CW I: 120–38, 481–2.
(1936) 'Some Remarks on Keynes' Theory', CW I: 223–32, 497–510.
(1937a) 'The Principle of Increasing Risk', CW I: 285–93.
(1937b) 'A Theory of Commodity, Income, and Capital Taxation', CW I: 319–25, 557–63.
(1937c) 'A Theory of the Business Cycle', CW I: 529–57.
(1938) 'The Determinants of Distribution of National Income', CW II: 3–20, 479–516.
(1939a) *Essays in the Theory of Economic Fluctuations*, London: Allen & Unwin, CW I: 233–318, 510–57.
(1939b) 'Money and Real Wages', CW II: 21–50, 516–21.
(1940) 'Wage Bill and Cash Circulation', CW VII: 38–44, 509.
(1941) 'What is Inflation?', CW VII: 83–8, 513–14.
(1942) 'The Minimum Essentials for Democratic Planning', CW III: 269–74.
(1943a) *Studies in Economic Dynamics*, London: Allen & Unwin, CW II: 117–90, 536–49.

(1943b) 'Political Aspects of Full Employment', CW I: 347–56, 571–8.
(1943c) 'The War Time Trend of Deposits', CW VII: 159–70, 517.
(1943) (and E.F. Schumacher), 'International Clearing and Long-term Lending', CW VII: 226–32, 521–3.
(1944a) 'Three Ways to Full Employment', CW I: 357–76, 578–82.
(1944b) 'Professor Pigou on "The Classical Stationary State": A Comment', CW I: 342–43, 566–70.
(1945) 'Full Employment by Stimulating Private Investment?', CW I: 377–86, 582.
(1946a) 'A Comment on "Monetary Policy"', CW I: 402–8, 592–3.
(1946b) 'Multilateralism and Full Employment', CW I: 409–16, 593–4.
(1949) 'Introductory Remarks on Inflationary and Deflationary Processes', CW VII: 575–85.
(1951) 'A Note on Long-Run Unemployment', CW I: 417–20, 594.
(1954a) *Theory of Economic Dynamics: An Essay on Cyclical and Long-Run Changes in Capitalist Economy*, London: Allen & Unwin, CW II: 205–348, 550–77.
(1954b) 'The Problem of Financing of Economic Development', CW V: 23–44, 206–8.
(1955/1962) 'A Model of Hyperinflation', CW II: 90–5, 527–8.
(1956) 'The Economic Situation in the United States as Compared with the Pre–war Period', CW VII: 279–86, 526–7.
(1957) (and A. Szeworski) 'Economic Problems of Production Automation in Capitalist Countries', CW II: 374–85, 584.
(1957–60) (ed.) *Studia z zakresu koniunktury współczesnego kapitalizmu* (Studies of Business Cycles in the Contemporary Capitalism) Vols. 1–4, Warsaw: Polish Academy of Sciences, PWN (Polish Scientific Publishers).
(1958) 'Central Price Determination as an Essential Feature of a Socialist Economy', CW III: 114–19, 344–5.
(1959) 'On the Methodology of Examining the Efficiency of Investment', CW IV: 293–6.
(1960a) 'Unemployment in Underdeveloped Countries', CW V: 3–5, 177–99.
(1960b) 'Financial Problems of the Third Plan: Some Observations', CW V: 122–8, 216–22.
(1962) 'The Economic Situation in the USA, 1956–1961', CW II: 386–401, 584–5.
(1963) 'Problems of Financing Economic Development in a Mixed Economy', CW V: 45–60, 208–10.
(1964) 'Observations on Social and Economic Aspects of "Intermediate Regimes"', CW V: 6–12, 199–204.
(1965) 'Theses on Technical Progress and Its Types', CW IV: 314–21.
(1966a) *Studies in the Theory of Business Cycles, 1933–1939*, Oxford: Blackwell.
(1966b) 'The Difference Between Crucial Economic Problems of Developed and Underdeveloped Non-Socialist Economies', CW V: 13–19, 204–5.
(1966) (and I. Sachs) 'Forms of Foreign Aid: An Economic Analysis', CW V: 61–91, 210–12.
(1968) 'Trend and Business Cycle Reconsidered', CW II: 435–50, 590–609.
(1969) *Introduction to the Theory of Growth in a Socialist Economy*, Warsaw: PWN (Polish Scientific Publishers), CW IV: 3–110, 237–86.
(1970a) 'Theories of Growth in Different Social Systems', CW IV: 111–17, 286.
(1970b) 'The Scope of the Evaluation of the Efficiency of Investment in a Socialist Economy', CW IV: 202–6, 329–34.
(1971a) *Selected Essays on the Dynamics of the Capitalist Economy, 1933–1970*, Cambridge: Cambridge University Press.
(1971b) 'Class Struggle and Distribution of National Income', CW II: 96–103, 528–9.
(1971) (and T. Kowalik) 'Observations on the Crucial Reform', CW II, 467–76, 610–15.
(1972) *Selected Essays on the Economic Growth of the Socialist and the Mixed Economy*, Cambridge: Cambridge University Press.
(1976) *Essays on Developing Economies*, Hassocks: Harvester.

(1986) *Selected Essays on Economic Planning* (ed. by J. Toporowski), Cambridge: Cambridge University Press.

References to other authors

Abdalla, I.S. (1979) 'Depaysannisation du developpement rural? Un choix lourd de consequences', *IFDA Dossier*, 9 July, pp. 3–15.

Abramovay, R. and Sachs, I. (1972) *Nouvelles configurations villes-campagnes*, Paris: Programme MOST de l'UNESCO.

Abramowitz, M. and David, P. (1996) 'Technological change and the rise of intangible investments: The US economy's growth-path in the twentieth century', in OECD (ed.), *Employment and Growth in the Knowledge-based Economy*, Paris: OECD.

Allsopp, C. (1993) 'Strategic policy dilemmas for the 1990s', *Oxford Review of Economic Policy*, 9(3), pp. 1–25.

Allsopp, C. and Vines, D. (1998) 'The assessment: Macroeconomic policy after EMU', *Oxford Review of Economic Policy*, 14(3), Autumn, pp. 1–21.

Appelbaum, E. and Schettkat, R. (1999) 'Are prices unimportant? The changing structure of the industrialized economies', *Journal of Post Keynesian Economics*, 21(3), Spring, pp. 387–98.

Ardeni, P. *et al.* (1996) 'La "nuova economia keynesiana": risultati e problemi aperti, in: Messori, M. (ed.), *La nuova economia keynesiana*, Milano, Il Mulino, pp. 49–144.

Arestis, P. (1996) 'Kalecki's role in post Keynesian Economics: An overview', in King, J. (ed.), *An Alternative Macroeconomic Theory: The Kaleckian Model and Post-Keynesian Economics*, Boston: Kluwer, pp. 11–34.

Arestis, P. and Marshall, M. (eds) (1995) *The Political Economy of Full Employment: Conservatism, Corporatism and Institutional Change*, Aldershot: Elgar.

Arestis, P. and Sawyer, M. (1999a) 'The macroeconomics of New Labour', *Economic Issues*, 4(1), March, pp. 39–57.

—— (1999b) 'The Economic and Monetary Union: Current prospects and alternative proposals', *Revista*, December.

Arestis, P. and Skuse, F. (1989) 'Austerity policies and the New Right: Recent UK experience', *Economie Appliquee*, XLII(1), pp. 171–202.

—— (1991) 'Wage and price setting in a post-Keynesian theory of inflation', *Economies et Societes*, Serie: *Monnaie et Production*, 11–12, pp. 91–106.

Arestis, P., Driver, C. and Rooney, J. (1985–6) 'The real segment of a UK ·post-Keynesian model', *Journal of Post Keynesian Economics*, 8(2), pp.161–81.

Arndt, H. (1972) 'Development economics before 1945', in Bhagwati, J. and Eckhaus, R. (eds), *Development and Planning: Essays in Honour of Paul Rosenstein-Rodan*, London: Allen & Unwin.

—— (1984) 'Introduction to economics', *Singapore Economic Review*, 29(2), October.

—— (1985) 'Origins of structuralism', *World Development*, 13(2), pp. 151–9.

Arunachalam, S. (1999) 'How the Internet is failing the developing world', *The Slab*, based on a talk to the Ninth International Conference of the International Federation of Science Editors, Egypt, June 1998, Australian Broadcasting Corporation, Sydney: http://www.abc.net.au/science/slab/infropoverty/story.htm.

Aschauer, D. (1998) *How Big Should the Public Capital Stock Be? The Relationship Between Public Capital and Economic Growth*. Public Policy Brief, 43, The Jerome Levy Economics Institute of Bard College, Annandale-on-Hudson.

Asimakopulos, A. (1975) 'A Kaleckian theory of income distribution', *Canadian Journal of Economics*, 8(3), pp. 313–33.

—— (1977) 'Profits and investment: A Kaleckian approach', in Harcourt, G. (ed.), *The Microeconomic Foundations of Macroeconomics*, Boulder, Col.: Westview Press, pp. 328–42.

Atkinson, A. (1999) 'Is rising income inequality inevitable? A critique of the Transatlantic Consensus', WIDER (World Institute of Development Economics Research) *Annual Lectures*, 3.

—— (2000) 'Increased income inequality in OECD countries and the redistributive impact of the government budget', WIDER (World Institute of Development Economics Research), Working Papers, 202.

Baddeley, M. (2001) 'Bubbles or Whirlpools? An empirical analysis of the effects of speculation and uncertainty on investment', mimeo, University of Cambridge.

Ball, L. and Mankiw, N. (1995) 'What do budget deficits do?', NBER, reprint No. 2046.

Bank of England Monetary Policy Committee (1999) *The Transmission Mechanism of Monetary Policy*, London.

Baran, P. and Sweezy P. (1968) *Monopoly Capital*, New York: Monthly Review Press.

Barro, R. (1994) 'What the Fed can't do', *Wall Street Journal*, 22 August.

Benassy, J.-P. (ed.) (1995) *Macroeconomics and Imperfect Competition*, Aldershot: Elgar.

Bernanke, S. *et al.* (1999) *Inflation Targeting*, Princeton: Princeton University Press.

Bettelheim, Ch. (1975) *On the Transition to Socialist Economy*, London: Harvester Press.

Bhaduri, A. (1973) 'A study of agricultural backwardness under semi-feudalism', *Economic Journal*, 83, pp. 120–37.

—— (1986) *Macroeconomics: The Dynamics of Commodity Production*, Armonk, NY: Sharpe.

—— (1991) 'Economic power and productive efficiency in traditional agriculture', in Gustafsson, S. (ed.), *Power and Economic Institutions*, Aldershot: Elgar.

Bhaduri, A. and Skarstein, R. (1996) 'Short period macroeconomic aspects of foreign aid', *Cambridge Journal of Economics*, 20, pp. 195–206.

—— (2003) 'Effective demand and the terms of trade in a dual economy: A Kaldorian perspective', *Cambridge Journal of Economics*, 27(4), pp. 583–95.

Bhaduri, A., Laski, K. and Riese, M. (1999) 'Effective demand versus profit maximization in aggregate demand/supply analysis: A dynamic perspective', *Banca Nazionale del Lavoro Quarterly Review*, September, pp. 281–93.

Bharadwaj, K. (1983) 'On effective demand: Some recent critiques', in Kregel, A. (ed.), *Distribution, Effective Demand and International Economic Relations*, London: Macmillan.

Bianchi, M. (1990) 'The unsatisfactoriness of satisficing: from bounded rationality to innovative rationality', *Review of Political Economy*, 2(2), pp. 149–67.

Bils, M. (1987) 'The cyclical behavior of marginal cost and price', *American Economic Review*, 77(5), pp. 838–55.

Binswanger, H. *et al.* (1985) 'Estimates of Agricultural Supply Response from Time Series and Cross-Country Data', Working Paper 1985/3, World Bank, EPOLS Division.

Binswanger, H., Khandker, S. and Rosenzweig, M. (1993) 'How infrastructure and financial institutions affect agricultural output and investment in India', *Journal of Development Economics*, 41, pp. 337–66.

Blanchard, O. and Kiyotaki, N. (1987) 'Monopolistic competition and the effects of aggregate demand', *American Economic Review*, September, pp. 647–66.

Bloch, H. and Sapsford, D. (1991–2) 'Post-war movements in prices of primary products and manufactured goods', *Journal of Post Keynesian Economics*, pp. 249–66.

—— (1996) 'Trend in the international terms of trade between primary producers and manufacturers', *Journal of International Development*, 14(1), pp. 53–67.

—— (2000) 'Whither the terms of trade? An elaboration of the Prebisch–Singer hypothesis', *Cambridge Journal of Economics*, 24, pp. 461–81.

Blundell, R. *et al.* (1992) 'Investment and Tobin's q', *Journal of Econometrics*, 51, pp. 233–57.

Boitani, A. *et al.* (1992) 'Concorrenza imperfetta, esternalita e spiegazioni delle rigidita nella Nuova Economica Keynesiana', *Economia Politica*, 9(2), pp. 299–361.

Borensztein, E. and Reinhart, C. (1994) 'The macroeconomic determinants of commodity prices', *IMF Staff Papers*, 41(2), pp. 236–67.

Bortis, H. (1997) *Institutions, Behaviour and Economic Theory: A Contribution to Classical-Keynesian Political Economy*, Cambridge: Cambridge University Press.

Boulding, K. (1950) *A Reconstruction of Economics*, New York: John Wiley.

Bowles, S. and Boyer, R. (1990) 'A wage-led employment regime: income distribution, labour discipline and aggregate demand in welfare capitalism', in Marglin, S. and Schor, J. (eds), *The Golden Age of Capitalism*, Oxford: Clarendon Press.

—— (1995) 'Wages, aggregate demand and employment in an open economy: An empirical investigation', in Epstein, G. and Gintis, H. (eds), *Macroeconomic Policy After the Conservative Era*, Cambridge: Cambridge University Press.

Bowles, S., Gordon, S. and Weisskopf, T. (1990) *After the Waste Land: A Democratic Alternative for the Year 2000*, Armonk, NY: Sharpe.

Boyer, R. (1988) 'Technical change and the theory of regulation', in Dosi, G. *et al.* (eds), *Technical Change and Economic Theory*, pp. 67–94.

Brenner, R. (1998) *The Economics of Global Turbulence: A Special Report on the World Economy, 1950–1998*, London: New Left Review, p. 229.

Britton, A. (1996) 'The goal of full employment', *National Institute of Economic and Social Research*, Report Series, 10.

Brouwer, E. and Kleinknecht, A. (1999) 'Keynes-plus?: effective demand and changes in firm-level R & D: an empirical note', *Cambridge Journal of Economics*, 23(3), May, pp. 385–89.

Brus, W. (1977) 'Kalecki's economics of socialism', *Oxford Bulletin of Economics and Statistics*, 39(1).

Bryant, K. and Wells, A. (eds) (1998) *A New Economic Paradigm?: Innovation-based Evolutionary System*, Discussions in Science and Innovation, 4, Dept. of Industry, Science and Resources, Canberra: Commonwealth of Australia.

Burchard, F. (1944) 'The causes of unemployment', in *The Economics of Full Employment*, Oxford: Blackwell.

Caniels, M. (1999) 'Regional growth differentials: The impact of locally bounded knowledge spillovers', unpublished thesis No. 99–42, Faculty of Economics and Business Administration, Maastricht University.

Cardoso, Eliana A. (1981) 'Food supply and inflation', *Journal of Development Economics*, 8, pp. 269–84.

Carpentier, R., Fazzari, S. and Petersen, B. (1994) 'Inventory investment, internal-finance fluctuations, and the business cycle', *Brookings Papers on Economic Activity*, 2, pp. 75–139.

Carvalho, F. (1988) 'Keynes, a instabilidade do capitalismo e a teoria dos ciclos economicos', *Pesquisa e Planejamento Economico*, December.

Caselli, F. (1999) 'Technological revolutions', *American Economic Review*, 89, March, pp. 78–102.

Chakravarty, S. (1994) *La planification du developpement: L'experience indienne*, Paris: Ed. de la Maison des Sciences de l'Homme.

—— (1997) 'M. Kalecki and development economics', *Writings on Development*, New Delhi: Oxford University Press, pp. 113–25.

Chapple, S. (1996) 'Kalecki and Keynes', in King, J. (ed.), *An Alternative Macroeconomic Theory: The Kaleckian Model and Post-Keynesian Economics*, Boston: Kluwer, pp. 35–54.

Chilosi, A. (ed.) (1979) *Kalecki: Antologia di scritti di teoria economica*, Bologna: Il Mulino.

—— (1982) 'Breit, Kalecki, and Hicks on the term structure of Interest rates, risk and the theory of investment', in Baranzini, M. (ed.), *Advances in Economic Theory*, Oxford: Blackwell.

—— (1988) 'Nessi e interpretazioni causali nella macro-economia di Kalecki', *Quaderni di storia dell'economia politica*, pp. 361–70.

—— (1989) 'Kalecki's quest for the microeconomic foundations of his macroeconomic theory', in Sebastiani, M. (ed.), *Kalecki's Relevance Today*, London: St Martin's Press, pp. 101–20.

Coddington, A. (1983) *Keynesian Economics: The Search for First Principles*, London: Allen & Unwin.

Committee on the Working of the Monetary System (1953) *Report*, Cmnd 827, London.

Costa, G. (1979) 'Il "principio della domanda effettiva" e la legge di Say?', *Rivista di politica economica*, LXIX(2), February, pp. 169–95.

Courvisanos, J. (1996) *Investment Cycles in Capitalist Economies: A Behavioural Kaleckian Contribution*, Cheltenham: Elgar.

—— (1998) 'Investment planning towards an innovative and sustainable environment', *School of Economics Discussion Paper*, 98–04, Hobart: University of Tasmania.

—— (2000) 'IT investment strategy for development: An 'instrumental analysis' based on the Tasmanian and New Brunswick Information Technology Strategies', *Prometheus*, 18(1), March, pp. 75–91.

—— (2001) 'Regional economic decay and regeneration under structural change', in Falk I. (ed.), *Learning to Manage Change*, Melbourne, NCVER, pp.13–22.

Courvisanos, J. and Verspagen, B. (2002) 'Innovation and investment in capitalist economies, 1870–2000: Kaleckian dynamics and evolutionary life cycles', paper presented at the 7th International Post Keynesian Workshop, University of Missouri, Kansas City, (June–July).

Cowling, K. (1982) *Monopoly Capitalism*, London: Macmillan.

Crotty, J. (1992) 'Neoclassical and Keynesian approaches to the theory of investment', *Journal of Post Keynesian Economics*, 14(4), Summer, pp. 483–96.

—— (1994) 'Are Keynesian uncertainty and macrotheory compatible? Conventional decision making, institutional structures, and conditional stability in Keynesian macromodels', in Dymski, G. and Pollin, R. (eds), *New Perspectives in Monetary Macroeconomics*, Ann Arbor: University of Michigan Press.

David, B. (1997) *Les transformations de l'agriculture bresilienne: une modernisation perverse (1960–1995)*, Paris: Ecole des Hautes Etudes en Sciences Sociales.

Davidson, P. (1978) *Money and the Real World*, 2nd edn., London: Macmillan.

Dell, S. (1977) 'Kalecki and the United Nations', *Oxford Bulletin of Economics and Statistics*, 39(1), pp. 40–2.

DIW (German Institute of Economic Research) (1997) 'Tendenzen der Wirtschaftsentwicklung, 1997/98', *DIW Wochenbericht*, 64(27–8).

Dixit, A. and Stiglitz, J. (1977) 'Monopolistic competition and optimum product diversity', *American Economic Review*, 67(3), June, pp. 297–308.

Dixon, H. and Rankin, N. (1994) 'Imperfect competition and macroeconomics: A survey', *Oxford Economic Papers*, 46, pp. 171–99.

Dobb, M. (1960) *An Essay on Economic Growth and Planning*, London: Routledge & Kegan Paul.

Dobrska, Z. and A. Szeworski (1958) 'Studia z zakresu koniunktury wspólczesnego kapitalizmu', Vol. 2. Polish Academy of Sciences, Panstwowe Wydawnictwo Naukowe, Warsaw.

—— (1959) 'Studia z zakresu koniunktury wspólczesnego kapitalizmu', Vol. 3. Polish Academy of Sciences, Panstwowe Wydawnictwo Naukowe, Warsaw.

Dobrska, Z. *et al.* (1960) 'Studia z zakresu koniunktury wspólczesnego kapitalizmu', Vol. 4. Polish Academy of Sciences, Panstwowe Wydawnictwo Naukowe, Warsaw.

Dodgson, M. and Rothwell, R. (eds) (1994) *The Handbook of Industrial Innovation*, Cheltenham: Elgar.

Dosi, G. *et al.* (eds) (1988) *Technical Change and Economic Theory*, London: Pinter.

Dow, J. (1964) *The Management of the British Economy 1945–60*, Cambridge: Cambridge University Press.

Duesenberry, J. (1958) *Business Cycles and Economic Growth*, New York, McGraw-Hill.

Dutt, A. (1987) 'Competition, monopoly power and the uniform rate of profit', *Review of Radical Political Economics*, 19.

—— (1992) 'A Kaldorian model of growth and development revisited: a comment on Thirlwall', *Oxford Economic Papers*, 44, pp. 56–72.

Dymski, G. (1996) 'Kalecki's monetary economics', in King, J. (ed.), *An Alternative Macroeconomic Theory: The Kaleckian Model and Post-Keynesian Economics*, Boston, Kluwer, pp. 115–40.

Eisner, R. (1996) 'The retreat from full employment', in Arestis, P. (ed.), *Employment, Economic Growth and the Tyranny of the Market: Essays in Honour of Paul Davidson*, Vol. 2, Cheltenham: Elgar.

Epstein, G. and Gintis, H. (1992) 'International capital markets and the limits of national economic policy', in Banuri, T. and Schor, J. (eds), *Financial Openness and National Autonomy*, Oxford: Oxford University Press.

—— (1995) 'Macroeconomic policies for sustainable growth', *Macroeconomic Policy after the Conservative Era*, Cambridge: Cambridge University Press.

—— (eds) (1995) *Macroeconomic Policy After the Conservative Era*, Cambridge: Cambridge University Press.

Erenburg, S. (1994) 'Linking public capital to economic performance. Public capital the missing link between investment and economic growth', Public Policy Brief, 14, Jerome Levy Economics Institute of Bard College, Annandale-on-Hudson.

European Commission: *Economic Data Pocket Book*, 12/1998.

Fazzari, S. and Athey, M. (1987) 'Asymmetric information, financing constraints and corporate investment', *Review of Economics and Statistics*, 69, pp. 481–7.

Fazzari, S. and Mott, T. (1986/7) 'The investment theories of Kalecki and Keynes: an empirical study of firm data, 1970–1982', *Journal of Post Keynesian Economics*, 9, pp. 181–7.

Fazzari, S., Hubbard, G. and Petersen, B. (1988) 'Financing constraints and corporate investment', *Brookings Papers on Economic Activity*, 1, pp. 141–206.

Feiwel, G. (1975) *The Intellectual Capital of Michal Kalecki: A Study in Economic Theory and Policy*, Knoxville: University of Tennessee Press.

Felix, D. (1998) 'Asia and the crisis of financial globalisation', in Baker, D., Epstein, G. and Pollin, R. (eds), *Globalization and Progressive Economic Policies*, Cambridge, Cambridge University Press.

Fischer, S. (1999) Statement in http://www.imf.org/external/np/speeches/1999/042899.htm.

FitzGerald, E. (1990) 'Kalecki on financing development: An approach to the macroeconomics of the semi-industrialised economy', *Cambridge Journal of Economics*, 14, pp. 183–203.

Flassbeck, H. (1996) 'Die Weltwirtschaft zu Beginn des 21 Jahrhunderts und die Herausforderungen fuer den Westen', in Lutz, Hartmann, Kreinsen (eds), *Produzieren im 21 Jahrhundert*, Muenchen, [Campus].

—— (1998) 'Realloehne und Arbeitslosigkeit: Eine einfache empirische Widerlegung der neoklassischen Beschaeftigungstheorie', DIW (German Institute of Economic Research), *Diskussionspapier*, 162, February.

Flassbeck, H. and Spiecker, F. (1998) 'Loehne und Arbeitslosigkeit', *Wirtschaftspolitische Diskurse der Friedrich Ebert Stiftung*, 118.

Flassbeck, H. *et al.* (1997) 'Unemployment in Europe and the US macroeconomics is the key', *Internationale Politik und Gesellschaft/International Politics and Society*, 4, ed. by Friedrich Ebert Stiftung.

Foss, N. (1994) 'Realism and evolutionary economics', *Journal of Social and Evolutionary Systems*, 17(1), pp. 21–40.

Freeman, C. and Perez, C. (1988) 'Structural crises of adjustment, business cycles and investment behaviour', in Dosi, G. *et al.* (eds.), *Technical Change and Economic Theory*, London: Pinter, pp. 38–66.

Freeman, C. and Soete, L. (1997) *The Economics of Industrial Innovation*, 3rd edn, London: Pinter.

Friedman, M. (1968) 'The role of monetary policy', *American Economic Review*, 58, pp. 1–17.

Galbraith, J. (1996) 'The surrender of economic policy', *The American Prospect*, 25, March–April, pp. 60–7.

—— (1998) *Created Unequal: The Crisis in American Pay*, New York: Free Press.

Geroski, P., Machin, S. and Van Reenen, J. (1993) 'The profitability of innovating firms', *Rand Journal of Economics*, 24(2), Summer, pp. 198–211.

Ghose, A. (1989) 'Rural poverty and relative prices in India', *Cambridge Journal of Economics*.

Gilbert, R. (1990) 'Primary Commodity Prices and Inflation', *Oxford Review of Economic Policy*, 6, pp. 77–99.

Glynn, A. (1995) 'Stability, inegalitarianism and stagnation: An overview of advanced capitalist countries in the 80s', in Epstein, G. and Gintis, H. (eds), *Macroeconomic Policy After the Conservative Era*, Cambridge, Cambridge University Press, pp. 18–57.

Godley, W. (1999) *Seven Unsustainable Processes, Special Report*, The Jerome Levy Economic Institute.

Goldsworthy, A. (1997) *The Global Information Economy: The Way Ahead*, Information Industries Task-force Report, Canberra, Dept. of Industry, Science and Tourism.

Goodwin, R. (1990) *Chaotic Economic Dynamics*, Oxford: Clarendon Press.

Gordon, D. (1995) 'Growth, distribution and the rules of the game: Social structuralist macro foundation for a democratic economic policy', in Epstein, G. and Gintis, H. (eds), *Macroeconomic Policy After the Conservative Era*, Cambridge, Cambridge University Press.

Gosh, A. (1996) *Paradigms of Economic Development*, Simla: Indian Institute of Advanced Study.

Gottschalk, P. and Smeeding, T. (1997) 'Cross national comparisons of earnings and income inequality', *Journal of Economic Literature*, 45, June, pp. 633–87.

Gray, J. (1999) *False Down: The Delusions of Global Capitalism*, London: Granta Books.

Greenwald, B. and Stiglitz, J. (1988) 'Money, imperfect information, and economic fluctuations', in Kohn, M. and Tsiang, S.-C. (eds), *Finance-Constraints, Expectations and Macroeconomics*, Oxford: Clarendon Press, pp.141–65.

—— (1993) 'Financial market imperfections and business cycles', *Quarterly Journal of Economics*, 108, pp. 77–114.

Greenwald, B., Stiglitz, J. and Weiss, A. (1984) 'Informational imperfections in the capital market and macroeconomic fluctuations', *American Economic Review, Papers and Proceedings*, 74, May pp. 194–9.

Gurley, J. and Shaw E. (1960) *Money in a Theory of Finance*, Brookings Institution.

Harcourt, G. (1972) *Some Cambridge Controversies in the Theory of Capital*, Cambridge: Cambridge University Press.

Harris, D. (1974) 'The price policy of firms, the level of employment and the distribution of income in the short run', *Australian Economic Papers*, 13, pp. 144–51.

Harrod, R. (1936) *The Trade Cycle*, Oxford: Oxford University Press (Clarendon).

Hart, O. (1982) 'A model of imperfect competition with Keynesian features', *Quarterly Journal of Economics*, February, pp. 109–38.

—— (1993) 'Financial market imperfections and business cycles', *Quarterly Journal of Economics*, 108, pp. 77–114.

Hart, O. and Weiss, A. (1984) 'Informational imperfections in the capital market and macroeconomic fluctuations', *American Economic Review, Papers and Proceedings*, 74, May pp. 194–9.

Hayek, F. von (1933) *Monetary Theory and Trade Cycle*, London: Jonathan Cape.

—— (1944) *The Road to Serfdom*, Chicago: University of Chicago Press.

Heller, W. (1966) *New Dimensions of Political Economy*, Cambridge, Mass.: Harvard University Press.

Hicks, J. (1967) *Critical Essays in Monetary Theory*, Oxford: Oxford University Press.

Hillinger, C., Reiter, M. and Weser, T. (1992) 'Micro foundations of the second-order accelerator of cyclical behaviour', in Hillinger C. (ed.), *Cyclical Growth in the Market and Planned Economies*, Oxford: Clarendon Press, pp. 167–80.

Hodgson, G. (1993) *Economics and Evolution: Bringing Life Back into Economics*, Cambridge: Polity Press.

—— (1997) 'Economics and evolution and the evolution of economics', in Reijnders, J. (ed.), *Economics and Evolution*, Cheltenham: Elgar, pp. 9–40.

Hollanders, H., Soete, L. and Weel, B. (1999) 'Trends in growth convergence and divergence and changes in technological access and capabilities', *MERIT Research Memorandum 99–019*, Maastricht University.

Horioka, C. and Feldstein, M. (1980) 'Domestic saving and international capital flows', *Economic Journal*, 90, June, pp. 314–29.

Hua, P. (1988) 'On primary commodity prices: The impact of macroeconomic monetary shocks', *Journal of Policy Modeling*, 20(6), pp. 767–90.

Huh, H. (1999) 'Australian Indicators', in *Quarterly Bulletin of Economic Trends*, 1, Melbourne Institute of Applied Economic and Social Research, University of Melbourne. Melbourne, pp. 15–19.

Husman, D. (1998) 'Problems with supply-side egalitarianism', in Bowles, S. and Gintis, H. (eds), *Recasting Egalitarianism*, London: Verso, p. 83.

International Commission on Peace and Food (ICPF) (1994) *Uncommon Opportunities: An Agenda for Peace and Equitable Development*, London: Zed Books.

International Monetary Fund (IMF) (1995) *World Economic Outlook* (Spring).

—— (1998) *World Economic Outlook*, (September).

Johnson, C. (1982) *MITI and the Japanese Miracle*, Stanford: Stanford University Press.

Jones, E. (1965) 'Agriculture and economic growth in England, 1660–1750: Agricultural change', *Journal of Economic History*, 25(1), pp. 1–18.

Jorgenson, D. (1963) 'Capital theory and investment behaviour', *American Economic Review*, 53, pp. 247–59.

—— (1967) 'The theory of investment behavior', in Ferber, R. (ed.), *Determinants of Investment*, New York: NBER.

—— (1971) 'Econometric studies of investment behaviour: A survey', *Journal of Economic Literature*, 9, pp. 111–47.

Kahn, R. (1931) 'The relation of home investment to unemployment', *Economic Journal*, 41, June, pp. 173–98.

Kaldor, N. (1939) 'Speculation and economic stability', *Review of Economic Studies*, VII(1), October, pp. 1–27.

—— (1954) 'The relation of economic growth and cyclical fluctuations', *Economic Journal*, 64, March, pp. 53–71.

—— (1955–6) 'Alternative theories of distribution', *Review of Economic Studies*, 23(2), reprinted in (1980) *Essays on Value and Distribution*, London: Duckworth, pp. 209–36.

—— (1967) *Strategic Factors in Economic Development*, Ithaca: Cornell University Press.

—— (1970) 'The case for regional policies', *Scottish Journal of Political Economy*, XVII(3), November; reprinted in (1978) *Further Essays on Economic Theory*, London: Duckworth, pp. 139–54.

—— (1976) 'Inflation and recession in the world economy', *Economic Journal*, 86, December, pp. 703–14.

—— (1978) 'What is wrong with economic theory', in *Further Essays on Economic Theory*, London: Duckworth, pp. 202–13.

—— (1982) *The Scourge of Monetarism*, Oxford: Oxford University Press.

—— (1983a) 'Keynesian policies after fifty years', in Worswick, D. and Threvithick, J. (eds), *Keynes and the Modern World*, Cambridge: Cambridge University Press.

—— (1983b) 'The role of commodity prices in economic recovery', *Lloyds Bank Review*, 149, July, pp. 21–34.

—— (1985) *Economics Without Equilibrium*, Cardiff: University College Press.

—— (1989) 'Equilibrium theory and growth theory', in Targetti, F. and Thirlwall, A. (eds), *The Essential Kaldor*, London: Duckworth, pp. 411–33.

—— (1996) *Causes of Growth and Stagnation in the World Economy*, R. Mattioli Lectures 1984, Cambridge: Cambridge University Press.

Keynes, J. (1930/1971) *A Treatise on Money*, London: Macmillan.

—— (1936/1973) *The General Theory of Employment, Interest and Money*, in *Collected Writings of John Maynard Keynes*, Vol. VII.

—— (1946) *Activities 1940–4: Shaping the Post-war World: The Clearing Union*, London: Macmillan.

Khalil, E. (1998–9) 'The Janus Hypothesis', *Journal of Post Keynesian Economics*, 21(2), Winter, pp. 315–42.

King, J. (ed.) (1996) *An Alternative Macroeconomic Theory: The Kaleckian Model and Post-Keynesian Economics*, Boston: Kluwer.

Klein, L. (1951) 'The life of John Maynard Keynes', *Journal of Political Economy*, 59, October, pp. 443–51.

—— (1964) 'The role of econometrics in socialist economics', in *Problems of Economic Dynamics and Planning, Essays in Honour of Michal Kalecki*, Warsaw: PWN, pp. 181–91.

—— (1966) *The Keynesian Revolution*, rev. edn, New York: Macmillan.

—— (1975) 'Foreword' to Feiwel, G. *The Intellectual Capital of Michal Kalecki*, Knoxville: University of Tennessee Press.

Korpi, W. (1991) 'Political and economic explanations for unemployment: A cross-national and long-term analysis', *British Journal of Political Science*, 21, part 3, p. 335.

Kowalik, T. (1964) 'Biography of Michal Kalecki', in *Problems of Economic Dynamics and Planning, Essays in Honour of Michal Kalecki*, Warsaw: PWN, pp. 1–l2.

Krawiec, A. and Szydlowski, M. (1999) 'The Kaldor–Kalecki business cycle model', *Annals of Operation Research*, 89, pp. 89–100.

Kriesler, P. (1987) *Kalecki's Microanalysis: The Development of Kalecki's Analysis of Pricing and Distribution*, Cambridge: Cambridge University Press.

—— (1989) 'From disequilibrium to the traverse in economic theory', *School of Economics Discussion Paper*, 89–13, Sydney: University of New South Wales.

Krugman, P. and Taylor, L. (1978) 'Contractionary effects of devaluation', *Journal of International Economics*, 8, August, pp. 445–56.

Kuh, E. (1963) *Capital Stock Growth: A Microeconometric Approach*, Amsterdam: North Holland.

Kumarappa, J. (1949) *The Gandhian Economy and Other Essays*, Maganvadi: Wardha, p. 5.

Kurien, C. (1996) 'Development with equity', *Economic and Political Weekly*, May 10, p. 1018.

Kuttner, R. (1997) *Everything for Sale: The Virtues and Limits of Markets*, New York: Knopf.

Laidler, D. (1985) *The Demand for Money: Theories, Evidence and Problems*, New York: Harper & Row.

Lange, O. (1939) 'Neoklasyczna szkola w ekonomii' (The Neoclassical School of Economics), in Lange, O. (1975), *Dziela* (*Works*), Vol. III, Warsaw: PWN Polish Scientific Publishers, pp. 64–92.

Lavoie, M. (1992) *Foundations of Post-Keynesian Economic Analysis*, Aldershot: Elgar.

—— (1996) 'Horizontalism, structuralism, liquidity preference and the principle of increasing risk', *Scottish Journal of Political Economy*, 43(3), pp. 275–300.

Legge, J. (1999) 'Created unequal: the crisis in American pay: a review', *Journal of Post Keynesian Economics*, 21(4), Summer, pp. 361–70.

Legge, J. and Hindle, K. (1997) *Entrepreneurship: How Innovators Create the Future*, South Melbourne: Macmillan.

Levy, J. (1943) *Economics is an Exact Science*, New York: New Economic Library.

Lindbeck, A. and Snower, D. (1987) 'Union activity, unemployment persistence and wage-employment ratchets', *European Economic Review*, 31, pp. 157–67.

Lipsey, R. (1972) 'The foundations of the theory of national income: An analysis of some fundamental errors', in Peston, M. and Corry, B. (eds), *Essays in Honour of Lord Robbins*, London: Weidenfeld & Nicolson, pp. 3–42.

López, J. (1998) 'Economic crisis and recovery in Mexico: a post-Kaleckian perspective', *Economia Aplicada*, Universidad Nacional Autonoma de Mexico, 45.

López, J. and Mott, T. (1999) 'Kalecki vs. Keynes on the determinants of investment', *Review of Political Economy*, 11(3), July, pp. 291–301.

Lowe, A. (1976) *The Path of Economic Growth*, Cambridge: Cambridge University Press.

Maddison, A. (2001) *The World Economy: a Millenial Perspective*, Paris: OECD.

Marglin, S. and Bhaduri, A. (1990) 'Profit squeeze and Keynesian theory', in Marglin, S. and Schor, J. (eds), *The Golden Age of Capitalism*, Oxford: Clarendon Press, pp. 153–87.

Martin, R. (1994) 'Innovation and industrial relations', in Dodgson, M. and Rothwell, R. (eds), *The Handbook of Industrial Innovation*, Cheltenham: Elgar, pp. 337–47.

Matthews, R.C.O. (1968) 'Why has Britain had full employment since the war?, *Economic Journal*, September.

Meyer, J. and Glauber, R. (1964) *Investment Decisions, Economic Forecasting and Public Policy*, Cambridge, Mass.: Harvard University Press.

Meyer, J. and Kuh, E. (1957) *The Investment Decision*, Cambridge, Mass.: Harvard University Press.

Michie, J. (1999) 'Globalisation, governance and public policy', Working Paper, Series, 99/06, Dept. of Management, Birkbeck College, University of London.

Michl, T. (1995) 'Assessing the costs of inflation and unemployment', in Arestis, P. and Marshall, M. (eds), *The Political Economy of Full Employment*, Aldershot: Elgar, pp. 54–78.

Minsky, H. (1957) 'Monetary systems and accelerator models', *American Economic Review*, 47, pp. 859–83.

—— (1963) 'Can "it" happen again?', in Carson, D. (ed.), *Banking and Monetary Studies*, Homewood, Ill.: Irwin, pp. 101–11.

—— (1975) *John Maynard Keynes*, New York: Columbia University Press.

—— (1982) *Can 'It' Happen Again? Essays on Instability of Finance*, Armonk, NY: Sharpe.

—— (1986) *Stabilizing an Unstable Economy*, New Heaven: Yale University Press.

Modigliani, F. and Miller, M. (1958) 'The cost of capital, corporation finance and the theory of investment', *American Economic Review*, 48, pp. 261–97.

Molana, H. and Vines, D. (1989) 'North–South growth and the terms of trade: a model on Kaldorian lines', *Economic Journal*, 99, June, pp. 443–53.

Moore, B. (1988) *Horizontalists and Verticalists: The Macroeconomics of Credit Money*, Cambridge: Cambridge University Press.

Mott, T. (1982) *Kalecki's Principle of Increasing Risk: The Role of Finance in the Post-Keynesian Theory of Investment Fluctuations*, PhD dissertation, Stanford: Stanford University Press.

—— (1985–6) 'Kalecki's principle of increasing risk and the relation among mark-up pricing, investment fluctuations, and liquidity preference', *Economic Forum*, 15, pp. 65–76.

—— (1992) 'In what sense does monopoly capital require monopoly?', in Davis, J. (ed.), *The Economic Surplus in Advanced Economies*, Aldershot: Elgar, pp. 114–29.

—— (1998) 'A Kaleckian view of New Keynesian Macroeconomics', in Rotheim, R. (ed.), *New Keynesian Economics/Post Keynesian Alternatives*, London: Routledge, pp. 262–72.

Mott, T. and Slattery, E. (1994) 'Tax incidence and macroeconomic effects in a Kaleckian model when profits finance affects investment and prices may respond to taxes', *Journal of Post Keynesian Economics*, 16, pp. 391–409.

Myrdal G. (1939) *Monetary Equilibrium*, London: W. Hodge & Co.

Needham, K. (2002) 'IT industry hit by rock-bottom gloom', *The Age*, 24 January, pp. 1, 5.

Nelson, R. (1995) 'Recent evolutionary theorizing about economic change', *Journal of Economic Literature*, XXXIII(1), March, pp. 48–90.

Nelson, R. and Winter, S. (1982) *An Evolutionary Theory of Economic Change*, Cambridge, Mass.: Harvard University Press.

Nowshirvani, V. (1977) 'A note on elasticity of marketable surplus of a subsistence-crop:

A comment', in Wadhva, C. (ed.), *Some Problems of India's Economic Policy*, New Delhi: Tata McGraw-Hill, pp. 389–92.

Nuti, D. (1986) 'Michal Kalecki's contribution to the theory and practice of socialist planning', *Cambridge Journal of Economics*, 10(4) pp. 333–53; and in Sebastiani, M. (ed.) (1989), *Kalecki's Relevance Today*, London: St Martin's Press, pp. 317–58.

Obstfeld, M. and Rogoff, K. (1996) *Foundations of International Macroeconomics*, Cambridge, Mass.: MIT Press.

Ocampo, J. (1999) 'Beyond the Washington consensus: an ECLA perspective', paper presented to the International Conference organized by Ecole des Hautes Etudes en Sciences Sociales in co-operation with MOST Programme of UNESCO.

OECD, (1970) *Inflation, The Present Problem*, Report by the Secretary General, Paris.

—— (1977) *Towards Full Employment and Price Stability*, Paris.

—— (1991) *Economic Outlook*, *World Development Report*, p. 137.

—— (1998) *Economic Outlook*, December.

—— (2002) *Economic Outlook*, 1, June, p. 71.

Osiatyński, J. (1988) *Michal Kalecki on Socialist Economy*, London: Macmillan.

Pasinetti, L. (1977) *Lectures on the Theory of Production*, New York: Columbia University Press.

Patinkin, D. (1982) *Anticipations of the General Theory? and Other Essays*, Oxford: Blackwell.

Persson, T. and Tabellini, G. (1994) 'Is equality harmful for growth?', *American Economic Review*, 84(3), June, pp. 600–21.

Polanyi, K. (1944/1962) *The Great Transformation: The Political and Economic Origins of Our Times*, Boston.

Pollin, R. (1991) 'Two theories of money supply endogeneity: some empirical evidence', *Journal of Post Keynesian Economics*, 14, pp. 366–96.

Porter, M.E. (1990) *The Competitive Advantage of Nations*, London: Macmillan..

Problems of Economic Dynamics and Planning, Essays in Honour of Michal Kalecki: (1964), Warsaw: PWN Polish Scientific Publishers.

Rehn, G. (1987) 'State and industrial relations in the 1980s: problems and trends, *Economic and Industrial Democracy*, No. 8.

Reijnders, J. (ed.) (1997) *Economics and Evolution*, Cheltenham: Elgar.

Reynolds, P. (1992) 'Macroeconomic policy co-ordination and commodity input prices', in Arestis, P. and Chick, V. (eds), *Recent Developments in Post-Keynesian Economics*, Aldershot: Elgar, pp. 160–84.

—— (1996) 'Kalecki's theory of prices and distribution', in King, J. (ed.), *An Alternative Macroeconomic Theory: The Kaleckian Model and Post-Keynesian Economics*, pp. 73–92.

Robinson, J. (1952) *The Rate of Interest and Other Essays*, London: Macmillan.

—— (1962) *Essays in the Theory of Economic Growth*, London: Macmillan.

—— (1964) 'Kalecki and Keynes', in *Problems of Economic Dynamics and Planning, Essays in Honour of Michal Kalecki*, Warsaw: PWN, and same author, *Collected Economic Papers*, Vol. III, pp. 92–9.

—— (1966a) 'Introduction', to Kalecki, M., *Studies in the Theory of Business Cycles, 1933–1939*, Cambridge: Cambridge University Press.

—— (1966b) *The Accumulation of Capital*, 3rd edn, London: Macmillan.

—— (1972) 'The second crisis of economic theory', *American Economic Review*, Vol. LXII, no. 2, May, pp. 1–10.

—— (1976) 'Michel Kalecki: A neglected prophet', *New York Review of Books*, 23(4), March, pp. 28–30.

—— (1977) 'Michal Kalecki and the economics of capitalism', *Oxford Bulletin of Economics and Statistics*, 39(1), pp. 7–17.

Rodrik, D. (1999) *The New Global Economy and Developing Countries: Making Openness Work*, Washington: John Hopkins University Press.

Rostow, W. (1990) *Theories of Economic Growth from David Hume to the Present: With a Perspective on the Next Century*, New York: Oxford University Press.

Rotemberg, J. and Saloner, G. (1986) 'A supergame model of price wars during booms', *American Economic Review*, 76(3), pp. 390–407.

Rothwell, R. (1994) 'Industrial innovation: Success, strategy, trends', in Dodgson, M. and Rothwell, R. (eds), *Handbook of Industrial Innovation,* Cheltenham: Elgar.

Rousseas, S. (1992) *Post Keynesian Monetary Economics*, Armonk, NY: Sharpe.

Rowthorn, R. (1977) 'Conflict, inflation and money', *Cambridge Journal of Economics*, 1.

Ruthven, P. (1998) 'Implications for business strategy and investment opportunities', in *Quarterly Bulletin of Economic Trends: Special Supplement Issue on the Asian Crisis*, Institute of Applied Economics and Social Research, University of Melbourne, October.

Sachs, I. (1962) *Patterns of Public Sector in Underdeveloped Economies*, New Delhi: Asia Publishing House.

—— (1963) *Foreign Trade and Economic Development in Underdeveloped Countries*, New Delhi: Asia Publishing House.

—— (1970) 'Selection of techniques: Problems and policies for Latin America', *Economic Bulletin for Latin America*, Santiago, 15(11), pp. 1–34.

—— (1971) 'Welfare states in poor countries', *Economic and Political Weekly*, VI(3/4), January.

—— (1993) *L'ecodeveloppement: Les strategies de l'ecodeveloppement au XXI siècle*, Paris: Syros.

Sachs, I. and Vinaver, K. (1979) 'Integration of technology in development planning: A normative view', in Sagasti, F. and Araoz, A. (eds), *Science and Technology for Development Planning in the STPI Countries*, Ottawa: International Development Research Center, pp. 117–36.

Sachs, I., Loske, W. and Linz, M. (1998) *Greening in the Nord: A Post-Industrial Blueprint for Ecology and Equity*, London and New York: Zed Books.

Sautter, Ch. (1987) *Les dents du dragon*, Paris: Orban.

—— (1996) *La France au miroir du Japon*, Paris: Odile Jacob.

Sawyer, M. (1982) 'Income distribution and the welfare state', in E. Boltho (ed.), *European Economy: Growth and Crisis*, Oxford: Oxford University Press.

—— (1985) *The Economics of Michal Kalecki*, London: Macmillan.

—— (1992) 'Prices and pricing in the post-Keynesian and Kaleckian traditions in the short run and in the long run', in Mongiovi, G. and Ruhl, C. (eds), *Macroeconomic Theory: Diversity and Convergence,* Aldershot: Elgar.

—— (1994) 'Prices, capacity utilization and employment in the post-Keynesian Traditions', in Dutt, A. (ed.), *New Directions in Analytical Political Economy*, Aldershot: Elgar.

—— (1995a) 'Obstacles to full employment in capitalist economies', in Arestis, P. and Marshall, M. (eds), *The Political Economy of Full Employment*, Aldershot: Elgar pp. 15–35.

—— (1995b) 'Overcoming the barriers to full employment in capitalist economies', *Economie Appliquee*, 48, pp. 185–218.

—— (1999a) 'Kalecki on money and finance', Leeds University Business School, Discussion Paper E.99/03; reprinted in (2001), *European Journal for the History of Political Economy.*

—— (1999b) 'The Kaleckian analysis and the new Millennium', *Review of Political Economy*, 11(3), pp. 303–19.

—— (1999c) Sawyer, M. (ed.), *The Legacy of Michal Kalecki*, Vol. 1, 2, Cheltenham: Elgar.

—— (2001) 'Kalecki on money and finance', *European Journal for the History of Political Economy*, 8(4), pp. 481–508.

Schäfer, H. (1997) 'Farm prices and agricultural production: An empirical study of 20 Indian districts', in Bhaduri, A. and Skarstein, R. (eds), *Economic Development* and *Agricultural Productivity*, Cheltenham: Elgar, pp. 98–116.

Schmookler, J. (1966) *Invention and Economic Growth*, Cambridge, Mass.: Harvard University Press.

Schulmeister, S. (1996) *Interest Rate, Investment, Growth and Public Debt, Summary*, Austrian Institute of Economic Research (WIFO), December.

—— (1998) *Employment Dynamics: A Comparison of the USA, Germany and Japan, Summary*, Austrian Institute of Economic Research (WIFO), April.

Schumpeter, J. (1912) *Theorie der wirtschaftlichen Entwicklung*, Leipzig: Duncker & Humbolt.

Sebastiani, M. (1989) (ed.), *Kalecki's Relevance Today*, London: St Martin's Press.

Sen, A. (1960) *Choices of Techniques*, Oxford: Blackwell.

Setterfield M. (1999) 'Expectations, path dependence and effective demand: A macroeconomic model along Keynesian lines', *Journal of Post Keynesian Economics*, 21(3), Spring, pp. 479–501.

Silverberg, G. and Verspagen, S. (1997) 'Economic growth: An evolutionary perspective', in Reijnders, J. (ed.), *Economics and Evolution*, Cheltenham: Elgar, pp. 137–70.

Skarstein, R. (1999) *Development Theory: A Guide to Some Unfashionable Perspectives*, New Delhi: Oxford University Press.

Skuse, F. (1995) 'Thatcherism and unemployment in the UK', in Arestis, P. and Marshall, M. (eds), *The Political Economy of Full Employment*, pp. 79–97.

Skuse, F.E. (1999) 'Kalecki's "Political Aspects of Full Employment" Revisited', in Daniel, S., Arestis, P. and Grahl, J. (eds), *Adjustment, Convergence and Economic Policy – Essays in Macroeconomics in Honour of Bernard Corry and Maurice Peston*, Vol. 1, Cheltenham: Edward Elgar.

Smith, K. (1998) 'Innovation as a systemic phenomenon: Rethinking the role of policy', in Bryant, K. and Wells, A. (eds), *A New Economic Paradigm?*, Discussions Papers, Dept. of Industry, Science and Resources, Canberra, pp. 17–51.

Snower, D. (1983) 'Imperfect competition, underemployment and crowding-out', *Oxford Economic Papers*, 35, pp. 245–70.

Soete, L. (1999) '"The New Economy': European Perspective', paper presented to the European Socio-Economic Research Conference, Brussels, 28–30 April.

Solow, R. and Taylor, J. (1998) *Inflation, Unemployment, and Monetary Policy*, Cambridge: Mass.: MIT Press.

Soros, G. (1998) *The Crisis of Global Capitalism*, New York: Public Affairs.

Stafford, G.B. (1970) 'Full employment since the war, comment', *Economic Journal*, with response by R.C.O. Matthews.

Steindl, J. (1941) 'On risk', *Oxford Economic Papers*, 5, June, pp. 43–53.

—— (1952/1976) *Maturity and Stagnation in American Capitalism*, New York: Monthly Review Press; Oxford: Oxford University Press; Oxford: Blackwell.

—— (1964) 'On maturity in capitalist economies', in *Problems of Economic Dynamics and Planning, Essays in Honour of Michal Kalecki*, Warsaw: PWN, pp. 423–32.

—— (1990) 'The role of household saving in the modern economy', in *Economic Papers 1941–1988*, London: Macmillan.

Stiglitz, J. (1984) 'Price rigidities and market structure', *American Economic Review*, 74(2), pp. 350–5.

—— (1998a) 'More instruments and broader goals: Moving toward the post-Washington Consensus', WIDER.

—— (1998b) 'Towards a new paradigm for development strategies, policies and processes', Geneva: UNCTAD Prebisch Lecture.

Stiglitz, J. and Weiss, A. (1981) 'Credit rationing in markets with imperfect information', *American Economic Review*, 71, pp. 393–410.

Sunkel, O. (ed.) (1993) *Development from Within: Toward a Neostructuralist Approach for Latin America*, Boulder, Col.: Lynne Reinner Publishers.

Sweezy, P. (1953) 'A crucial difference between capitalism and socialism', in Horowitz, D. (ed.) (1968), *Marx and Modern Economics*, London: MacGibbon & Kee.

—— (1958) 'Veblen on American capitalism', in Dowd (ed.), *Thorstein Veblen: A Critical Appraisal*, Ithaca, NY: Cornell University Press.

Sylos-Labini, P. (1979) 'Prices and income distribution in manufacturing industry', *Journal of Post Keynesian Economics*, 2(1), Autumn, pp. 3–25.

—— (1982) 'Rigid prices, flexible prices and inflation', *Banca Nazionale del Lavoro, Quarterly Review*, 140, pp. 37–68.

Szeworski, A. (1965) *Cykl koniunkturalny a interwencja państwa* (The Trade Cycle and Government Intervention), Warsaw: PWE.

Szydlowski, M., Krawiec, A. and Tobola, J. (2001) 'Non-linear oscillations in: business cycle model with time lags', *Chaos, Solitons and Fractals*, 12, pp. 505–17.

Targetti, F. (1985) 'Growth and the terms of trade: a Kaldorian two sector model', *Metroeconomica*, 36(1), February, pp. 79–96.

Taylor, L. (1982) 'Food price inflation, terms of trade and growth', in Gersovitz, M. *et al., The Theory and Experience of Economic Development*, London: Allen & Unwin, pp. 60–77.

—— (1988) *Varieties of Stabilization Experience*, Oxford: Clarendon Press.

Tchaianov, A. (1990) *L'organisation de l'economie paysanne*, Paris: Librairie du Regard.

Tepicht, J. (1973) *Marxisme et agricullture: Le paysan polonais*, Paris: A. Colin.

The Economics of Full Employment: Six Studies in Applied Economics, prepared at the Oxford University Institute of Statistics (1944), Oxford: Blackwell.

Thirlwall, A. (1986) 'A general model of growth and development on Kaldorian lines', *Oxford Economic Papers*, 38, pp. 199–219.

Thurow, L. (1998) 'Wage dispersion: Who done it?', *Journal of Post Keynesian Economics*, 21(1), Autumn, pp. 25–37.

—— (1999) *Building Wealth: The New Rules for Individuals, Companies and Nations in a Knowledge-based Economy*, New York: HarperCollins.

Tobin, J. (1966) 'Adjustment responsibilities of surplus and deficit countries', in Fellner, W., Machlup, F. and Triffin, R. (eds), *Maintaining and Restoring Balance in International Payments*, Princeton: Princeton University Press.

—— (1981) 'The monetarist counter-revolution today: An appraisal', *Economic Journal*, 91(1), pp. 29–42.

Toivanen, O., Stoneman, P. and Diederen, P. (1996) 'Uncertainty, macroeconomic volatility and investment in new technology', unpublished paper, Warwick Business School Research Bureau, University of Warwick, UK, 29 October.

Toporowski, J. (1996) 'Kalecki, Marx and the economics of socialism', in King, J. (ed.), *An Alternative Macroeconomic Theory: The Kaleckian Model and Post-Keynesian Economics*, Boston: Kluwer, pp. 168–86.

Tsuru, S. (1993) *Japan's Capitalism: Creative Defeat and Beyond*, Cambridge: Cambridge University Press.

United Nations (2001) *World Economic Report*, New York: United Nations.

United Nations Development Program (UNDP) (1999), *Human Development Report*, New York: United Nations.

Veblen, T. (1899) *The Theory of the Leisure Class*, New York: Macmillan.

—— (1904) *The Theory of Business Enterprise*, New York: Scribner's Sons.

—— (1906) 'The socialist economics of Karl Marx', in *The Place of Science in Modern Civilisation and Other Essays*, New York: Viking Press.

—— (1919, 1921) 'The technicians and the revolution', in Lerner, M. (1948) (ed.), *The Portable Veblen*, New York: Viking Press.

Verspagen, B. (1999) 'Evolutionary macroeconomics: A synthesis between neo-Schumpeterian and post-Keynesian lines of thought', *The Electronic Journal of Evolutionary Modeling and Economic Dynamics*, No. 1007.

—— (2002) 'Structural change and technology, a long view', Druid Summer Conference, Copenhagen.

Wade, R. (1990) *Governing the Market: Economic Theory and the Role of Government in East Asian Industrialization*, Princeton: Princeton University Press.

Weitzman, M. (1985) 'The simple macroeconomics of profit sharing', *American Economic Review*, 75(5) pp. 937–53.

von Weizsaecker, E., Lovins, E. and Lovins, L. (1997) *Factor Four: Doubling Wealth, Halving Resource Use*, The New Report to the Club of Rome, London: Earthscan.

Wells, J. (1995) 'Unemployment: Job creation and job destruction in the UK since 1979', in Arestis, P. and Marshall, M. (eds), *Political Economy of Full Employment*, pp. 98–126.

van Wijnbergen, S. (1985) 'Interdependence revisited: A developing countries perspective on macroeconomic management and trade policy in the developing' world', *Economic Policy*, 1, pp. 82–137.

Wycoff, A. (1996) 'The growing strength of services', *OECD Observer*, 2000, June.

Index